Java EE 8 and Angular

A practical guide to building modern single-page applications
with Angular and Java EE

Prashant Padmanabhan

BIRMINGHAM - MUMBAI

Java EE 8 and Angular

Commissioning Editor: Merint Mathew
Acquisition Editor: Chaitanya Nair
Content Development Editor: Zeeyan Pinheiro
Technical Editor: Ruvika Rao
Copy Editor: Safis Editing
Project Coordinator: Vaidehi Sawant
Proofreader: Safis Editing
Indexer: Tejal Daruwale Soni
Graphics: Jason Monteiro
Production Coordinator: Nilesh Mohite

First published: January 2018

Production reference: 1100118

Published by Packt Publishing Ltd.
Livery Place
35 Livery Street
Birmingham
B3 2PB, UK.

ISBN 978-1-78829-120-0

www.packtpub.com

To my father, Padmanabhan S, whose guidance had helped me navigate the course of this book. To my wife, Pallavi, for being crazy enough to love me and to my daughters, Tanisha and Samayra, who are my world of happiness.

— Prashant Padmanabhan

`mapt.io`

Mapt is an online digital library that gives you full access to over 5,000 books and videos, as well as industry leading tools to help you plan your personal development and advance your career. For more information, please visit our website.

Why subscribe?

- Spend less time learning and more time coding with practical eBooks and Videos from over 4,000 industry professionals

- Improve your learning with Skill Plans built especially for you

- Get a free eBook or video every month

- Mapt is fully searchable

- Copy and paste, print, and bookmark content

PacktPub.com

Did you know that Packt offers eBook versions of every book published, with PDF and ePub files available? You can upgrade to the eBook version at `www.PacktPub.com` and as a print book customer, you are entitled to a discount on the eBook copy. Get in touch with us at `service@packtpub.com` for more details.

At `www.PacktPub.com`, you can also read a collection of free technical articles, sign up for a range of free newsletters, and receive exclusive discounts and offers on Packt books and eBooks.

Contributors

About the author

Prashant Padmanabhan is a professional Java developer and solutions architect. He has been developing software since 2002 and is still loving it. Professionally, he has over a decade of experience and considers himself a coding architect, building enterprise-scale software using Java, JEE, and open source technologies put together.

Writing a book is a big commitment and I would like to share my heartfelt thanks to my family, who allowed me to be immersed in my thoughts without getting distracted. I couldn't have written this book without my wife Pallavi's unconditional support and my father's guidance.

I'm grateful to editors, Zeeyan Pinheiro, Ruvika Rao, and the team at Packt.

About the reviewer

Sukma Wardana comes from a small city in East Java, Indonesia, and his curiosity for computers took him to Brawijaya University, where he got his computer science degree. His love for programming and problem solving helped him become a software developer, mostly works with legacy enterprise applications built on top of Java Enterprise Edition/Spring technology.

Sukma still spends his time working with those old legacy enterprise applications with the hope to delete more unnecessary code, and he relentlessly helps people who want to update their legacy applications or start new green field projects for their startup ideas, with Java EE. He is familiar with Java EE and the backend, but he would love to talk more about the world of frontend, which consists mainly of JavaScript frameworks.

Packt is searching for authors like you

If you're interested in becoming an author for Packt, please visit `authors.packtpub.com` and apply today. We have worked with thousands of developers and tech professionals, just like you, to help them share their insight with the global tech community. You can make a general application, apply for a specific hot topic that we are recruiting an author for, or submit your own idea.

Table of Contents

Preface

The demand for modern and high performing web enterprise applications is growing rapidly. No more is a basic HTML frontend enough to meet customer demands. This book will be your one-stop guide to build outstanding enterprise web applications with Java EE and Angular. It will teach you how to harness the power of Java EE to build sturdy backends while applying Angular on the frontend. Your journey to building modern web enterprise applications starts here!

The book starts with a brief introduction to the fundamentals of Java EE and all the new APIs offered in the latest release. Armed with the knowledge of Java EE 8, you will go over what it's like to build an end-to-end application, configure database connection for JPA, and build scalable microservices using RESTful APIs running in Docker containers. Taking advantage of the Payara Micro capabilities, you will build an Issue Management System, which will have various features exposed as services using the Java EE backend. With a detailed coverage of Angular fundamentals, the book will expand the Issue Management System by building a modern single page application frontend. Moving forward, you will learn to fit both the pieces together, that is, the frontend Angular application with the backend Java EE microservices. As each unit in a microservice promotes high cohesion, you will learn different ways in which independent units can be tested efficiently.

Finishing off with concepts on securing your enterprise applications, this book is a hands-on guide for building modern web applications.

Who this book is for

If you are a Java developer wanting to update your knowledge on the latest Java EE trends and explore Angular, then you are at the right place. The book takes a pragmatic approach toward these concepts, while helping you explore the examples on your own.

By the end of this book, you'll be armed with knowledge to write high performance, secure Angular and Java EE applications.

What this book covers

Chapter 1, *What's in Java EE 8?*, walks us through the enhancements that make the Java Enterprise Edition (EE) 8 release an important one.

Chapter 2, *The CDI Advantage Combined with JPA*, covers the usage of JPA for modeling our domain objects and structuring our code with CDI's powerful set of services. This chapter will get us through the basics of JPA and CDI, which are fundamental to writing Java EE applications.

Chapter 3, *Understanding Microservices*, lets you step back and understand the broader picture of a solution before using it as a silver bullet for every problem. We explore some of the key fundamentals when implementing a microservice architecture while comparing it with its peers.

Chapter 4, *Building and Deploying Microservices*, helps us get our hands on to build our own services. Along the way, we look at the current solutions available, such as containers and frameworks, that help write scalable applications.

Chapter 5, *Java EE Becomes JSON Friendly*, JSON has made inroads into the Java EE world, finally making it a first-class citizen. Here, we cover the enhancements to JSON-P and look at the new standard JSON-B, both of which play an influential role for RESTful API development.

Chapter 6, *Power Your API with JAXRS and CDI*, covers these standards that are the most widely used ones for writing RESTful APIs. You will understand, how HTTP-centric mapping between URI and corresponding API classes, marked with annotations are used to work with this style.

Chapter 7, *Putting It All Together with Payara*, makes use of our knowledge of various Java EE capabilities. We build an end-to-end application based on a Microservice architecture. We not only write code but also document, run, and deploy it in Docker containers.

Chapter 8, *Basic TypeScript*, talks about how JavaScript rules the world of Web but does have its own challenges when writing complex client-side code. This chapter explores writing TypeScript code and its relation with JavaScript.

Chapter 9, *Angular in a Nutshell*, shows you how to leverage TypeScript and write single page applications in Angular. You will learn how to use Angular CLI and build components that make up an Angular application.

Chapter 10, *Angular Forms*, teaches the angular way of dealing with data submission, validation, capturing submitted value, and some rich features of Angular forms over the course of this chapter.

Chapter 11, *Building a Real-World Application*, helps us start building a frontend business application using our Angular skills. We explore the various facets of Angular templates and components that will be used to build an Issue Management System as a sample.

Chapter 12, *Connecting Angular to Java EE Microservices*, combines both worlds of Angular and Java EE as we put together the Issue Management System frontend and backend. We will look at how the HttpModule of Angular can be used for connecting to RESTful APIs.

Chapter 13, *Testing Java EE Services*, explores the fundamentals of testing and its relevance in an microservice architecture.

Chapter 14, *Securing the Application*, leverages token authentication for securing our frontend and backend application. This chapter goes over JSON Web Token and its usage in Angular and Java EE.

To get the most out of this book

The following is a descriptive list of the requirements to test all the codes in the book:

- **Hardware**: 64-bit machine with minimum 2 GB of RAM (4 GB preferred) and at least 5 GB of free disk space
- **Software**: JDK 8, Git, Maven, Payara Micro Server, Docker, Node, npm, Angular CLI
- **Oracle JDK 8**: All the codes are tested on Oracle JDK 8, but OpenJDK should work fine as well
- **Docker**: Docker CE and Docker Compose
- **More details**: Latest version of Git and Maven (Apache Maven 3.5 or above), Payara Micro 5 (`https://www.payara.fish/downloads`)

 The book is being written considering Java EE 8 and Payara. But a compatible/stable version of Payara for the latest EE 8, hasn't been released yet. So the code has been verified against Payara Micro 5 Alpha releases (`https://www.payara.fish/upstream_builds`)

Download the example code files

You can download the example code files for this book from your account at www.packtpub.com. If you purchased this book elsewhere, you can visit www.packtpub.com/support and register to have the files emailed directly to you.

You can download the code files by following these steps:

1. Log in or register at www.packtpub.com.
2. Select the **SUPPORT** tab.
3. Click on **Code Downloads & Errata**.
4. Enter the name of the book in the **Search** box and follow the onscreen instructions.

Once the file is downloaded, please make sure that you unzip or extract the folder using the latest version of:

- WinRAR/7-Zip for Windows
- Zipeg/iZip/UnRarX for Mac
- 7-Zip/PeaZip for Linux

The code bundle for the book is also hosted on GitHub at https://github.com/ PacktPublishing/Java-EE-8-and-Angular. We also have other code bundles from our rich catalog of books and videos available at https://github.com/PacktPublishing/. Check them out!

Download the color images

We also provide a PDF file that has color images of the screenshots/diagrams used in this book. You can download it here: https://www.packtpub.com/sites/default/files/ downloads/JavaEE8andAngular_ColorImages.pdf.

Conventions used

There are a number of text conventions used throughout this book.

CodeInText: Indicates code words in text, database table names, folder names, filenames, file extensions, pathnames, dummy URLs, user input, and Twitter handles. Here is an example: "AppModule is a root module with the @NgModule decorator that's used for defining a module."

A block of code is set as follows:

```
@NgModule({
    declarations: [ AppComponent, PositivePipe ],
    exports:      [ AppComponent ],
    imports:      [ BrowserModule, AppRoutingModule ],
    providers:    [ DashboardService ],
    bootstrap:    [ AppComponent]
})
export class AppModule { }
```

When we wish to draw your attention to a particular part of a code block, the relevant lines or items are set in bold:

```
this.stats = {
        bookings: 100,
        cancellations: 11,
        sales: 5000
    }
```

Any command-line input or output is written as follows:

```
ng new hello-ng-dashboard --routing
cd hello-ng-dashboard
```

Bold: Indicates a new term, an important word, or words that you see onscreen. For example, words in menus or dialog boxes appear in the text like this. Here is an example: "The page presents a form where you can specify the maven projects **Group ID**, **Artifact ID**, and **Dependencies**."

 Warnings or important notes appear like this.

 Tips and tricks appear like this.

Get in touch

Feedback from our readers is always welcome.

General feedback: Email `feedback@packtpub.com` and mention the book title in the subject of your message. If you have questions about any aspect of this book, please email us at `questions@packtpub.com`.

Errata: Although we have taken every care to ensure the accuracy of our content, mistakes do happen. If you have found a mistake in this book, we would be grateful if you would report this to us. Please visit `www.packtpub.com/submit-errata`, selecting your book, clicking on the Errata Submission Form link, and entering the details.

Piracy: If you come across any illegal copies of our works in any form on the Internet, we would be grateful if you would provide us with the location address or website name. Please contact us at `copyright@packtpub.com` with a link to the material.

If you are interested in becoming an author: If there is a topic that you have expertise in and you are interested in either writing or contributing to a book, please visit `authors.packtpub.com`.

Reviews

Please leave a review. Once you have read and used this book, why not leave a review on the site that you purchased it from? Potential readers can then see and use your unbiased opinion to make purchase decisions, we at Packt can understand what you think about our products, and our authors can see your feedback on their book. Thank you!

For more information about Packt, please visit `packtpub.com`.

1
What's in Java EE 8?

Java in general has enjoyed a successful run in the enterprise space for nearly two decades, but we all understand that being successful today doesn't guarantee success tomorrow. Businesses have become more demanding compared to how things used to be 10 years ago. The need for flexible, robust, and scalable solutions delivered over the internet using the web and mobiles is only growing. While Java addresses most of these needs, change is inevitable for it to adapt to newer challenges. Fortunately for Java, with a large community of developers around it, there are a plethora of tools, libraries, and architectural patterns being established to deliver solutions for these business complexities. Java EE standardizes these solutions and allows the Java developer to leverage his existing skills in building enterprise applications.

Just like a hammer can't be the solution for every problem, using the same technology stack can't be the solution to every business challenge. With the web becoming faster, there's been a rise in client-side frameworks that are very responsive. These web client frameworks rely on enterprise services to utilize the underlying business capabilities of an enterprise. Java EE enables teams to deliver cloud-ready solutions using architectural patterns such as microservices.

Java EE, which stands for Enterprise Edition, can be considered an umbrella specification for defining the entire Java EE platform. EE 8 is the latest specification, which itself relies upon several other specs and groups them together into a unified offering. These changes are meant to simplify, standardize, and modernize the technical stack used by developers to make them more productive in building next-generation applications.

The enterprise space for business applications has never been more vibrant than now. Java EE 8 brings with it newer APIs and improvements to existing ones. This chapter will try to provide you with a clear understanding of what this release train of Java comprises. There's a fair bit to cover, so brace yourself as we dive into the world of Java EE.

We will cover the following topics in this chapter:

- Improvements in EE 8
- Overview of Java SE 8
- CDI 2.0
- JSON Processing 1.1
- JSON Binding 1.0
- JAXRS 2.1
- Servlet 4.0
- JSF 2.3
- Bean Validation 2.0
- Java EE Security API 1.0

Improvements in EE 8

Java EE has always tried to move common infrastructure tasks to container-based models. In recent times, these have been further simplified, allowing for developers to focus on the business logic rather than worry about the ceremonious code necessities. Java EE 7 focused on WebSockets and JSON, which helped build HTML 5 support. Java EE 8 continues to build upon EE 7, with a focus on building modern cloud-ready web applications with ease of development in mind.

Here's a quick summary of changes for the impatient. But don't get overwhelmed, as we will be going over these in more detail in the follow-up sections. So, what has changed, you may ask? Well, let's begin with JSON. Just like you can process XML documents and map XML to objects or objects to XML, now you can do the same with JSON too by using JSON-P and JSON-B. Java EE 8 now supports HTTP/2 with the Servlet 4.0 update and brings with it some exciting options to use. REST APIs are only growing stronger; now we have the support for server-sent events and we can use concurrency utilities available with SE 8 along with a reactive client API. Authentication and authorization support gained a standard way of doing things with the introduction of the new Java EE Security API. Bean validation now leverages SE 8 features to extend its range of options. CDI is no longer confined to the boundaries of EE, as it's now going to be made available for SE as well, along with new capabilities such as `Async` events, observer ordering, and more.

In the next few sections to follow, we will go over these changes in more detail, and what they mean when building an application.

Overview of Java SE 8

One of the goals of Java EE 8 was better alignment with Java SE 8. SE 8 was a major update; it was released in March 2014 and brought with it some major changes to the language and APIs. Lambdas, streams, default methods, and functional-style programming were introduced and were the highlights of the release. With these capabilities, the method of writing code was no longer going to be the same. A few other noteworthy additions in this release were optionals, repeating annotations, the date/time APIs, type annotations, and CompletableFutures.

If you would like to dig deeper into this release, then considering reading a book specific to Java 8. Here, we will cover just enough for getting to grips with some of the language features.

Lambdas, streams, and default methods

Lambdas have been the biggest change in the language since generics were introduced in Java 5. This was a fundamental change that impacted many of the APIs to follow. Anonymous classes are very useful to pass code around, but they come at the cost of readability as they lead to some boilerplate code (think Runnable or ActionListener). Those wanting to write clean code that is readable and void of any boilerplate would appreciate what lambda expressions have to offer.

In general, lambda expressions can only be used where they will be assigned to a variable whose type is a functional interface. The arrow token (->) is called the **lambda operator**. A functional interface is simply an interface having exactly one abstract method:

```
Runnable run = new Runnable() {
    @Override
    public void run() {
        System.out.println("anonymous inner class method");
    }
};
```

With lambdas similar to those in the preceding code, the code can be rewritten as follows, where the empty parenthesis is used for the no args method:

```
Runnable runWithLambda = () -> System.out.println("hello lambda");
```

To understand some of the enhancements, let us look at an example. Consider the `Hero` class, which is a plain Java object with two properties, telling us the name of the `Hero` and whether the hero can fly or not. Well, yes there are a few who can't fly, so let's keep the flag around:

```java
class Hero {
    String name;
    boolean canFly;
    Hero(String name, boolean canFly) {
        this.name = name;
        this.canFly = canFly;
    }
    // Getters & Setters omitted for brevity
}
```

Now, it's typical to see code that iterates over a collection and does some processing with each element in the collection. Most of the methods would typically repeat the code for iterating over a list, but what varies is usually the condition and the processing logic. Imagine if you had to find all heroes who could fly and find all heroes whose name ends with man. You would probably end up with two methods—one for finding flying heroes and another for the name-based filter. Both these methods would have the looping code repeated in them, which would not be that bad, but we could do better. A solution is to use anonymous inner class blocks to solve this, but then it becomes too verbose and obscures the code readability. Since we are talking about lambdas, then you must have guessed by now what solution we can use. The following sample iterates over our `Hero` list, filtering the elements by some criteria and then processing the matching ones:

```java
List<String> getNamesMeetingCondition(List<Hero> heroList,
Predicate<Hero> condition) {
        List<String> foundNames = new ArrayList<>();
        for (Hero hero : heroList) {
            if (condition.test(hero)) {
                foundNames.add(hero.name);
            }
        }
        return foundNames;
}
```

Here, `Predicate<T>` is a functional interface new to Java 8; it has one abstract method called test, which returns a Boolean. So, you can assign a lambda expression to the `Predicate` type. We just made the condition a behavior that can be passed dynamically.

Given a list of `heroes`, our code can now take advantage of lambdas without having to write the verbose, anonymous inner classes:

```
List<Hero> heroes = Arrays.asList(
        new Hero("Hulk", false),
        new Hero("Superman", true),
        new Hero("Batman", false));

List<String> result = getNamesMeetingCondition(heroes, h -> h.canFly);
result = getNamesMeetingCondition(heroes, h -> h.name.contains("man"));
```

And finally, we could print the hero names using the new `forEach` method available for all collection types:

```
result.forEach( s -> System.out.println(s));
```

Moving onto streams, these are a new addition along with core collection library changes. The Stream interface comes with many methods that are helpful in dealing with stream processing. You should try to familiarize yourself with a few of these. To establish the value of streams, let's solve the earlier flow using streams. Taking our earlier example of the hero list, let's say we wanted to filter the heroes by the ability to fly and output the filtered hero names. Here's how its done in the stream world of Java:

```
heroes.stream().filter(h -> h.canFly)
             .map( h -> h.name)
             .forEach(s -> System.out.println(s));
```

The preceding code is using the `filter` method, which takes a `Predicate` and then maps each element in the collection to another type. Both `filter` and `map` return a stream, and you can use them multiple times to operate on that stream. In our case, we map the filtered `Hero` objects to the `String` type, and then finally we use the `forEach` method to output the names. Note that `forEach` doesn't return a stream and thus is also considered a terminal method.

If you hadn't noticed earlier, then look again at the previous examples in which we already made use of default methods. Yes, we have been using the `forEach` method on a collection which accepts a lambda expression. But how did they add this method without breaking existing implementations? Well, it's now possible to add new methods to existing interfaces by means of providing a default method with its own body. For collection types, this method has been defined in the `Iterable` interface.

These capabilities of Java 8 are now powering many of the EE 8 APIs. For example, the Bean Validation 2.0 release is now more aligned to language constructs such as repeatable annotations, date and time APIs, and optionals. This allows for using annotations to validate both the input and output of various APIs. We will learn more about this as we explore the APIs throughout the book.

CDI 2.0

What would the world be like if there was only a single object with no dependencies? Well, it certainly wouldn't be called object-oriented, to begin with. In programming, you normally have your objects depend on other objects. The responsibility of obtaining these other dependencies is owned by the owing object itself. In **Inversion of Control** (**IoC**), the container is responsible for handing these dependencies to the object during its creation. **Context and Dependency Injection** (**CDI**) allows us to set the dependencies on an object without having to manually instantiate them; a term often used to describe this is called **injection**. It does this with the added advantage of type-safe injection, so there's no string matching done to get the dependency, but instead its done based on the existing Java object model. Most of the CDI features have been driven by the community and input from expert group members. Many of the features in CDI have been influenced by a number of existing Java frameworks such as Seam, Guice, and Spring.

While Java EE developers have enjoyed this flexible yet powerful API, SE developers were deprived of it, as CDI was part of Java EE alone. That's changed since this version, as this powerful programming model is now going to be available for Java SE as well. As of the 2.0 release, CDI can be used in both Java SE and Java EE. To make use of CDI in SE, you can pick a reference implementation such as **Weld** to get started. CDI can be broken down into three parts:

- Core CDI
- CDI for Java SE
- CDI for Java EE

Given how important CDI has become to the Java EE platform, it's a key programming model to familiarize oneself with. It can be considered the glue between the other specifications and is heavily used in JAXRS and Bean Validation specs. It's important to note that CDI is not just a framework but a rich programming model with a focus on loose coupling and type safety. A reference implementation for CDI is Weld, which is an open source project developed by JBoss/Red Hat. The primary theme for this release was to add support for Java SE, as earlier versions were targeted specifically at Java EE alone. CDI provides contexts, dependency injection, events, interceptors, decorators, and extensions. CDI services provide for an improved life cycle for stateful objects, bound to well-defined contexts. Messaging between objects can be facilitated by using event notifications. If all this sounds a little overwhelming then don't worry, as we will be covering all of it and much more in the next chapter.

If there's any feature that might draw developers towards CDI, then that in all probability must be the event notification model of CDI. CDI events are pretty much what you would refer to as an implementation of the *observer pattern*. This feature largely influences the decoupling of code to allow for greater flexibility in object communication. When we talk about events in CDI, this mainly involves two functions; one is to raise an event and the other would be to catch an event. Now isn't that simple? Events can be synchronous or asynchronous in nature. Event firing is supported by the Event interface; the earlier version was only supported by firing synchronous events, but with the 2.0 release you can now fire async events as well. Now, in case you are wondering what this event is and why we would use it, an event is just a Java object that can be passed around. Consider a plain old Java object called LoginFailed. Based on a certain scenario or method invocation, we want to notify an observer of this event, what just happened. So, here's how you can put this together in code:

```java
public class LoginFailed {}

public class LoginController {
 @Inject Event<LoginFailed> loginFailedEvent;

 public void loginAttempt() {
  loginFailedEvent.fire(new LoginFailed());
 }

}
```

We will discuss the specifics of events and more in the next chapter, which is dedicated to CDI and JPA. For now, we have just scratched the surface of what CDI has to offer, but nevertheless this should serve as a good starting point for our journey into the exciting world of CDI-based projects.

JSON Processing 1.1

Most languages provide support for reading and writing text files. But when it comes to special types of documents such as XML, CSV, or JSON, processing requires handling them differently to traditional text files. Java has historically had support for XML-based, documents but the support for JSON was provided via third-party libraries. JSON itself is a lightweight data-interchange format which is a well documented standard and has become extremely successful; it has become the default format for many systems. Java had the support for processing XML documents using **Java API for XML Processing (JAXP)** and JSON-P, which was introduced in Java EE 7. You can now process JSON documents as well. So, JSON-P does for JSON what JAXP does for XML. The 1.1 version was an update to the earlier JSON-P specification called JSON-P 1.0. This was to keep it updated with the JSON IETF standards. While this might sound like the other JSONP (notice the lack of hyphen), which stands for JSON with Padding, this is *not* that. JSONP is a format used to deal with cross origin AJAX calls using GET, while JSON-**P** is the specification defined within Java EE, used for JSON Processing and written as JSON-P.

When dealing with any Java EE API, you would have a public API and a corresponding reference implementation. For JSON-P, here are some useful references:

JSON-P official web site	https://javaee.github.io/jsonp
JSR-374 page on the JCP site	https://jcp.org/en/jsr/detail?id=374
API and reference implementation	https://github.com/javaee/jsonp

The API includes support for parsing, generating, and querying JavaScript Object Notation data. This is made possible using the object model or the streaming model provided by the JSON-P API. You can consider this a low-level API, which is different to the higher level declarative JSON binding API which is also part of Java EE 8. The streaming model can be considered similar to StAX for XML for creating and reading JSON in a streaming manner, while the object model can be used to work with JSON, similar to DOM for XML.

Working with JSON documents

To get an understanding of how this works, consider the following JSON document saved in a file called demo.json (it can be any file), which contains an array of JSON objects with the name and priority key-value pairs:

```
[
  {
    "name": "Feature: Add support for X",
    "priority": 1
  },
  {
    "name": "Bug: Fix search performance",
    "priority": 2
  },
  {
    "name": "Feature: Create mobile page",
    "priority": 3
  }
]
```

Now, before looking at the API, it is important to understand how we need to perceive this JSON document. JSON defines only two data structures, one being an array that contains a list of values and the other an object that is just a name key-value pair. There are six value types in JSON, namely:

- String
- Number
- Object
- Array
- Boolean
- Null

In the previous document, the square brackets around the content denote an array that has multiple objects as its values. Let's take a look at the first JSON object, as follows:

```
{
  "name": "Feature: Add support for X",
  "priority": 1
}
```

The curly braces, { }, denote a JSON object that contains a key-value pair. The key must be a string in quotes followed by the value, which must be a valid JSON data type. In the previous case, we have the string in quotes, `"Feature: Add support for X"`, and this maps to a String data type. The value of the `"priority"` key is a number data type, given as 1. Since the value can be any JSON data type, you could also have nested objects and arrays as values of the JSON object. Here's an example of that, showing the `"ticket"` key having an array as its value, which contains objects:

```
{
  "name": "Feature: Add support for X",
  "priority": 1,
  "ticket": [
    {
      "name": "Feature: add new ticket",
      "priority": 2
    },
    {
      "name": "Feature: update a ticket",
      "priority": 2
    }
  ]
}
```

Having built an understanding of this document structure, let's look at the API.

JSON Processing API

JSON-P can be considered as having two core APIs:

`javax.json`	JSON Object Model API for a simpler way of working with JSON documents in memory.
`javax.json.stream`	JSON Streaming API, which parses a document and emits events without loading the entire document in memory.

Let's look at what the parsing API looks like when trying to parse the previous sample document. First we need to obtain a parser using the `Json` class. This class is a factory class for creating JSON processing objects:

```
JsonParser parser =
Json.createParser(Main.class.getResourceAsStream("/sample.json"));
```

Next, we use the returned `JsonParser` object to loop over all the entries using the `hasNext()` method, similar to an iterator, and in turn invoke the `next()` method, which emits a `JsonParser.Event` instance. This instance will hold the current JSON entry which can be a key or value:

```
while (parser.hasNext()) {
            JsonParser.Event e = parser.next();
            System.out.print(e.name());
            switch (e) {
                case KEY_NAME:
                    System.out.print(" - " + parser.getString());
                    break;
                case VALUE_STRING:
                    System.out.print(" - " + parser.getString());
                    break;
                case VALUE_NUMBER:
                    System.out.print(" - " + parser.getString());
            }
            System.out.println();
}
```

Using the preceding loop, we will be able to parse and examine each entry as we go through the entire document.

Apart from creating parsers using the `Json` class, we can also obtain a `JsonObjectBuilder` instance which is used to create JSON object models from scratch. A one line demo is shown as follows, and creates a `JsonObject`:

```
JsonObject json = Json.createObjectBuilder().add("name", "Feature
ABC").build();
```

More advanced usage is possible by nesting calls to the `add(...)` method, which we will look at later on. There have been many noteworthy enhancements with JSON-P 1.1, such as:

- **JSON Pointer**: Allows for finding specific values in a JSON document
- **JSON Patch**: Allows for modifying operations on a JSON document
- **JSON Merge Patch**: Allows for using patch operations with merge
- **Addition of JSON Collectors**: Allows for accumulating JSON values from streams

Additionally, `JsonReader` has a new method called `readValue()` which returns a JSON value from the underlying input source. Similarly, `JsonWriter` was updated with another new method called `write(JsonValue value)`, which allows for writing the JSON value to an output source. These additions were possible without breaking the earlier APIs because default methods were introduced in Java 8. We will go through more details about parsing and various other APIs in another chapter, but for now this should give you a starting point to begin exploring the APIs further.

JSON Binding 1.0

As the version number 1.0 suggests, this is one of the new additions to the Java EE specification group. It's also probably the most welcomed addition, as it brings with it the much awaited ability to bind any Java object to a JSON string in a standard way. As the predominant way of exchanging information is JSON, most developers would look for solutions to convert their APIs' input and output values to and from JSON. JSON-B does for JSON what JAXB did for XML—it acts as a binding layer for converting objects to JSON and JSON string to objects. While the default mapping mechanism should serve us well, we all know that there's always a need for customization. Thus, there are customization options available when the defaults aren't good enough for a use case. This can be done using annotations on your Java classes.

The **Yasson** project is the reference implementation for JSON-B. For JSON-B, here are some useful references:

JSON-B official web site	`https://javaee.github.io/jsonp`
JSR-367 page on the JCP site	`https://jcp.org/en/jsr/detail?id=367`
API and spec project	`https://github.com/javaee/jsonb-spec`
Yasson RI project	`https://github.com/eclipse/yasson`

One of the reasons why JAXB, and now JSON-B, are so popular is because they almost hide the complexity of working with the document. As a developer, you get to focus on the business objects or entities while letting these binding layers take care of the complexities of mapping an object to/from their document representation. The API provides a class called `Jsonb`, which is a high-level abstraction over the JSON Binding framework operations. There are mainly two operations that you would perform using this class; one is to read JSON input and deserialize to a Java object and the other is to write a JSON output by serializing an object. To get an instance of the `Jsonb` class, you need to obtain it from a `JsonbBuilder`. An example of its usage follows:

```
Jsonb jsonb = JsonbBuilder.create();
```

The builder also allows for passing in custom configurations that can change the processing behavior. Once you have obtained the `Jsonb` instance, you can use any of the `toJson` or `fromJson` overloaded methods for performing any operation. This instance is thread-safe and can be cached for reuse. Consider this sample to see the API in action:

```
class Ticket {
    public String name;
    public Integer priority;
}
```

Here are the lines of code required for converting Java objects to/from JSON:

```
Ticket t = new Ticket();
t.name = "Feature ABC";
t.priority = 2;

/* Create instance of Jsonb using builder */
Jsonb jsonb = JsonbBuilder.create();

/* Ticket to this  {"name":"Feature ABC","priority":2} */
String jsonString = jsonb.toJson(t);

/* {"name":"Feature ABC","priority":2} to a Ticket */
Ticket fromJson = jsonb.fromJson(jsonString, Ticket.class);
```

As you can see, this is very different to working with the JSON-P APIs, which are low-level. The JSON-B API allows for working with JSON with a much simpler API. There are times when you can even combine the two APIs (JSON-P and JSON-B) to perform certain operations. Imagine you are given a large JSON file from which you need to selectively extract a nested object to use that object in your code. You could use the JSON-P API and use the JSON Pointer to extract the needed object, and then later use JSON-B API to deserialize it to a Java object. When working with JSON, single object types aren't enough—you often run into a collection of objects that you need to work with. In our sample, think instead of one ticket. You may be reading and writing a collection of tickets. As you might expect, JSON-B has built-in support for collections too. As a matter of fact, it also supports generic collections for working with JSON. Generics, as you may recall, is for compile time type checking, but is implemented by the compiler using a technique called type erasure. Thus, the type information is not present at runtime. Hence, to correctly perform deserialization, the runtime type of the object needs to be passed to JSON-B.

JSON-B also offers some options in the form of compile time customization using annotations and runtime customization using the `JsonbConfig` class. The annotations can be placed on classes that you need to do the custom changes, and that's it. The customization options don't end there, though, as there might be times when you may not have access to the source code for some reason. In such cases, you can make use of an adapter, which allows for writing your custom code to perform the mapping; this allows more fine-grained control over data processing. These options are very handy for a developer to have at their disposal in today's age where JSON is prevalent.

JAXRS 2.1

Java EE has always been good at supporting various over the network communication options, right from binary RPC, XML-based RPC or now XML and JSON-based communication via JAXRS over HTTP/1 and HTTP/2 protocols. In recent times, REST-based web services have become the de facto choice for developing web APIs. There are broadly two standards that can be followed when developing web services, one being SOAP and the other REST. Initially, the SOAP-style APIs dominated the enterprise space and it seemed there was no room for any other, but the REST style had its own appeal. As mobile applications grew, so did the demand for server-side APIs. Clients required more flexibility and weren't exactly a fan of the verbosity of SOAP XMLs.

REST APIs are less strict and thus more flexible and simpler to use, which added to their appeal. While a SOAP document primarily focused on XML and had to conform to SOAP standards, REST APIs enjoyed the freedom of choice in terms of data format. The dominant choice of data format in REST for communication is JSON documents, but it can be XML too, or any other. The published APIs in REST are known as resources. There are suggested design guidelines when building a REST API, and while these aren't going to prevent you from doing it your way, its best to stick to the guidelines for the most part. Think of them as a design pattern, which you may follow. REST in itself is an architectural pattern and widely adopted in the industry.

JAXRS 2.0 was imagined as a single client request and a single server response. But with 2.1 and the underlying HTTP/2 updates, you can now think of single requests as having multiple responses. The new API update allows for non-blocking interceptors and filters as well.

A JAXRS project would typically have one or more resources along with some providers. Building a REST endpoint or resource, as they are called, is as simple as creating a class with a few annotations and writing a resource method. There will be one class to bootstrap the REST resources, and then you will define the actual resource and providers that are needed by your application. Bootstrapping is done by creating a subclass of the Application class, which serves to configure your REST resources. This is similar to the following snippet:

```java
/**
 * To bootstrap the REST APIs
 */
@ApplicationPath("/resources")
public class JaxrsActivator extends Application { }

@Path("heroes")
public class HeroResource {
    @GET
    @Path("{id}")
    public Hero getSingleHero(@PathParam("id") String id) {
        return new Hero(id);
    }
}
```

With those annotations added to the class, the `HeroResource` class has just been transformed into a REST resource. The class will be deployed within a web application (WAR file) and can be run locally on any JEE compliant server. As REST resources are accessed via `http(s)`, this resource will now be available at a URL, given its called **heroapp**. Notice that `/resources` is actually defined by the subclass of the `javax.ws.rs.core.Application` class. So, you define the prefix for all the REST endpoints using the `@ApplicationPath` annotation. Typically, naming conventions include `/api`, `/resources`, or `/rest`:

```
http://localhost:8080/heroapp/resources/heroes/1
```

The matching of request to resource methods is done internally by the container using an algorithm which is implementation specific, but the output is defined by the specification. What this means to a developer is that they can rely on the standards and not worry about different implementations.

In the 2.1 release, which was updated from the earlier JAXRS 2.0 version, came a Reactive Client API. The reactive style of programming is for the client side, which allows for a more reactive way of handling a request/response. This is not done by replacing the existing Client API, but instead by extending it to support this new style of programming. A noticeable change includes the `rx()` method on the Client Fluent API. Additionally, there's better async support as it embraces the concurrency features of Java 8. CDI updates have also been leveraged along with underlying Java 8 alignment. Server Sent Events is a popular web transport technique used for pushing one-way asynchronous updates to the browser. SSE is supported in both client and server APIs. With SSE, it's possible to have a communication channel kept open from the server to the clients, such that subsequent communications from the server to connected clients can be sent. With SSE and WebSocket its time to stop polling. While polling occasionally isn't that bad an idea, there are better alternatives at our disposal. Polling in general adds to unnecessary resource usage and undue complexity, which we can avoid now. The growing need for a real-time push has led to new standards such as SSE, which is an HTTP-based solution for one-sided communication and WebSockets an exciting standard allowing for bidirectional communication between both client and server.

The idea of SSE can be applied whenever a client needs to subscribe to updates from the server, such as a stock quote update that the server may send to the client when there's any change in the price. WebSockets, on the other hand, can be used for more complex use cases as it supports two-way communication, such as messaging or collaboration tools which require updates going in both directions. Needless to say, these can be used to replace the age old polling solutions that always fall short. Now that we understand the differences between SSE and WebSockets, it's also worth noting that HTTP/2 Push is unrelated to the two. Simply put, HTTP/2 Push is a mechanism to push assets to the web browser in advance to avoid multiple round trips.

JAXRS uses *Providers,* which are classes that you annotate with the `@Provider` annotation. These classes are discovered at runtime and can be used to register filters, interceptors, and more. You may think of these as layers that sit between the originating request and your REST resource. These can be used to intercept the incoming request and thus allow for applying any cross-cutting concerns across the application. Now, this is a good idea to make use of given it promotes the separation of concerns. Imagine polluting your code with redundant checks or validations for each request, which are part of the infrastructure or protocol-related logic. This feature allows us to separate the infrastructure code from the actual business logic that your component should focus on. We will go over more details in the later chapters, but this should serve as a good reference regarding what JAXRS has to offer.

Servlet 4.0

For the majority of developers, this may not impact the way you write servlet code, but it does offer some performance benefits along with new abilities such as server push. HTTP/2.0 is a binary protocol based on frames and is the new standard for the web. HTTP/2 standard was approved around February 2015 and is supported by most modern day browsers. While the web has been evolving at a fast pace, the same can't be said about HTTP itself. For years, developers had to work around the limitations of HTTP 1.x, but the wait is finally over, as this version has better alignment with modern day demands. Some of the HTTP/2 benefits include the ability to reuse the same TCP connection for multiple requests, more compressed header information, priority and packet streaming, and server push to send resources from the server to the client. This results in reduced latency with faster content downloads. For the uninformed, this change won't be a crucial change and your applications will continue to function as they did before with the added benefit of faster performance.

So, there are no new HTTP methods and no new headers or URL changes that you need to worry about. Since Java EE servlets are primarily based on the HTTP protocol, it was only logical for it to get updated to meet the changes in the HTTP standards. The 4.0 update is mainly focused on adding support for the HTTP/2.0 standard, and thus is a 100% compliant implementation for the HTTP/2 specification. What this update should bring with it is increased performance.

Some of the features of HTTP/2 are:

- Request/response multiplexing (bi-directional support)
- Optimized headers (uses HPACK header compression)
- Binary frames (this solves the HOL blocking problem present in HTTP/1.1)
- Server Push
- Stream prioritization
- Upgrade from HTTP/1.0

Servlet 4.0 serves as an abstraction of the underlying protocol, allowing us to focus on the high-level APIs that shield us from the intricacies of HTTP. It's also interesting to note that the servlet specification itself is relied upon by other specs, such as JSF, which will be utilizing these updates to their benefit. Typically, you can think of an HTTP request/response cycle as one request and one response, but that just changed. Now one request can be used to send out multiple responses. To put this into perspective, remember the earlier workarounds of HTTP 1.1, such as domain sharding or where we tried to save multiple requests in order to reduce the TCP connection overhead, such as using CSS Sprites (one image combined with multiple images), well that's no longer needed.

Server Push

There's a new **Push builder API** that can be used for server push features. Armed with the server push ability, a server can push a resource to the client. This doesn't mean that there's no request needed in the first place. You need to obtain a `PushBuilder` from the request object and then use this for constructing a push request. Thus, there's always a request, based on which, the push feature is enabled.

A sample of this is as follows:

```
PushBuilder pushBuilder = httpServletRequest.newPushBuilder();
```

Once a `pushBuilder` instance is obtained from the request, you can use it to set the required URI path, which is to be used for sending the push request. A sample is shown here:

```
request.newPushBuilder()
.path("/assests/images/product.png")
.push();
```

Here, the paths beginning with / are considered absolute paths. Without the / prefix, the path would be considered to be relative to the context of the request used to create the instance of `PushBuilder`. While the short code shown here is handy, it must be used with caution since there's a possibility that the call to `newPushBuilder()` may return `null` if push is not supported.

If you are wondering how we put that `newPushBuilder` method on the request object, remember that Java 8 has default methods. So, the signature of the method looks like the following:

```
default PushBuilder newPushBuilder()
```

Building a push request involves setting the request method to GET and setting the `path` explicitly, as that won't be set by default. Calling the `push` method generates the push request from the server and sends it to the client, unless the push feature is not available for some reason. You may add headers or query strings to the push request by using the `addHeader` or `queryString` methods.

With the preceding code, the server will send a push to the client that made this request. The client may already have the resource and thus can tell the server that it has this cached from a previous request, and in turn will inform the server to not bother sending this resource over the wire. You might have guessed by now that it's the client who can dictate whether a resource should be pushed or not. Thus, the client can explicitly disable the server push.

Let's imagine we need to push the logo to the client from our servlet. Here's how we might write this code:

```
protected void processRequest(HttpServletRequest request,
    HttpServletResponse response)
        throws ServletException, IOException {
    PushBuilder pushBuilder = request.newPushBuilder();
    if (pushBuilder != null) {
        pushBuilder.path("images/logo.png")
            .addHeader("Content-Type", "image/png")
            .push();
```

```
    }
    try (PrintWriter writer = response.getWriter();) {
        writer.write(new StringBuilder()
                .append("<html><body>")
                .append("<img src='images/logo.png'>")
                .append("</body></html>").toString());
    }
}
```

The Servlet API already provides Java SE 9 support for HTTP/2. There's broadly just two classes, `HttpRequestGroup` and `HttpRequest`. These are just enough to solve the most common use cases but not exhaustive enough to replace a more established HTTP client library. It will support both the earlier HTTP/1 version along with the newer HTTP/2 version.

JSF 2.3

There has been a rise in frontend frameworks, and these have competed with each other to become dominant frameworks for the web. **JavaServer Faces** (**JSF**), while it isn't the new kid on the block, still has a fairly large community and is the primary framework in the Java EE space for building UIs, which makes it a force to be reckoned with.

JSF is the standard user interface for building applications with Java EE. It takes a component-based approach to building the UI, which is different to the traditional request-based model. While it has been around for over a decade, it didn't gain much traction, arguably, until the 2.x release. There have been supporting frameworks and libraries built around JSF, and thus it enjoys good community support. Frameworks such as **PrimeFaces**, **RichFaces**, and **IceFaces**, along with libraries such as **OmniFaces** and more, have made it a popular choice among developers. That doesn't mean there aren't any critics; a framework this old is bound to have an opinionated community. With new client-side solutions making their mark, including **Angular** and **React**, the competition has only grown tougher. That's good news for developers, as it leads to a richer selection of choices for building your next web application.

The latest update of 2.3 brings with it many enhancements and refinements and makes it aligned with Java 8. Some of the major features include:

- CDI integration, which makes it easy for injecting JSF artefacts into classes and EL expressions
- The confusion of Managed Bean annotations is finally resolved
- Supports Java 8 date/time APIs

- `f:websocket`, which allows for easy usage of the WebSocket protocol
- Validation and conversion enhancements
- Lots of API updates and fixes

When writing a JSF application, its fairly routine to obtain references to certain context-based objects. Earlier versions didn't have any easy way to obtain these, and developers had to look up the instances by using some statically chained methods, such as the following:

```
FacesContext.getCurrentInstance().getExternalContext(). [ get request map,
get request header map, and more get stuff]
```

This issue is solved by CDI, as it allows for injecting these artefacts directly in your classes. Additionally, it's also possible to use these via the EL expression. All of this is possible because JSF now provides some default providers for common use cases. A few handy ones are listed in the following table:

Before	EL variable available	Using Inject
`FacesContext.getCurrentInstance()`	`#{facesContext}`	`@Inject` `FacesContext` `facesContext;`
`FacesContext.getCurrentInstance()` `.getExternalContext()` `.getRequestMap();`	`#{requestScope}`	`@Inject` `@RequestMap` `Map<String, Object>` `map;`
`FacesContext.getCurrentInstance()` `.getExternalContext()` `.getRequestHeaderMap();`	`#{header}`	`@Inject` `@HeaderMap` `Map<String, Object>` `map;`
`FacesContext.getCurrentInstance()` `.getExternalContext()` `.getRequestParameterMap();`	`#{param}`	`@Inject` `@RequestParameterMap` `Map<String, Object>` `map;`

It's important to note that the general reference types, such as Map or others, would require specifying a qualifier (RequestMap, HeaderMap, and so on), to assist in resolving the required type. With CDI integration support, it's also possible to inject your own custom validator and converter, too.

JSF 2.0 brought it's own set of annotations, but as soon as CDI arrived, those annotations had to be revisited. Since CDI has universal appeal in terms of managed beans, it conflicts with JSF's own annotations. It was finally decided with the 2.3 release to deprecate the JSF defined annotations in favour of the more flexible and universal CDI annotations. Thus, Managed Bean annotations were deprecated in favor of CDI annotations.

There's support for Java 8 date/time APIs in the 2.3 release, with an update to the existing converter tag, called `<f:convertDateTime>`. The `type` attribute now takes more values along with earlier ones, such as both, `date`, `time`, `localDate`, `localTime`, `localDateTime`, `offsetTime`, `offsetDateTime`, and `zonedDateTime`. If we have a bean with a `LocalDate` property, then the same can be referenced in the facelets view, as follows:

```
<h:outputText value="#{ticketBean.createdDate}">
    <f:convertDateTime type="localDate" pattern="MM/dd/yyyy" />
</h:outputText>
```

The WebSocket protocol offering full bi-directional communication support, as well as developers wanting to utilize these abilities, has led to the inclusion of web socket integration in JSF standard. It's now possible to register a WebSocket with the client using the `f:websocket` tag, pushing messages to the client from the server using `PushContext`. You can get this running with very little code; all you need to do is name the channel, which is a required attribute for this tag, and then register a JavaScript callback listener through the `onmessage` attribute. That's it for the client side. This callback would be invoked once the server sends a message to the client. In case you are wondering, the message is encoded as JSON and sent to the client. Here are a few snippets to help you understand this better.

This is the JSF view part, which registers the WebSocket:

```
<f:websocket channel="jsf23Channel"
onmessage="function(message){alert(message)}" />
```

Then, on the server side, the `PushContext` is injected and later used for sending the push messages to the client:

```
@Inject @Push
private PushContext jsf23Channel;

public void send() {
    jsf23Channel.send("hello websocket");
}
```

A few other enhancements include support for importing constants for page authors using the `<f:importConstants/>` tag. Also, there will be support for the `c:forEach` method of iteration using `ui:repeat`. While we are on the iterating point, it's worth mentioning that support for map-based iteration has also been added, and this means you can now use `ui:repeat`, `c:forEach`, and `h:dataTable` to iterate over the entries in a map. The `@FacesDataModel` annotation allows for supplying your own custom registrable `DataModel` objects that can then be used in `ui:repeat` or `h:dataTable`. This can be utilized by library providers to add more flexibility to their components. An example of `ui:repeat` using a map is shown here:

```
<ui:repeat var="anEntry" value="#{ticketMapOfFeatures}">
    key: #{anEntry.key} - value: #{anEntry.value}
</ui:repeat>
```

AJAX method calls are now supported—you can invoke a `JavaScript` method which in turn will invoke a server-side bean method in an Ajax call. Those familiar with the PrimeFaces `p:remoteCommand` can relate to this feature, with the difference being that it's included as a standard now. This can be done using the `h:commandScript` component tag. Similar to invoking the server-side code from JavaScript, you can also invoke JavaScript from server-side code as well, which is made possible using API enhancement. This is done by referencing the `PartialViewContext` and invoking the `getEvalScripts` method for adding your JavaScript code to the response. With so many additions, JSF has once again become worth adding to a developers arsenal when building web applications for Java EE.

Bean Validation 2.0

With the advent of so many technical choices such as microservices, rich front end applications, data stores like NoSQL, and a plethora of systems always communicating with each other and exchanging data, it's vital to get the data validation done right. There's a growing need for data validation services; most APIs typically have some input and output as part of their contract. The input and output are usually the candidates for applying some validation on.

Imagine you are trying to register a user in the system but the client didn't send the username or email which was required by your business logic. You would want to validate the input against the constraints defined by your application. In an HTML-based client, if you were building a HTML form, you would want the input to meet certain criteria before passing it down for further processing. These validations might be handled in the client-side and/or in your server-side processing. Validation is such a common requirement for any API that there's room for standardizing these constraints and applying them in an intuitive way on your APIs. Bean Validation specification defines a set of built-in validations that can be used on your APIs in a declarative way using annotations. It would be naive to think this covers every possible case, thus there's a way to use your own custom validators when the built-in ones just won't do.

As you might have guessed, this kind of validation is not only restricted to JAXRS web services but can be applied across various specs such as JSF, JPA, CDI and even third-party frameworks such as **Spring**, **Vaadin**, and many more. Bean Validation allows for writing expressive APIs with constraints defined in a declarative manner, which get validated on invocation.

Now, if you are familiar with the earlier version, then you might be wondering what's changed in 2.0. Well, the main driving factor for the 2.0 release involved leveraging the language changes brought in by Java 8 for the purpose of validation. We have new types, such as `LocalTime` or `LocalDate`, as well as the possibility to repeat annotations or use lambda expressions. So, an update to support and leverage these changes was only logical.

Let's assume we have a REST resource (web service) that takes a team as input to be added into the system and outputs the updated list of teams. Here, we want a name to be provided for a team and this can't be null. So, here's the code for doing just that:

```
public class Team {
      private Long id;
      //NotNull suggest the name of a team can't be null
      @NotNull
      private String name;
      //Rest of the code can be ignored
      ...
}

@Path("teams")
public class TeamResource {
      /* A method to add new team, which requires the input
       of Team to be Valid
      */
      @POST
      @Produces(MediaType.APPLICATION_JSON)
```

```
public List add(@Valid Team team) {
  //Rest of the code can be ignored
  ...
}
}
```

Let's assume we have the preceding JAXRS resource running on a server. If you invoke this API and supply team data as input, then it must have a name in order for the input to pass the validation constraint. In other words, valid team input has the name field satisfying the NotNull constraint. Similarly, it's possible to put a constraint on the result as well. A rewritten method signature is shown as follows, which puts a NotNull constraint on the response:

```
@POST
@Produces(MediaType.APPLICATION_JSON)
public @NotNull List<Team> add(@Valid Team team) { ... }
```

With Bean Validation 2.0, a whole new set of possibilities have been added. One of the biggest features is validating collections. It's now possible to validate the contents of a type-safe collection. We could, for instance, add type annotations to validate the contents of generic collections such as List<@NotNull Team>, or even better, List<@NotNull @Valid Team>:

```
@POST
@Produces(MediaType.APPLICATION_JSON)
public @NotNull List<@NotNull @Valid Team> add(@Valid Team team)
{ ... }
```

You could also use the @Email annotation on a collection like this, List<@Email String>, to ensure the emails present within the list are conforming to the email validation constraint. The API also allows you to supply your own regex to validate the input. Also, it's interesting to note that @Email validation doesn't mean the value cannot be null. What it means is that if a string is present, then it must be a valid email but can be null, too. It's best to separate concerns from the core validation of the email and the NotNull validation for the input.

A few more examples are:

- List<@Positive Integer> positiveNumbers;
- Map<@Valid Team, @Positive Integer> teamSizeMap;

In the preceding example, we want our map to have valid team instances as the key, and the value must be a positive integer:

```
@Size(max=10)
private List<String> only10itemsWillBeAllowed;
```

In the preceding case, we want to have a list containing a maximum of 10 items.

A more complex case would be validating a player list with a maximum of 11, and each player must be a valid instance. Valid would mean meeting all validation constraints put on a player class:

```
@Size(max=11)
private List<@Valid Player> players;
```

The preceding constraints provide for a very natural way to put constraints declaratively on your code, which is much more readable and closer to the definition where it's used.

Another way of validating a collection of items is to put the validation constraint near the type parameter. So, while both the following approaches would work, the latter is preferred:

```
@Valid
private List<Player> players;
```

It can also be:

```
private List<@Valid Player> players; //Preferred
```

Now, Bean Validation also makes use of the Optional class, where you can put validation on the type it holds. For example:

```
public Optional<@Valid Team> getTeam() { ... }
```

A few more built-in constraints worth checking out are @NotBlank, @Future, @Past, @Negative, @Pattern, @Min, and @Max. By default, the Bean Validation API has very nice integration with key life cycle events of other specifications. This allows for all of the validation to happen at key stages of an object's life cycle, such as that of JPA or JSF managed beans.

Java EE Security API 1.0

Security, while arguably not close to every developer's heart, sooner or later becomes a critical topic that needs attention. In Java EE, security has generally been supported by servers and also provided by third-party solutions. This is also one of the reasons why Java EE security is considered confusing or non-portable at times. Security is not something new to any of us, and put simply, web applications in general need to establish the identity of the user and then decide if the user is allowed to see or perform an operation. This is called **authentication** and authorization of resources. Security has evolved over the years from simple form-based authentication or BASIC auth to LDAP and OAuth-based solutions.

If you are wondering why there's a need for security standards in Java EE, then couple of reasons are to standardize the security mechanism and avoid vendor-specific configurations when working with security, as well as meeting modern day demands. This being a new specification and owing to various other reasons, the specification doesn't change things drastically but instead will be focusing on standardization of existing security features offered by various Java EE vendors. To ensure what is already out there doesn't break, the enhancements have been modified to provide alternative options when configuring security, rather than replacing what might already be in use.

This initiative will simplify the API by allowing for sensible defaults where applicable, and will not require server configuration changes, which becomes a challenge with today's PaaS or cloud-based delivery models. Another feature is using annotation defaults and integration with other specs such as CDI. There is now an API for authentication and authorization, along with an identity store API. An identity store can take the form of a database, LDAP, or some other custom store. If you haven't heard of LDAP, then its just a protocol to access data from a directory server which basically stores users. From an API perspective, `IdentityStore` would be an abstraction of a user store. This would be used by `HttpAuthenticationMechanism` implementations to authenticate users and find their groups. Here, a group is used to denote a role to which the user belongs, but unlike a role, think of a group as a more flexible option to map users in and out of. There will be two methods provided by the `IdentityStore` API:

- `validate(Credential)`
- `getGroupsByCallerPrincipal(CallerPrincipal)`

Support may be provided for either one or both based on the underlying implementation. So, if the implementation only supports authentication but not authorization then only the `validate(Credential)` method would be supported.

The feature list also includes additions related to password aliasing and role mapping and excludes CDI support. The reference implementation for security in Java EE is provided by the project Soteria.

The link to GitHub project is `https://github.com/javaee-security-spec/soteria`.

Summary

We have covered quite a few aspects of the Java EE 8 release train, while catching up on new and existing changes. As a developer working on Java EE solutions, these capabilities provide a big boost to one's productivity. The growing adoption of REST APIs with JSON as its preferred data-interchange format has led to better support of JSON in the platform. JSON now enjoys the same status as XML for support in Java EE. The widely used Servlets API has been updated to be aligned with the HTTP/2 standards and its offerings. Other noteworthy enhancements include updates to JAXRS, JSF, WebSockets, Server-Sent Events, and a new reactive client API for JAXRS. Many of these APIs are influenced by Java 8 changes, which have played an influential role in updates.

CDI standard is now very well integrated in all the other specifications offered by Java EE. The influence of CDI is not limited to EE alone, and it's a welcome entry into Java SE as well. Bean Validation updates have made constraint additions to code an ease to work with. Additionally, there have been maintenance updates to existing APIs and new additions including Java security and JSON-B, which are now available under the umbrella spec of Java EE.

2
The CDI Advantage Combined with JPA

In this chapter, we will go over CDI, which has become a ubiquitous API for dependency injection and context management in Java EE. We will be looking at the new CDI 2.0 features along with the earlier ones, which are shipped with Java EE 8. Having completed the CDI journey, we will move onto the standard persistence solution, **Java Persistence API (JPA)** for Java applications.

The topics covered will be:

- The CDI programming model:
    - CDI for Java SE 8
    - RequestContext activation
    - Event enhancements:
        - Asynchronous events
        - Ordered events
    - Annotation Literals
- JPA:
    - Entities
    - Performing CRUD operations with entities
    - Entity listeners
    - Validations in entities

Introduction to context and dependency injection

CDI caters to a very fundamental design idea, as that of dependency injection. When writing any application, you would typically define multiple classes and some relationship between them. Thus, to work with one object you would need to hand it its dependencies during its creation. When using CDI, these dependencies are provided to the object, rather than the owning object fetching them for itself. **Dependency Injection** (**DI**) leads to the owning object becoming independent of the dependency creation and lookup code, which makes it loosely coupled, and the code is testable. Both qualities, while difficult to pull off, are worth striving for.

Now, before we get into the nuts and bolts of CDI and how it helps to structure the code, let's explore what dependency injection is and what problems it helps solve with an example. Consider a business scenario where we are building an issue management system. It will facilitate collaboration between all members to look at various issue tickets that have been created in the system and work on them as tasks. To begin with, we will have a `Task` class which holds the current ticket number. To obtain this ticket number, we need to somehow reach into the database and fetch the latest ticket that was assigned to a user. Here's what the `Task` class looks like:

```
public class Task {
    private String ticketId;
    private String status;

    public Task(User member) {
        DataSource ds = DatabaseResource.getDS();
        TicketPersistence ticketPersistence =
                new TicketPersistence(ds);
        this.ticketId = ticketPersistence
                .getLatestAssignedTicket(member);
    }
}
```

Now, this code is fairly simple to read as it takes a `User` instance during the `Task` construction and fetches the `ticketId` value from the database. But in order to get the `ticketId`, which is what the `Task` class really needs, it has to obtain an instance of the `TicketPersistence` class, which requires a `DataSource` for the lookup of the latest assigned ticket. There are quite a few things which aren't quite right about this code. Spend a minute thinking about what you think is not right, then have a look at the points listed here:

- The instantiation of a `Task` has multiple dependencies, such as `DataSource` and `TicketPersistence` class, making its construction complex.
- The testing of a `Task` class would require setting up all the dependencies as well, such as passing a `User` as a dummy object and setting up a test database for the `DataSource`. But we are still left with using the real `TicketPersistence`, which can't be swapped.
- The `Task` class knows too much about `TicketPersistence` and its internal dependency on a `DataSource`, while all it really wanted was the `ticketId`.
- There may be other code that requires a `Task` object to be passed, such as a `TaskStatusReport` class, which simply checks the status of a `Task` class for reporting. Here, `TaskStatusReport` doesn't care about the `ticketId`, yet it has to deal with the complexity of the `Task` creation, which occurs due to the `ticketId` property.

Whenever the instantiation of an object becomes complex due to either a constructor or static block initialisers, it hinders the testability of such objects. As a first step, we could certainly move the construction of dependencies to some kind of factory class and then pass the objects required to `Task`. Here's a refactored constructor of the `Task` class:

```
public Task(User member, TicketPersistence ticketPersistence) {
        this.ticketId = ticketPersistence
                      .getLatestAssignedTicket(member);
}
```

While this is better than the earlier code, this would still leave us with the option of passing both the `User` and `TicketPersistence` dependencies as mocks in order to test a `Task`. Knowing that neither `User` nor `TicketPersistence` is actually being saved as local field members of the `Task` class for referencing later, we can do away with these as well. A cleaner and testable `Task` code looks like the following:

```
public class Task {
     private String ticketId;
     private String status;
```

```
public Task(String latestTicket) {
    this.ticketId = latestTicket;
}
```

With the preceding code, it's much easier to work with a `Task` object. Instead of concerning itself with how to look up the `ticketId` value from the database, this code is asking for what it needs, which is the `ticketId` value. The responsibility of looking up the `ticketId` value from some repository can be moved to a factory or builder, or even a DI. The two key points to take away from the preceding example are:

- Ask for a dependency rather than getting it yourself
- Don't use an intermediate object to get to the object that you really want

Going back to our `Task` class, which did have dependency on `TaskPersistence`, the same could have been injected into the `Task` class or a even a `Factory`, with the following code as a part of applying DI:

```
@Inject TaskPersistence persistence;
// Field injection
```

The following code could also be used:

```
@Inject Task(TaskPersistence persistence) { ... }
//Constructor injection
```

Here, DI (CDI) would create an instance of `TaskPersistence` and inject it into the calling object, in this case `Task` would be provided as its dependency. Notice the type of object injected is `TaskPersistence`, as that's the simplest form of injection.

When talking about dependency injection, another term that comes up is **Inversion of Control (IoC)**. It simply means to delegate the responsibility of finding the dependency to another piece of code or container, which injects the object being asked for. Having given you an understanding of dependency injection, let's explore CDI and how it helps to write code when you do have dependencies to work with.

CDI programming model

This programming model unifies the various approaches taken by existing dependency injection frameworks such as Spring, Guice, and Seam. It has been designed considering the scope of objects as well. CDI was introduced in Java EE 6, and now with Java EE 8, we have the latest CDI 2.0 version, which offers Java SE support as well. While Java EE 5 did make resource injection possible, it did not have the support for general purpose dependency injection for objects. With CDI, we have beans that are container managed, and these managed beans are **Plain Old Java Objects (POJOs)** whose life cycle is controlled by the Java EE container. The idea of the bean has been presented in Java for ages in various forms, such as JSF bean, EJB bean, and so on. CDI takes this idea and provides a unified view to managed beans across the entire Java platform, which is relied on by every other specification including JSF, EJB, Servlet, JPA, and more. This allows you to take advantage of this specification together with the services offered by other Java EE specifications. While writing a trivial application, you may not find the benefits of DI appealing enough, but the moment your code grows, as well as its dependencies, it can certainly benefit from using CDI.

While CDI can be used in both SE and EE environments, there are few considerations to be noted for its usage in the Java EE environment, which is component-based. CDI enhances the EJB model by providing contextual life cycle management. While session beans can be injected into other beans, the same can't be said for message driven Beans and entity beans as they are considered non-contextual objects. Since CDI allows for defining any bean with a name, this feature allows you to reference the bean in JSF applications as well.

This specification defines five built-in scopes, which are:

- RequestScoped
- SessionScoped
- ApplicationScoped
- ConversationScoped
- DependentScoped

It's also possible to define custom scopes if needed using portable extensions. Apart from contextual scopes, we get a flexible event notification model and the ability to use interceptors for cross-cutting concerns and decorators.

It's not possible to cover all of what CDI has to offer in a single chapter, but we will go through enough features to be proficient in utilizing CDI to our advantage. Those wanting to explore further can do so by looking up the references mentioned later ahead.

A few of the services offered by CDI are listed here:

- Type-safe dependency injection with the ability to swap a dependency for another during deployment using metadata placed in XML
- EL expression integration to allow for resolving beans in JSF or JSP pages.
- Addition of interceptor bindings and decorators
- Powerful event notification model which makes use of the observer pattern
- Ability to extend CDI with portable extensions using its **Service Provider Interface (SPI)**

CDI for Java SE 8

The 2.0 version does not mark the start of using CDI in SE, as that support was already provided in a non-standard way. Both Apache **OpenWebBeans** and **Weld** did support the SE mode, and these have been standardized now for use with CDI in Java SE. There are also other projects that support CDI such as **Apache DeltaSpike**, which offers portable extensions that are handy features for Java developers.

To get started, you can create a Maven project and declare a dependency on a CDI implementation such as JBoss Weld. If Maven isn't your cup of tea, you can use other means to get the `weld-se-core` library added to your standalone SE project. Your `pom.xml` should have a dependency declaration, as shown here:

```
<dependency>
      <groupId>org.jboss.weld.se</groupId>
      <artifactId>weld-se-core</artifactId>
      <version>3.0.0.Final</version>
</dependency>
```

Additionally, create a `beans.xml` file located under `src/main/resources/META-INF/`, with the following contents:

```
<?xml version="1.0" encoding="UTF-8"?>
<beans xmlns="http://xmlns.jcp.org/xml/ns/javaee"
      xmlns:xsi="http://www.w3.org/2001/XMLSchema-instance"
      xsi:schemaLocation="http://xmlns.jcp.org/xml/ns/javaee
      http://xmlns.jcp.org/xml/ns/javaee/beans_2_0.xsd"
      bean-discovery-mode="all">
</beans>
```

From an API perspective, this library provides an implementation of CDI 2.0, and its basic dependency graph is shown here for a maven project named **cdi2-se-app** (a few additional dependencies have not been shown to keep it simple):

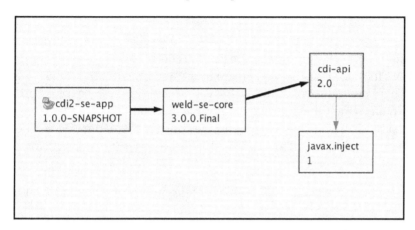

With the `weld-se-core` library added, we can now begin writing a CDI powered application.

Let's look at some sample code of the CDI in action:

```
public class BootCDI {
    public void doSomething() {
        System.out.println("do something called");
    }

    public static void main(String... args) {
        try (SeContainer container = SeContainerInitializer
                        .newInstance().initialize()) {
            BootCDI appInstance = container
                            .select(BootCDI.class)
                            .get();
            appInstance.doSomething();
        }
    }
}
```

The `SeContainerInitializer.newInstance().initialize()` call starts up the CDI container. This returns an `SeContainer` instance, which is our handle to the CDI container. This class also allows for some basic looking up of beans without having to go through the underlying `BeanManager`. As we used *try-with-resources*, the container resource will be closed at the end of the `try` block.

The `select` method on the `SeContainer` instance will obtain the `BootCDI` bean instance in a type-safe manner by returning an `Instance<BootCDI>` object, which is further used to get the dynamically returned object of `BootCDI` type. That's all it takes to boot up CDI in your SE application in a standard way.

The `SeContainerInitializer.newInstance()` also allows programmatic configuration by invoking methods such as `addPackages` and `disableDiscovery` to restrict the runtime behavior to only look for classes that you are interested in, without having to work with `beans.xml`. There are more possibilities that can be configured by exploring the APIs of the `Weld` container, allowing for a highly configurable environment. Dependency injection itself can be achieved by simply using `@Inject` in the code for the dependency. The annotation can be used on method, constructor, and field. This allows setter, constructor, and field injection support respectively.

We can now use classes such as `Task` with annotations, binding them to well-defined contexts such as `ApplicationScoped`, `SessionScoped`, or `RequestScoped`. The `Task` class in turn can use a constructor-based dependency on `TaskPersistence`, which will be injected by the CDI. The scope of `TaskPersistence` will be bound to the scope of the `Task` bean. If `Task` is declared as `ApplicationScoped`, then the dependency of `TaskPersistence` is bound to the scope of `Task`, which is the owning object in this situation. Thus, multiple calls to retrieve the `Task` bean would return the same `Task` instance along with the same `TaskPersistence` object as its dependency. Here's what the refactored `Task` using the CDI looks like:

```
class TaskPersistence {
  //Code omitted for brevity
}

@ApplicationScoped
public class Task {
    private final TaskPersistence persistence;
    @Inject Task(TaskPersistence persistence) {
        this.persistence = persistence;
    }
    //Rest of the code omitted for brevity
    ...
}
```

If an application code directly uses the `new` operator to instantiate a bean, then no parameters or dependencies are injected for that bean and its life cycle is not managed by the container.

RequestContext Activation

When we talk about context in Java EE, we are presented with various options, such as **Application**, **Request**, **Session**, and **Conversation** context, but not everything makes sense in an SE environment. While the `Application` context can be present in SE, which starts with the container boot and lives till the container is shutdown, there isn't support for any other context. The only additional context which is supported in CDI 2.0 is the request context. There are two approaches to obtain the request context it can be framework managed or it can be programmatically managed by the developer.

For programmatic access, you need to inject the `RequestContextController` instance in your class and then use its `activate()` and `deactivate()` methods to work with the request context in the current thread. Calling `activate()` within a thread will activate the request context if not already active. Similarly, `deactivate()` will stop the active request context if it exists, but may throw a `ContextNotActiveException` otherwise. Here's the API-based method of `request` context control:

```
@ApplicationScoped
public class Task {
    @Inject
    private RequestContextController requestContextController;
    public void doWorkInRequest(String data) {
        boolean activated = requestContextController.activate();
        //some work here
        if(activated) requestContextController.deactivate();
    }
}
```

For the container to automatically start a request context, an interceptor binding annotation of `@ActivateRequestContext` can be used, which is bound to the method execution. Here's an example of this in action:

```
@ApplicationScoped
public class Task {
    @ActivateRequestContext
    public void doWorkInRequest(String data) {
            //some work here, with request context activated
    }
}
```

With the preceding code, if you had a `RequestScoped` bean injected into the `Task` class, then the same would be created for each invocation of the `doWorkInRequest` method.

In a Java SE application, the notion of `request` may not sound right, as Java EE developers would typically talk of requests as HTTP requests. But if you consider some GUI applications where a button is clicked, then you can relate this to a click event which is fired as part of the button click request.

Enhancing events

CDI 1.1 had an event notification model, which has become popular among developers as it helps with the decoupling of code, following the observer pattern. Version 2.0 builds on this model and adds more enhancements, such as asynchronous event processing along with the ordering of events. To observe an event, the bean simply defines a method that has the `@Observes` annotation, and a parameter type that is used by CDI to identify the event type (class type), which should be passed to this method:

```
public void process(@Observes Task task) { }
```

Further restrictions on which events are passed to the observer method can be applied by using qualifiers at the injection point. Interestingly, the observer can work with generic types as well. Given the following two observers, the container will invoke the appropriate method based on the parameterized type of the event:

```
public void processTaskList(@Observes List<Task> taskList) { }
public void processTaskIds(@Observes List<Integer> taskIdList) { }
```

The raising of events is done using the `Event` interface methods for firing either synchronous or asynchronous events with a payload. The order in which the observers are called is not defined, unless the ordered events approach mentioned later is followed. It's also possible to change the data in an observer, since the data (or payload) passed is not mandated to be immutable. Here's the relevant portion of the code snippet used for firing an event:

```
@Inject Event<Task> event;

public void doSomething() {
      event.fire( new Task() );
}
```

The corresponding observer would be as follows:

```
public void handle(@Observes Task task) {
// can update the task instance
}
```

With CDI 2 offering asynchronous events and ordered events, let's explore each in more detail.

Asynchronous events

These were introduced as part of CDI 2.0, and allow for raising events in an asynchronous way. The earlier version 1 had only synchronous event firing support, leading to the event firing code having to wait for all the observers to finish execution, and only then could the next line of code execute. It also meant that an exception in one observer would prevent other observers from getting called. This was because all the observer calls were made within the same thread.

With CDI 2, there's support for asynchronous observer invocation. The observers will be running in different threads than the thread which fires the event. Owing to the nature of different threads, the async events won't allow mutation of the payload. None of the CDI built-in contexts will be propagated across these threads, other than the Application context which is shared across. Async event firing is achieved by using the `fireAsync` method on the `Event` interface and is observed by using the new `@ObservesAsync` annotation. The `fireAsync` method returns a `CompletionStage` instance that was introduced in Java 8, allowing for the handling of exceptions which are made available after a completion of calls in a suppressed manner.

Having understood how synchronous and asynchronous events behave, let's look at a summary of the difference between the two methods, provided by the `Event` interface, namely `fire` and `fireAsync`:

`public void fire(T event)`	Synchronous call within same thread, where payload is mutable. Exception in any one observer breaks the next observer.
`public <U extends T> CompletionStage<U> fireAsync(U event)`	Asynchronous call with immutable payload. Exceptions are suppressed and available after completion.
`public <U extends T> CompletionStage<U> fireAsync(U event, NotificationOptions options)`	Same as `fireAsync`, with additional options to configure the observer methods notification, for example, supplying an executor for async delivery.

Ordered events

This basically orders the observers using the `@Priority` annotation. This feature can be made use of when there are multiple observer methods and you need to control which ones are called first and which ones are called later:

- The lowest value would be the first observer method that gets called
- The highest value would be called last
- If there's no priority specified then this event will be considered mid-range priority
- For observer methods with the same priority, the ordering is undefined
- No priority is applicable for asynchronous events, since they're not sequential

The usage of the ordered event is shown here:

```
public void observer1(@Observes @Priority(1) Payload event) { }
public void observer2 (@Observes @Priority(2) Payload event) { }
```

Given the behavior of ordered events using `@Priority`, along with the mutable state of the payload, one could utilize this feature for certain use cases. Consider a fairly common scenario in which the system should lock the user account based on the number of failed login attempts. Additionally, send out a notification to the user, such as an SMS, if the account gets locked in the process. In this case, we could define two ordered observers for this type of event, with the first observer checking for failed attempts and setting the lock status on the payload object. The second observer would then be able to see the changes made to the payload by the first observer and thus, based on this change in status, it would send the notification. Let us see, how this can be tackled in the sample code explained next.

A login service will raise a `LoginEvent` containing a user's ID and attempt count. Take a look at the `LoginEvent` code:

```
public class LoginEvent {
    private final Integer attemptsMade;
    private final String userId;
    private boolean lockAccount = false;
    public LoginEvent(Integer count, String userId) {
        this.attemptsMade = count;
        this.userId = userId;
    }
    ...
}
```

The relevant code snippet for the `AccountService`, a class responsible for signing in the user and raising an event, is shown here:

```
@Inject private Event<LoginEvent> event;

/* A login method on this class, raises the event for failed login attempts
using below line. */
event.fire(new LoginEvent(attemptsMadeCount, byUserId ));
```

The first observer is responsible for checking and locking the account based on attempts made:

```
public class MonitorAccountAccess {
    public static final Integer MAX_ATTEMPTS = 3;
    public void lockForFailedAttempts(
            @Observes @Priority(1) LoginEvent event) {
        if(event.getAttemptsMade() >= MAX_ATTEMPTS) {
            event.setLockAccount(true);
            //do more work to push status in database
        }
    }
}
```

The second observer is responsible for sending an SMS when an account gets locked. This code relies on the lock account status update being changed in the `MonitorAccountAccess` code block:

```
public class AccountLockNotification {
    public void sendSmsOnAccountLock(@Observes @Priority(2) LoginEvent
event) {
        if(event.isLockAccount() == false) return;
        sendAccountLockSms(event.getUserId());
    }
}
```

When the event is fired synchronously from the `AccountService` code, `MonitorAccountAccess` will be called first, as it has `@Priority(1)`. Later, the `AccountLockNotification` code gets called, along with `@Priority(2)` and the updated `LoginEvent` object.

Annotation literals

Before exploring annotation literals, let's look at @Qualifiers. For multiple implementations of a bean type, the qualifiers can help specify which type to inject with the help of qualifier annotation. These can be used to aid the container in injecting the correct type of bean, as shown here:

```
interface OrderProcessor { ... }

@OrderPlaced
class OrderPlacedProcessor implements OrderProcessor {...}

@OrderCancelled
class OrderCancelledProcessor implements OrderProcessor {...}
```

Since there is more than one implementation of OrderProcessor, we can make use of a qualifier to specify which implementation to inject. This would be used when implementing classes as well as at the injection point:

```
@Inject @OrderPlaced    private OrderProcessor processor;
@Inject @OrderCancelled private OrderProcessor processor;
```

There's an additional annotation called @Alternative, which is used to define an alternate implementation. It is disabled by default and can be activated via deployment configuration in beans.xml.

Qualifiers can also be added to the Event instance using either a qualifier annotation at the injection point of the event or by passing the qualifier to the select method of the Event interface:

```
@Inject @OrderPlaced  private Event<ShopOrder> placedEvent;
```

Here, every event fired using placedEvent would have the qualifier ShopOrder. This would invoke every observer that:

- Has a type to which the event object ShopOrder is assignable
- Does not have any event qualifier other than the one specified at the injection point, such as OrderPlaced

It's not difficult to realize that soon we may end up having multiple qualifiers when dealing with cases. For example, you may end up with event instances annotated with qualifiers such as `OrderPlaced`, `OrderCancelled`, `OrderShipped`, and so on. Apart from the verbosity that it adds to the code, this is also a challenge when you need to specify the qualifier dynamically.

CDI allows for the creation of annotation instances. CDI 1 already had support for this, but CDI 2 has brought in a more convenient method to create these using some helpers. These will reduce the amount of code required to create an annotation literal. It provides an option to subclass the `AnnotationLiteral` class and then pass the qualifier dynamically:

```
event.select(new AnnotationLiteral<OrderPlaced>() {})
     .fire( shopOrder );
```

A point to note here is that the `select` method can take multiple `Annotation` options, thus allowing for multiple event qualifiers to be passed.

There are built-in annotation literals provided as well, as mentioned in the specification:

- `javax.enterprise.inject.Any`
- `javax.enterprise.inject.Default`
- `javax.enterprise.inject.New`
- `javax.enterprise.inject.Specializes`
- `javax.enterprise.inject.Vetoed`
- `javax.enterprise.util.Nonbinding`
- `javax.enterprise.context.Initialized`
- `javax.enterprise.context.Destroyed`
- `javax.enterprise.context.RequestScoped`
- `javax.enterprise.context.SessionScoped`
- `javax.enterprise.context.ApplicationScoped`
- `javax.enterprise.context.Dependent`
- `javax.enterprise.context.ConversationScoped`
- `javax.enterprise.inject.Alternative`
- `javax.enterprise.inject.Typed`

Annotations that don't have any members can be instantiated using the constant named INSTANCE, available on the static nested class Literal:

```
RequestScoped reqScopedLiteral = RequestScoped.Literal.INSTANCE;
```

Annotations with members have a different approach, as they provide a static factory method for obtaining the instance:

```
Named literalObject = NamedLiteral.of("beanName");
```

With all these and more, CDI provides the Java developer with a solid programming model, promoting loosely coupled communication between objects and allowing for better structuring of code.

Here are a few references:

CDI 2.0 page on the JCP site	https://jcp.org/en/jsr/detail?id=365
CDI 2.0 specification	http://docs.jboss.org/cdi/spec/2.0/cdi-spec.pdf
CDI reference implementation	http://weld.cdi-spec.org/

Java Persistence API (JPA)

Before we start wielding JPA and CDI together, let's get the basics out of the way for JPA. The Java Persistence API allows for the modelling of the domain objects for accessing, persisting, and managing data between POJOs and a relational database. JPA is the standard for working with **object-relational mapping** (ORM) solutions. Popular ORM solutions include Hibernate, EclipseLink (the reference implementation for all JPA versions), Apache OpenJPA, and DataNucleus. JPA puts the focus back on the domain model for retrieving and persisting data without having to deal with resource management and vendor specific SQL.

Most developers would be accustomed to hearing about Hibernate in articles and projects; it also shows up as a skill sought by employers. While Hibernate and the like can be used directly, using JPA helps us avoid falling in the vendor lock-in pit and in turn maintains portability. Hibernate is bundled as the default **ORM** for **RedHat/JBoss** servers, while **EclipseLink (RI)** is bundled as part of **Glassfish** and **Payara**. Similarly, **Apache OpenJPA** is used in **TomEE**.

JPA has been tagged as a maintenance release, which has led to minor but noteworthy updates in JPA 2.2. This release brings with it support for Java 8 and better CDI integration.

It all starts with an `EntityManager`. To work with JPA, you must obtain an `EntityManager` instance, which acts as the gateway to perform any database operation. The steps are outlined here:

1. Create `persistence.xml` and define one or more `persistence-unit` in it:

```xml
<?xml version="1.0" encoding="UTF-8"?>
<persistence version="2.1"
xmlns="http://xmlns.jcp.org/xml/ns/persistence"
xmlns:xsi="http://www.w3.org/2001/XMLSchema-instance"
xsi:schemaLocation="http://xmlns.jcp.org/xml/ns/persistence
http://xmlns.jcp.org/xml/ns/persistence/persistence_2_1.xsd">

    <persistence-unit name="taskDb" transaction-type="JTA">
    <jta-data-source>jdbc/AppDS</jta-data-source>
    <exclude-unlisted-classes>false</exclude-unlisted-classes>
    <properties>
    <property name="javax.persistence.schema-generation.database.action"
     value="drop-and-create"/>
    <property name="eclipselink.logging.level" value="FINE"/>
    </properties>
    </persistence-unit>

</persistence>
```

2. Obtain an `EntityManager` in a non-managed environment (using CDI):

```java
@Produces public EntityManager create() {
        return Persistence.createEntityManagerFactory("taskDb")
                .createEntityManager();
}

public void close(@Disposes EntityManager em) {
    em.close();
}
```

3. Obtaining an `EntityManager` in a managed environment can be done like so:

```java
@PersistenceContext(unitName="taskDb") EntityManager em;
```

4. Use the `EntityManager` instance within a transaction to perform the operations on an entity.

Entities

To activate Java persistence on a bean class, we can use the @Entity annotation, which lets us map the bean to a database table. The identifier field denoted by @Id is used to map the primary key column of the table. The mapping of a bean to a table can be done using annotations or XML, but here we will stick to using annotations. One entity instance can be considered as representing one row of a table.

 XML mapping can be used to override the values defined by annotations. This can be useful for deployment-based configuration changes without changing the code.

An entity mapping structure is shown here:

JPA Entity class	Database Create Table structure
| ```
@Entity
 @Table(name="task_detail")
 public class Task {
     @Id private Long id;
     private String name;
     private LocalDate assignedon;
     private LocalDateTime createdon;
   //Getters are setters omitted
 }
``` | ```
CREATE TABLE `task_detail` (
 `id` int(11) NOT NULL AUTO_INCREMENT,
 `name` varchar(30),
 `assignedon` date,
 `createdon` timestamp,
 PRIMARY KEY (`id`)
 )
``` |

The mapping defines an entity called Task, which is mapped to a table named "task_detail". While JPA would use default names based on class and member names to map it to corresponding tables and columns, there are times when you need to handle the differences. Here, we have used the @Table annotation since our class name is Task but the table name is task_detail. Similarly, if the field names are different then we could make use of the @Column annotation. An example is as follows:

```
@Column(name = "last_modified")
LocalDateTime lastModified;
```

As of JPA 2.2, we now have support for these date/time classes:

- `java.time.LocalDate`
- `java.time.LocalTime`
- `java.time.LocalDateTime`
- `java.time.OffsetTime`
- `java.time.OffsetDateTime`

Prior to JPA 2.2, while there was no support for the date/time APIs, we could have still managed the conversion of `LocalDate` or `LocalDateTime` using an `AttributeConverter`, as shown here, which is applied automatically to all entities having such fields due to `autoApply=true`:

```
@Converter(autoApply = true)
public class LocalDateConverter
                implements AttributeConverter<LocalDate, Date> {
  @Override
  public Date convertToDatabaseColumn(LocalDate entityDate) {
    return (entityDate == null ? null : Date.valueOf(entityDate));
  }

  @Override
  public LocalDate convertToEntityAttribute(Date dbDate) {
     return (dbDate == null ? null : dbDate.toLocalDate());
  }
}
```

It's now also possible to inject a bean within an `AttributeConverter` instance; this can be useful to fetch a configuration object which may hold the needed format or other useful information. Consider using a converter when you need to map the database representation of a value to a Java representation that can't be mapped by default.

A few common use cases could be:

- Mapping a number value such as `one` or `zero` to a Boolean field
- Encryption of password for saving and decryption during fetch
- Mapping a value to a corresponding enum type

When defining the entities, it's also common to put named queries in the entity itself, which can later be referenced when querying the database using `EntityManager`. An example is shown here:

```
@Entity
@Table(name="task_detail")
@NamedQuery(name = "Task.findById",
            query = "SELECT t FROM Task t WHERE t.id = :id")
@NamedQuery(name = "Task.findByName",
            query = "SELECT t FROM Task t WHERE t.name = :name")
public class Task {
    // code omitted
}
```

This can then be referenced during querying:

```
TypedQuery<Task> query = em.createNamedQuery("Task.findById", Task.class);
query.setParameter("id", 1);

//With TypedQuery you don't need a cast to Task type below
query.getSingleResult().getName();
```

When mapping an entity to a table, it's best to use the `@Table` annotation, rather than changing the `Entity` name itself. The reasons are:

```
@Entity(name="tasks") class Task { ... }
em.createQuery("SELECT t FROM Task t"); // won't work
em.createQuery("SELECT t FROM tasks t"); // is correct, since we changed
the entity name
```

You may have noticed that we didn't use the `NamedQueries` container annotation. Well, JPA 2.2 makes use of repeatable annotations; this means you can leave out the superfluous container annotation and just repeat the one you need, such as `NamedQuery`. In the previous versions, you needed to use a container annotation such as `NamedQueries` which would then wrap multiple `NamedQuery` annotations. But that's no longer needed since JPA 2.2 takes advantage of the repeatable annotation feature introduced in Java 8:

Earlier versions of JPA	With repeatable annotations support

`@NamedQueries({`
`    @NamedQuery(name = ...),`
`    @NamedQuery(name = ...)`
`})`
	`@NamedQuery(name = ...)`
	`@NamedQuery(name = ...)`

Most annotation are repeatable, such as:

- NamedStoredProcedureQuery
- NamedNativeQuery
- NamedEntityGraph
- AttributeOverride
- PersistenceContext

It's fairly common to see fields such as created, last_modified in most if not all tables in a database. When mapping such tables to entities, we can use a super class with the annotation @MappedSuperclass and define the common mapping fields and associations, which all subclasses inherit. The super class itself is not persisted and only used for field inheritance. Here's an example of that:

```
@MappedSuperclass
public class MappedSuperEntity implements Serializable {
    @Id
    @GeneratedValue(strategy = GenerationType.IDENTITY)
    protected Long id;
    @NotNull
    @Size(min = 1, max = 4000)
    @Column(name - "name")
    protected String name;
    @NotNull
    @Column(name = "created")
    protected LocalDateTime created;
    @Column(name = "last_modified")
    protected LocalDateTime lastModified;
    // code omitted
}
```

A subclass can override the basic mappings by using the AttributeOverride annotation. Notice we have used annotations such as @Size to put further validation constraints on our bean. These are from the Bean Validation API that we looked at earlier.

When working with multiple entities, you may need to define a relationship between them. In JPA, this is done by using annotations which support bidirectional and unidirectional relations. The following four annotations can be applied on relational members of a class:

- @ManyToMany
- @ManyToOne
- @OneToMany
- @OneToOne

It's no surprise that a table in a relational database is not designed with object-oriented thinking. Often, when mapping a entity to an table, we may want to group certain fields/members and use a composition rather than declaring all the fields in a single class. JPA provides `@Embeddable` to do just that.

Here's an example showing how we create a user entity with a *has-a* credential. The database has all the fields present in a single table:

Entity with embedded object	Single table in database
`@Entity` `public class User {` `@Id Long id;` `@Embedded Credential credential;` `//other fields omitted` `}` `@Embeddable class Credential {` `String email;` `String password;` `}`	`CREATE TABLE ``user`` (` ` ``id`` int(11) NOT NULL AUTO_INCREMENT,` ` ``email`` varchar(50),` ` ``password`` varchar(30),` ` PRIMARY KEY (``id``)` `)`

We have covered three major types of classes that you would typically create when working with JPA:

- **Entity**: This is the basic unit of bean which is used for persistence
- **MappedSuperclass**: Class without its own table, but used for common field inheritance by entities
- **Embeddable**: Class without its own table, properties of which can be persisted via embedding it in another entity

Performing CRUD operations with entities

The basic usage of an `EntityManager` is to execute the **create, read, update, and delete** (**CRUD**) operations for the entity. These operations are performed using a transaction, and JPA supports two kinds:

- **JTA container managed transactions:** Demarcation of transactions are handled by the container, such as using a method with a transaction required attribute as part of a stateless bean. On completion of the method, the transaction will be committed.

- **Resource local transactions**: Demarcation of transactions must be done programmatically. For example, using the `EntityTransaction` instance and invoking its `begin` and `commit` operations.

Methods with read-only operations need not be performed within a transaction, although in a JEE environment there is hardly any overhead for a transaction with modern day containers. It's still best to measure this for your use case and decide.

Once you have an `EntityManager` obtained, as described in the text, *It all starts with an EntityManager*, then we can start performing the CRUD operations using it.

Creating an entity within the database is done using the `persist` operation on an `EntityManager`, which creates a record in the table for the entity. This operation is performed only on new entities which have no entry in the database.

In its simplest form, a `persist` operation can be done like so:

```
Task theTask = new Task(100L, "Work on next big thing");
em.persist(theTask);
```

The `persist` method inserts the non-managed entity into the database by firing an `INSERT` statement. Once the entity is persisted, it enters a managed state and thus any changes made to the entity within a transaction are tracked and updated in the database during the commit. If the entity being persisted has an embedded annotation reference to an embeddable class, then fields of that class are persisted as well. For example, a `User` having a composition relation with the `Credential` class, as shown before.

Updating an entity is done by simply performing field changes on a managed entity within a transaction and posting the transaction commits. The changes are automatically synchronized with the database. The transaction can be container managed using the EJB method within transactional bounds, or user managed, as shown here:

```
em.getTransaction().begin();
Task theTask = em.find(Task.class, 4L);
theTask.setAssignedon(LocalDate.of(2018, 7, 21));
em.getTransaction().commit();
```

It would be a mistake to follow this strategy to conditionally perform `persist` for a managed entity, as shown next:

```
@Stateless
public class TaskService {
    @Inject EntityManager em;
```

```
public void update() {
    Task task = em.find(Task.class, 2L); // Get existing task
    task.setName("updated name here");
    if( some condition ) {
        em.persist(task); //Line won't make a difference
    }
}
}
```

Here, the changed name of the task, will be synced to database irrespective of whether `em.persist` call is executed or not. For updating a `managed` entity, it's not required to call the `persist` method, as the entity will be saved as part of the transaction completion.

When working with detached entities, a `merge` operation is performed first, to synchronize the changes done to the entity in its detached state.

Removing an entity is done by using the `remove` method of `EntityManager`. This is done by first finding the entity, putting it into the `managed` state, then invoking the `remove` operation. A detached entity (which is a `non-managed` entity) cannot be passed to `remove`, and if passed it will throw an exception:

```
em.getTransaction().begin();
em.remove(theTask); // theTask is a reference to Task object
em.getTransaction().commit();
```

Reading an entity is very common and there are a variety of options available to perform a `read` operation, such as using the APIs or using JPQL, which is the query language for Java persistence. JPQL is similar to SQL but instead of working on tables and their columns, it works on the entities and their associations. We already looked at one example a little earlier when we used `TypedQuery` to find an entity by referencing a named query. Here's a similar snippet using `createQuery`:

```
TypedQuery<Task> query = em.createQuery("SELECT t FROM Task t",
Task.class);
List<Task> tasks = query.getResultList();
```

The preceding code can be further expanded to restrict the data being fetched, such as in the case of fetching a paginated list of records. For such use cases, the `Query/TypedQuery` provides methods for result restrictions:

```
query.setFirstResult(start); //: Result would be fetched from the offset of
the start number.
query.setMaxResults(pageSize); //: Results can be less or the same as the
pageSize number.
```

If you don't need the flexibility of writing a query and need to just find an entity by its primary key, then the same can be done using the `find` method with `EntityManager`:

```
Task task = em.find(Task.class, 100L);
```

With JPA 2.2, there's now support for getting a `Stream<X>` from the result set. Both `javax.persistence` and `TypedQuery` / `Query` support the `getResultStream` method. This returns a `Stream` instance. An example usage is shown here:

```
TypedQuery<Task> query = em.createQuery("SELECT t from Task t",
                                         Task.class);
List<String> names = query.getResultStream().map(Task::getName)
                          .collect(Collectors.toList());
```

It's thus possible to use the usual methods of stream, such as `filter` and `map`, to work with the result set. But it's best to rely on your database/SQL for operations that can be performed within the database, rather than trying to process it in the JVM. A WHERE clause or an aggregate function such as *sum* or *count* are more efficiently done in SQL, rather than trying to load the entire list in JVM and processing it using streams.

Before concluding CRUD aspects when using JPA, it's also worth noting that the read operations are pulling in all the fields of an entity. There are times when you would require a subset of fields, or fetching some aggregate value rather than loading the whole entity. In those cases, an approach called projection is a better fit. It can be considered as having a select query return only the required fields, and then using a constructor expression to map it to a data transfer object or value object, rather than getting the entity directly.

Entity listeners

The listeners can be put to use for performing interception on entity life cycle operations. We can also inject CDI managed beans into an entity listener for performing any additional processing. Here are the seven life cycle callback annotations that can be used:

`PostLoad`	This can be used to track the read calls made on an entity.
`PrePersist` `PreRemove` `PreUpdate`	These are called before performing the corresponding save, remove, or update operation on an entity. These annotations can be combined and placed in a single method as well.
`PostPersist` `PostRemove` `PostUpdate`	As the name suggests, these are performed after the corresponding save, remove, or update operation on an entity. These annotations can be combined and placed in a single method as well.

The Task entity has an entity listener associated with it, thus during its life cycle events, the listener callback methods would be invoked. If there is more than one listener, then the invocation is done in the order of the listener declaration:

```
@Entity
@Table(name="task_detail")
@EntityListeners({TaskAudit.class})
public class Task extends MappedSuperEntity {
 // code omitted
}
```

During each life cycle event of the Task entity, our TaskAudit class methods would be invoked, which are listening to the event. Thus, to listen to the post persist event, the following code declares a trackChanges method with the @PostPersist annotation:

```
public class TaskAudit {
    @PersistenceContext private EntityManager em;
    @PostPersist public void trackChanges(MappedSuperEntity entity)
    { ... }
}
```

While the listeners are handy to use for simple cases, they fall short for handling more complex requirements. There are modules, such as **Hibernate Envers**, which provide support for auditing capabilities with more capable features, but these are not part of the standard JPA specification.

Validations the entity

The Bean Validation API defines many validation constraints that can be applied together on the JPA entities. These are provided in the javax.validation.constraints package.

To apply validations on an entity, you can put the constraints on its fields. Consider our Task entity with validations defined as follows:

```
@Entity
@Table(name="task_detail")
public class Task {
  @Id
  @GeneratedValue(strategy = GenerationType.IDENTITY)
  private Long id;

  @NotNull
  @Size(min = 1, max = 5)
  private String name;
```

```
@Pattern(regexp = "[a-zA-Z]")
private String title;

@Future
private LocalDate targetDate;
// Getters & Setters to follow
}
```

Given the validation constraints defined here, the fields of the `Task` class will have the following constraints:

- `name`: A name cannot contain a `null` value and must be a minimum length of one and a maximum length of five characters.
- `title`: This is constrained by the regular expression pattern, suggesting that only letters of the alphabets are allowed if a value is present. But the value of title may be set to `null`.
- `targetDate`: The valid value can be null or a date in the future, if present.

When trying to persist the bean using an `EntityManager`, the Bean Validation takes place, and for any value that doesn't meet the defined constraints, there is a violation detected, resulting in a `javax.validation.ConstraintViolationException`.

These validations are triggered as part of the life cycle of the event, such as pre-persist, pre-update, or pre-remove. These can be controlled by configuring them in the `persistence.xml` file. Here's a code that tries to save a `Task` object, but doesn't conform to the constraints listed previously. It would result in an `ConstraintViolationException`, which we can catch and print to the console:

```
public void save() {
    Task theTask = new Task();
    theTask.setName("A longer name than allowed");
    try {
        em.persist(theTask);
    } catch (ConstraintViolationException violation) {
        violation.getConstraintViolations().forEach(
                v -> System.out.println("violation " + v)
        );
    }
}
```

Since the `name` field has a constraint of `@NotNull` and `@Size` defined, this code would result in the following output, as `persist` would fail:

```
Info: violation ConstraintViolationImpl{
    interpolatedMessage='size must be between 1 and 5',
    propertyPath=name,
    rootBeanClass=class org.company.project.domain.Task,
    messageTemplate='{javax.validation.constraints.Size.message}'
}
```

It's also possible to override the constraint message by using the message parameter on the annotation during declaration. For example, `@NotNull(message = "The task name must not be null")`.

Now that we have looked at how JPA can trigger these constraint checks as part of the life cycle of events, let's explore validating a entity programmatically. Consider that you have an entity, perhaps as a result of a REST API input, and would like to validate the bean. Here, you can inject a `javax.validation.Validator` instance and use its `validate` method to find any `ConstraintViolation` instances. Here's the snippet to do just that:

```
@Inject Validator validator;
...
// Some method which takes Task object and validates
Set<ConstraintViolation<Task>> flaws = validator.validate(theTask);
flaws.stream()
     .map(ConstraintViolation::getMessage) // Get message string
     .forEach(System.out::println);        // Print message string
```

If any violations are found, then the `validate` method will return a non-zero set of items. That shows you how we can use the programmatic approach when you need more fine-grained control over constraint checks.

Summary

As you may have noticed, getting started with JPA and CDI isn't that complex. With an understanding of both, it's possible to build large applications which utilize these technologies for various business cases. We looked at how dependency injection promotes writing loosely coupled and testable code and how CDI, a ubiquitous API for dependency injection and context management in Java EE, helps us do that.

CDI 2 brings ordered and asynchronous events to further enrich this programming model. As of the 2.0 release, CDI is available for Java SE as well. JPA has been updated for utilizing Java 8 Streams, repeatable annotations, and date/time APIs along with better CDI integration support. The JPA entities are defined as classes using `@Entity`, `@MappedSuperclass`, and `@Embeddable` annotations. To track state changes, we get to use entity listeners that can be used with CDI as well. Bean Validation 2.0 can be leveraged when defining constraints on JPA entities; this declarative method makes adding validations a fairly easy task to do.

Having learnt about CDI and JPA, which are two fundamental APIs that are used for building Java EE solutions; we can now switch our focus to microservices as we explore API-driven architecture.

3
Understanding Microservices

The world of software is an ever-changing one, and within it there is an ever-increasing need for faster deliveries. With businesses trying to reduce time-to-market for each application, the onus of meeting such demands is with the engineering team, who also need to maintain a balance between quality and speed.

There are many useful principles and patterns defined in the software ecosystem that help meet these business needs to some extent. However, as neither business needs nor systems remain constant, architectures must evolve as well to address these challenges. Maintaining the competitive edge is vital for the survival of any business. Microservices have been grabbing points for delivering software that meets these modern-day demands. It's also a unique architectural pattern, as it makes **development and operations (DevOps)** part of its architecture. In the sections that follow, we will build an understanding of what microservices mean and how Java EE developers and architects can leverage this new paradigm using their enterprise Java skills.

Here are two definitions of microservices:

"Microservices are a loosely-coupled service-oriented architecture with bounded context."

– Adrian Cockroft (cloud architect at Netflix)

"Small autonomous services, that work together, modelled around a business domain."

– Used by Sam Newman (author of Building Microservices)

Microservices is a term that has been around for a while but has gained momentum only in recent years. This is an architectural style that can be considered as a variant or specialisation of **service-oriented-architecture** (**SOA**). It's an architecture that talks about how to go about building complex systems composed of fine grained services. There are many theories and books published on this subject, concerning why you should be doing it or why you shouldn't be. This is the only chapter of this book that will focus on the concepts of microservices; the rest of the book will focus on the how-to.

Companies delivering large scale web solutions such as Netflix, Amazon, and eBay have adopted the microservices way and have been successful in implementing it. It's worth noting that these companies didn't start with this architectural style; instead, they had to carefully carve out their microservices from their monolith applications. Before we grab our sculpting tools, let's understand the problems we are trying to solve using this approach. Let's consider the differences between approaches by first considering a traditional monolithic application and then seeing how a microservice-based architecture solves some of the shortcomings of the former.

What we will cover:

- Traditional monoliths
- Multiple small units of work
- Single responsibility
- The need for REST
- Scale only what needs to scale
- The bad parts, yes, there are few

Traditional monoliths

When building modern enterprise web applications, it's common to build it as a monolith. In this architectural style, applications can be built as modules which are bundled as a single deployable unit and executed in a single runtime process. Deploying a monolith can be done by simply packaging the application as a **web archive** (**WAR**) file and publishing the artifact to a server. Starting a project with the monolith approach is much easier than trying to build a service-oriented or microservice architecture from the start. This approach does have some benefits, such as the following:

- Monoliths are simpler to work with, as even though developers may not get the correct boundaries defined between the modules, it's not that hard to refactor

- Testing a monolith is simpler as there's less moving parts when compared to a service-oriented architecture
- Not much thought is needed for what to scale, as you can add more boxes and the entire monolith application will scale horizontally
- It's easier to enforce constraints on the team by means of centralised governance

Let's consider an example where you may be building an issue management system, which has various modules such as document manager, users, audit, and ticket management. Audit could be a web service API, but for convenience, it's bundled along with the same application. Here, the application would be deployed as a single unit (WAR) and run on a Java EE application server. If any of the modules are unable to cope with the load, then the entire application is scaled to meet this demand. Here's what a scaled monolith looks like:

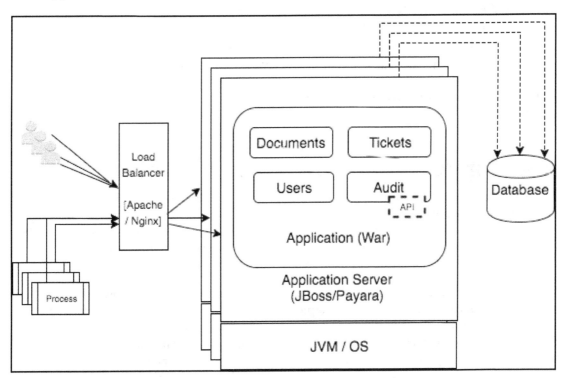

While the monolith is good for simpler projects, it does have drawbacks when used for larger complex applications. It is critical for architects and developers to understand the benefits and drawbacks that each architecture brings with it. Here are the drawbacks of a monolith:

- As the code base grows, changes are difficult to make without impacting other parts of the system.
- Making changes in one area needs to be followed with testing the entire monolith, so the duration of an iteration can't be kept short.
- As both code and team size grow, it becomes a challenge for anyone to fully understand the application.
- Even for small changes, the entire application must be deployed.
- It isn't possible to tailor the hardware resources specifically to module needs.
- Changing a library or framework is a daunting task and can't be done often. This results in outdated libraries lying around due to legacy code.
- Hard to find root causes, with many collaborators but no ownership.

As we move through the evolution of software development, things are getting more complex and the drawbacks of the traditional monolith start to outweigh its benefits.

Need for delivering new features quicker

In a competitive market where software is ubiquitous, businesses are realizing that success depends on being able to deliver good quality software at a fast pace. There are various practices and development methodologies that facilitate efficient delivery of software. The drawbacks of a traditional monolith prevent it from meeting the demands of complex large-scale applications, which require rolling releases at a fast pace.

Microservice architecture, meanwhile, promotes small modules focused towards business capabilities that can be independently deployed as services. These smaller services can subsequently be combined together to act as one large enterprise-level application. The communication between the services can happen using HTTP or messaging, which is a typical choice for lightweight communication. Successful microservice architecture is best achieved with a small cross-functional team, as it aids in delivering solutions faster. By keeping the code base small, it's often easier for the team to perform a refactor or rewrite from scratch, if the situation so demands; this wouldn't be feasible in a monolith application. The services are built as a separate application and interface with each other via published service contracts. Thus, it is easier to change the implementation details of a service without impacting other services, as long as the contract is honored.

In the case of the issue management system, we would decompose the application by breaking it into smaller services focused around a business capability. This process is known as **functional decomposition**.

This would create a logical isolation for each service, which will have its own database, potentially different from others such as relational or NoSQL as per the need of that service. This is called **polyglot persistence**, which here means allowing your service to embrace the persistence solution that is right for its needs. The impact of one service choosing a different data-store is confined to that service itself, as none of the other services are affected by this choice.

Here's how that would look in the microservices world:

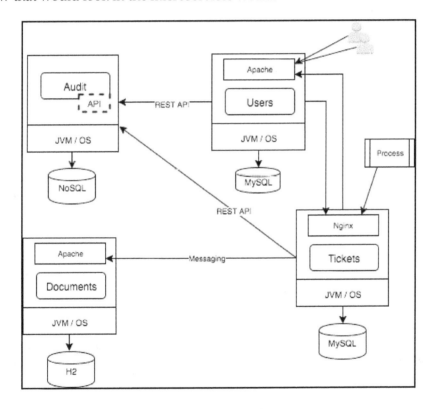

It's also possible, if not mandatory, to use container based solutions to deploy these services. Container solutions such as **Docker** are the means to meet **DevOps** standards for consistent and fast deployments. There are benefits to be gained when using this architecture, such as:

- Ability to scale individual components/services.
- Small business capability focused services are easier to maintain and refactor.
- Business logic is confined to the context of a service and not spread across the whole application.
- Deploying a single service need not require testing the entire application.
- Each service can be allocated an appropriate server instance as per its memory or CPU needs. For example, a service such as *audit* could be CPU intensive, while the *tickets* service may be memory intensive.
- Production issues can be delegated to the right people, by knowing which cross-functional team owns the service.
- Since it's easy to deploy a single service with negligible impact to other services, production fixes and changes can be rolled out faster.

When working with a microservice architecture, tooling becomes an essential ingredient for success. Thus, it also promotes the adoption of DevOps practices such as:

- **Continuous Deployment**:
    - Automated deployments are a must. Imagine having to deploy 20 or 100 services manually!
    - Unit/integration testing automation to allow for faster feedback on builds.

- **Automated Infrastructure**:
    - Tooling for logging, monitoring, performance metrics
    - Quick provisioning and de-provisioning of instances

This approach solves many of the scalability issues inherent in a monolith, but for it to be effectively implemented, we need to look at how teams are structured. Switching to a microservices architecture will require the creation of a cross-functional team that owns a product (not project) focused towards the business need and adopting the DevOps methodology. DevOps can be considered as a cultural change, an extension of agile development practices. It tries to bridge the gap between the developers who build the software and the IT operations that maintain it. This culture promotes teams to own the build, test, and deploy cycle for the product they are responsible for delivering.

Team size and dependency

Melvin Conway doesn't refer to software systems alone. For the information technology world, his observation means that the design of a code base gets largely influenced by the way an organisation structures its own teams. You might be wondering as to why we are discussing team structures here. This has to do with certain characteristics of a microservices architecture, which advocates the decentralizing of all things.

Conway's law :

Organisations that design systems are constrained to produce designs that are copies of the communication structures of these organisations.

Traditionally, the choice of technology to be used is decided and applied organisation wide, so you belong to either a Java camp or some other, such as Ruby or Golang. Similarly, the choice of database is influenced primarily by the resource skills and not necessarily by the need of the business. These choices get passed on to the teams, who are responsible for building the solution. This is not necessarily a bad idea, as it ensures that the organisation is aligned to a particular choice and usually has resources that are skilled in the chosen technology. The problem lies in the *one size fits all* approach, which gets further aggravated in a monolith as different business modules typically get clubbed into a single unit of work. What may have been chosen as a right solution to begin with may not remain right as things evolve.

In traditional monolithic applications, the development team would build a large enterprise application, pass it on to the testers for quality checks, and then push it to operations for deployment and maintenance work. Within a large development team, there can be further silos created as developers are responsible for different modules and they often share libraries built by other developers. Under such conditions, the question of who provides the support and fix when an issue occurs often becomes a challenging one to answer. Here, teams operate on multiple service or projects and are functionally separated. This can be visualized, as shown in the following image:

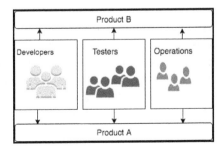

Greater success can be achieved with cross-functional teams, working on a common goal, than with functional teams with a *us versus them* mind-set. This small team would include people with different functional expertise such as development, testing, operations, and others, who can promote innovation through collaboration, which can be critical to the success of a business. In traditional organisational structures, work is passed from one large team to another and the responsibility for building and maintaining a project is spread across multiple teams.

Another notion that is promoted in microservice architecture is that of product not project. This implies that the team should consider themselves to be working on a product and owning it throughout its lifetime. A project, on the other hand, is executed and handed over to operations on completion. In the cross-functional team, the onus of building and maintaining the product throughout its lifetime will be on this single team. Having all the necessary expertise in one team makes it highly productive and self-directed. This can be visualized as follows:

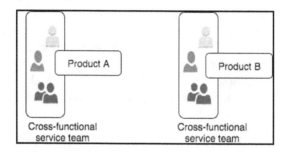

Amazon has popularized the term two-pizza teams, for describing the maximum size of a team responsible for a service. The idea being, that your team should be no larger than a dozen people (they did have a large pizza). There will be times when you need to share certain resources, as certain specialist roles need to be rotated. An infra engineer, for example, won't always be occupied for a single service and may be able to contribute more to others. A lead or architect can pitch in on various microservices and doesn't need to be confined within one team. Thus, teams can depend on other specialized teams which comprise of specialists like architects, managers, and others. These specialized teams would probably have leads and in turn can publish standards and perform reviews, to ensure everyone has the broader goal covered. But introducing too many external checks can have a negative effect, as it would hamper the team's ability to progress and deliver fast. Thus, it's important to give people enough control do their job, yet have a sense of balance between governance of teams to help them when needed. A blanket rule for how to build teams cannot be made, as that largely depends on how your organisation is currently structured.

Multiple small units of work

The idea is to take a complex problem and try to break it into smaller pieces. As mentioned in one of the advantages of microservices—*Small business capability focused services are easier to maintain and refactor*, we should build our microservice as a fine-grained service. This even allows for replacing the service without having to spend weeks or months attempting to do so. Each of these small units (microservices) should be capable enough to:

- Provide for its own private datastore
- Be independently deployable with its own runtime process
- Publish the public interface for others to use in the form of a API contract
- Be fault tolerant, so failure in one should not affect other services
- Be confined to a bounded context (from **Domain driven design (DDD)**)

Smaller code base

When working on any code base, its size is a detrimental factor in forming an understanding of the application. Given the principle of having a separate team that owns the microservice and its build, test, and deploy cycles, it is logical to maintain a separate repository (Git or any VCS). A separate code repository allows for a smaller code base, leading to reduced code complexity, and also avoids merge conflicts, which pester larger code bases with multiple collaborators.

The small code base brings with it compelling advantages for the developers. Imagine having chosen a tech stack only to realize that it isn't the right stack to use. Sounds familiar, right? Mistakes will be made, and our only hope is to use an architecture that allows us to dispose of the code and redo it using another choice. If your code base is small, then a rewrite is no longer a distant dream. It's easier to squeeze performance out of this code base than try to speed up a larger bundle of code modules put together.

The term *micro* in microservices doesn't mean less lines of code. Lines of code is a very misleading measure and cannot be relied upon to keep your services small. As discussed in the coding practices and single responsibility sections that follow, there are a few design guidelines that should be followed to keep your services small.

Coding practices

There are many best practices that are followed by developers around the world. Some of these can be as simple as following a code convention, or applying a more advanced pattern, principle, or general guideline. When building a microservice, its public APIs need to be designed carefully. The internal structure of a microservice is an implementation detail that doesn't get exposed to others.

You cannot ignore the fact that you are publishing a service, which is the face of your API. REST APIs have certain best practices, which should be followed. It's beyond the scope of this book to cover each of these practices, but standardizing on the resources and the request and response formats will go a long way in making the code consistent and easy to work with. Consider the following practices, which are focused towards this type of architecture:

- Follow DDD
- Document it
- Build for failure
- Infrastructure as part of code

Follow domain-driven design

Focus on the responsibility that the microservice is trying to meet. The scope of the service is more important than the lines of code used to build it. Teams would usually sit together and build an understanding of the domain from the domain experts. Once the domain is understood, then it is modeled as domain objects, which can be further grouped as sub-domains. In a monolith, the entire domain model is within a single application, but the microservice architecture would lead your domains to be used within different business contexts.

Bounded Contexts is a term used in DDD, which maps the domain entities within the context of its usage. A payment microservice might require a domain entity such as User, to be used for billing purposes, and thus the User entity may need to have payment details associated with it. But if the same domain entity is used in a notification service, then the payment information is an additional detail, which shouldn't get leaked into this service.

The idea of a bounded context is further explained in the section on *Single Responsibility*.

Document it

The service must be well-documented for it to be useful. The **Web API** contract of a service can be published via documents which are manually built or generated automatically using various build tools. SOAP APIs have a **WebService Description Language (WSDL)** used to describe the service, but REST APIs do not have an equivalent. Given the growing popularity of REST, there are other solutions that have come up to fill this gap. A possible choice for documenting REST resources is *Swagger*. There is the **Open API Initiative (OAI)** that is working to standardize REST API documentation. The specification is based on Swagger, which defines the metadata that is used for documenting APIs.

Developers can make use of the maven Swagger plugin to generate an API document for their microservice. There are other options to generate or document your APIs, but Swagger does bring compelling features that make it an appealing choice. It potentially frees up the developer from having to update the documents manually. There are some goodies it offers, such as the ability to generate API information in a readable format that contains the REST resource name, URL, HTTP method, and request and response formats. It also generates JSON or YAML files which can be used by other tools to provide easy generation of client libraries tailored to the service.

Some good qualities to have in documentation are:

- It should be easy to generate and rely on the code itself, which is the best source of truth.
- The presentation of the document should be readable for humans and available over the web for browsing.
- Should contain samples, describing the service.
- The ability to try out a service based on its documentation can be a valuable addition.
- Separation should be maintained between what is public API and what is private API. Things which are to be used by others can be termed public API, but APIs that are internal to a service should be flagged accordingly.
- Clearly state the current and previous versions of the APIs published.

When using document generation tools, the generated documentation can itself be hosted in some source repository or Docker registry (more on this later). This allows it to be versioned and referenced by the team when required.

References:

- **Swagger**: http://swagger.io/
- **Open API Initiative (OAI)**: https://www.openapis.org/
- **Maven plugin**: https://github.com/kongchen/swagger-maven-plugin

Build for failure

The demand of distributed computing requires services to be written so that they are capable of handling failures. The failure of one service can lead to a cascading effect across all and can be the biggest bottleneck in the application. When invoking REST APIs, consider using *time outs,* as waiting for long periods will have an adverse effect on the response times. When a response doesn't meet the defined **service level agreement** (**SLA**), you could have a default response kept available for such cases.

If a service is timing out, then there's a good chance that it may be down or it may not be available for a longer period. Using a circuit breaker allows you to avoid calling the service that is timing out frequently. If a service is timing out beyond a defined number of times, then the circuit breaker would prevent any further calls. After a defined interval, the circuit-breaker would retry the target service, thereby allowing it time to recover.

These patterns can be written in plain Java code without relying on libraries to do it for you. As an example, you could create an interceptor for all external calls made, which keeps track of failures. Once the threshold of failures is reached, the interceptor can have logic that tells it to not make any further calls to the target service until a defined period. After the configured period is over, the interceptor can start allowing new calls to the service.

Infrastructure tooling as part of code

With containerisation solutions such as **Docker**, you can make the infrastructure part of your code. Most environments require some form of configuration setup to work with. With virtualisation support for cloud applications running on AWS and other cloud providers, it's become a lot easier to build/test/deploy your code on server instances which can be spun up and removed within seconds. Infrastructure as part of your code means to be able to setup a server instance without having to go through the manual process of getting all the needed OS libraries and versions figured out. You can use scripts, which can be written in a readable language, to spin an instance that has the needed setup ready for your actual application. This makes DevOps simpler for the developer who can now utilize tooling like Ansible, Puppet, Docker, and so on to provision the infrastructure when needed.

We will explore more on Docker and how to use it in practice in the next chapter. For now, here's a quick reference of a Docker file; don't worry if you haven't seen this before, we will be covering the details soon.

Take a look at the Dockerfile snippet, shown as follows:

```
FROM prashantp/centos-jdk:8

ADD wildfly-10.0.0.Final /opt/wildfly
EXPOSE 8080 9990
ENV WILDFLY_HOME /opt/wildfly

CMD ["/opt/jboss/wildfly/bin/standalone.sh", "-b", "0.0.0.0"]
```

This is a simple sample of a Docker file that can be used to run a JBoss/Wildfly instance on your local machine.

Single responsibility

Your services should strive to achieve a single responsibility and not get tangled with many, which leads to more reasons for it to change than are necessary. This is one of the principles of SOLID design principles. The single responsibility principle is strictly speaking not about microservices, but instead about classes and objects and maybe too simplistic for it to be applied here. This principle, in the context of a microservice, results in each of the components being highly cohesive and staying focused around one business capability.

When organizing code, Java developers often use packages to create modules. In a layered architecture, modules are generally created by technical concerns, such as presentation, business, and persistence. Packaging by layers has certain disadvantages, such as changes to functionality usually requiring a change across all the layers involved. Another strategy to organise code is to package by business domain or features. This approach results in packages named *tickets*, *users*, and so on, which are created as feature modules. When modules are organised after the domain, it helps developers who are looking at the code structure build a quick understanding of what the application is about. It also tends to promote high cohesion and loose coupling between modules.

In microservice architecture, a service should focus on a single business capability. When building an *issue management system* for working with tickets that are assigned to users, we may choose to create a *tickets microservice* responsible for creating and fetching tickets. Similarly, we may also build a *users microservice* for creating and getting the users within the system. These services should be kept independent of one another and must have well-defined boundaries. It's not enough to keep the business logic separated; even the domain objects should be modeled to meet the purpose of a given microservice.

Typically, the domain entities are grouped as one big shared module (bundled as JAR), which gets added as a dependency to the service. The moment a tickets service fetches a `Ticket` entity (think JPA entity or a domain object), it inadvertently pulls in all related entities along with it. Assume a `Ticket` entity references a `User` entity and `User` references an `Address` entity; we would be polluting our tickets service with information it shouldn't get coupled with, such as an `Address`.

The idea of a bounded context is described by Eric Evans in his seminal book, *Domain Driven Design*. When crafting your domain model, you should identify the domain boundaries and align them to the business capability the service caters to. As you develop a model, you should identify its bounded context. Boundaries help prevent leaking of information in unwanted parts of your code. Going back to *issue management system*, both the *users* and *tickets* microservices may reference a `Ticket` object. Within the context of the users service, a `Ticket` object may have just the **Id** and **Name** properties, which are required. But the tickets service will require more details about the `Ticket` object, such as the status, dates, priority, and so on. So even though the `Ticket` entity may mean the same thing, it will be created as different classes, used by two different applications, with its own database:

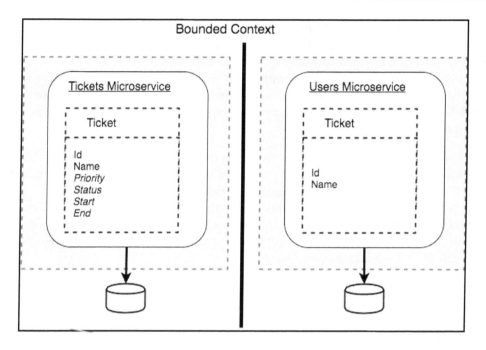

This idea is very difficult to apply in a monolithic architecture, as most of the code base is collocated. But if you have a separate cross-functional team with its own database in a microservices architecture, this very same idea of bounded context is far more achievable. Even if you don't hit perfection, it's an idea worth trying.

The need for REST

REST is a dominant communication style used in SOAs. The business domain model is exposed as resources, where each resource is a published web service that has a defined API contract. These APIs take input using a message format such as JSON and share a response compliant to the protocol used. The microservice itself will have additional external dependencies, such as other APIs for which it acts as the REST client. Since the communication is over the network, it adds to the latency of a service call and thus it's vital to keep this communication lightweight. Each service would also need to be resilient to failures in other services.

To deal with failures and performance issues in other services, a service may incorporate strategies to overcome such cases. As an example, a users service may invoke the tickets API/resource for fetching the latest tickets. For some reason, if the tickets resource is unable to return a response (due to being slow or just not available), then the users service may use a default list which is kept internally for such cases. There are other strategies such as **Bulkhead**, **Circuit-breaker**, and **Timeout** that aid in dealing with the complexity of distributed communication.

Since microservices are fine-grained and modeled around business capabilities, they need to communicate with other services to get work done. In a large, complex application, a request often gets processed by more than one service. When processing a use case such as opening a new *ticket* or assigning a *ticket* to a *user*, there can be multiple services that will participate in this request. Microservices typically communicate with each other using REST. REST APIs facilitate lightweight communication over HTTP with flexible message formats, such as JSON/XML/text, and so on.

Each service publishes a API, which is then consumed by other services which act as its REST Client. Communication among the services can be point-to-point, or based on the use case, it can be asynchronous publish-subscribe model, which is also lightweight. Here's how the communication between our *issue management* microservices can be visualized:

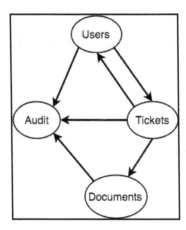

As you can see, while this is an acceptable practice, as the number of services grow, so will the complexity inherent with point-to-point communication. Here's where an **API Gateway** adds value to microservices by providing certain benefits:

- A single entry point for external calls which gets routed to your services internally
- Acts as a layer of security, preventing any attacks from external sources
- Can act as an adapter, allowing for the handling of different message protocols
- Can provide monitoring and logging across services
- It also takes away the problem of service discovery from the clients
- The gateway can also apply the *Circuit-breaker* pattern for fault tolerance:

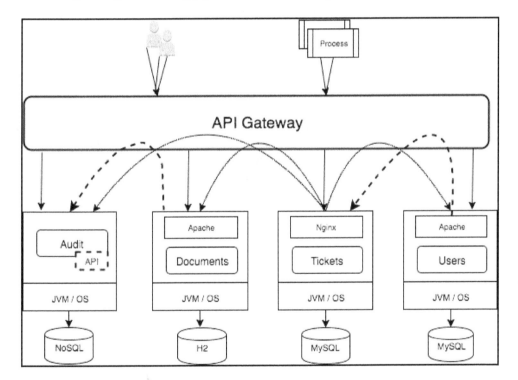

While the gateway does act as a layer for routing and message translations (almost similar to an enterprise service bus), it's important to keep it dumb and not add any business logic to it. This would allow the endpoints to evolve, without having to worry about part of its logic residing on the gateway.

Scale only what needs to scale

The ability to scale a particular application service is one of the greatest benefits of using this architectural style. A business's ability to meet its growing demands depends on the ability of its application to scale as needed. While breaking the application into microservices gives us flexibility in scaling individual services, it also adds the complexity of knowing which service to scale. You can pick microservices that deal with critical business aspects, such as an eCommerce checkout service, and equip them with more hardware resources.

When packaging a microservice, you can bundle it as an executable JAR file. Solutions such as **Spring Boot**, **Wildfly Swarm**, and **Dropwizard** support this. With these approaches, you can bundle your application along with a server which starts as part of your application. You can also use Payara Micro, which provides a cleaner solution by separating the infrastructure (server) and your code. You can start a Payara Micro instance using `java -jar payara-micro-xxx.jar` and specify the WAR file that needs to be deployed on start by using a command line argument. All these options result in a single runtime process, hosting your microservice application.

In simple terms, scaling a microservice means you need to deploy more than one instance of it. With a container based solution, you can replicate the container instance using an image of your service and spawn a new instance with it. An **API Gateway** can act as the front for your services and a load balancer would then route the requests to a cluster of microservice instances:

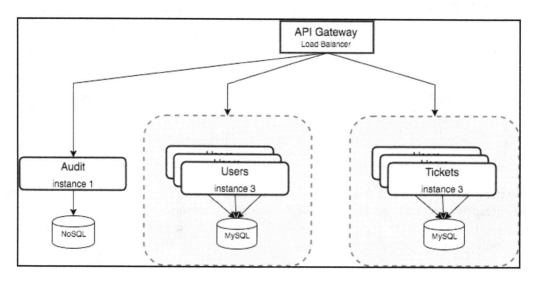

A practice often seen in enterprises is using a single machine to host multiple services (think multiple JBoss/Payara instances on a single box). The problem with this is that if even one of those processes goes haywire, it will end up taking all the services running on that machine down with it. Docker containers, on the other hand, allow you to isolate each running process, thereby mitigating the risk of one rogue service killing the others. In microservices, you would want to take advantage of a container environment, to protect you from such failures.

There are more advanced techniques to scaling, such as a three dimension scalability model, as described in the book, *The Art of Scalability*. Once you have containerized an application using Docker and produced a Docker image, you can use *Kubernetes* to manage the scaling needs of your microservice applications. **Kubernetes** is an open source platform that helps with deploying and scaling containerized applications. The project was originally developed by Google for their internal applications. The application Google used was called **Borg**, which can be considered a predecessor to Kubernetes.

The bad parts, yes, there are a few

Implementing the microservices architecture leads to a change in organisational culture, and it is not an easy one to make. Seeing a few large companies achieving success by following this model doesn't necessarily mean it's the right option for your company's need. Before making any changes, it's best to make careful considerations of the benefits and challenges ahead. SOA or having a monolith haven't become obsolete patterns, and neither is microservices the ultimate solution. These points do not intend to drive you away from using microservice architecture, but to make you aware of the disadvantages and certain pitfalls that you'll need to pay attention to. You are probably going to run into rough edges when trying this out at first, but it's essential to be able to learn from your mistakes and decide what works and what doesn't for your team.

Modular services that are defined by business capabilities are not easy to do. There are concepts of DDD, such as bounded context and single responsibility, that help guide us, but these aren't easy to get right first time. It sometimes helps to start off by writing a monolith and then refactor it into microservices later. This helps with defining the business boundaries and modules to build, which is never clear at the beginning of a project.

Having multiple databases can be challenging. Transactions across services which affect various databases are not easy to work with. When a single request is made into the application, the same is often passed downstream to other services which participate in the request handling. Identifying the issue with a request becomes difficult when multiple services are involved. To allow tracing of such requests within the application, a correlation ID is generated at the start of the request and gets passed as a header to each service. The idea is not unique to microservices, and is often used in SOA or other service orchestration solutions.

No matter how much developers love to rewrite code following the next technology buzz, not all projects are candidates for migrating to microservices. With any form of distributed computing, there are challenges that are well-known in the computing world, such as:

- Administering and monitoring dozens or hundreds of services is hard
- Development and testing of distributed systems is not easy; thus, automation of testing and deployment is essential to have
- Decomposing may lead to violation of the *DRY principle* (duplication of code), which needs some analysis
- Another general issue is referenced as *Fallacies of distributed computing*, which is also well-documented in material found on the internet

When doing microservices development, it's best to avoid some common mistakes. Here are few *Dos* and *Don'ts* to consider, before we move on:

Dos	Don'ts
A service is responsible for only one business capability.	A service is responsible for more than one business capability.
Single repository per microservice. All logs and branches are focused on supporting this one service.	Putting more than one microservice in the same repository. Tracking release branches and history becomes convoluted and introduces complexity for build tools as well.
All communication between services are done only via its published interfaces such as API contracts.	A microservice communicates with another services repository directly without going through its API contract.

Avoid sharing database with multiple microservices. Use one database per service.	Multiple microservices share a database. While seemingly okay, it can lead to cross dependencies, which in turn complicates deployment and scalability.
Maintain the database SQL scripts or infrastructure scripts, like Docker files and so on, as close to the service as possible. For example, use the same repository to store all related artifacts for a service.	Maintaining infrastructure or database scripts separately rather than associating it with code repositories.
You are going to have multiple machines and independent processes to work with.	One Tomcat/JBoss with two or more WAR files.

Summary

We walked through the difference between building a traditional monolith application and how a microservice-based architecture can add value to large complex applications. Now, you know how a cross-functional team can help deliver software faster using DevOps and other practices. Distributed computing has its own challenges and the solution is to not think of it as an afterthought, but instead make it part of your requirement.

We saw how microservices are made by decomposing a monolith into functional capabilities. This requires an understanding of the domain, which helps build the bounded context for our domain model. We also covered a few of the disadvantages of using this as a silver bullet, as one-size-fits-all is certainly not true.

Microservices can be considered a subset of SOA. Using this architecture for large applications has many benefits such as a lower learning curve due to a smaller code base. This allows for refactoring within short time frames. Testing of individual services can be done without having to run a large test suite for the entire application.

4
Building and Deploying Microservices

With an understanding of what makes a microservice, we can now take a deep dive into bundling microservices and deploying them. We will make use of the containerization solutions available and see how they can be used when working with this architectural style.

Java EE has a rich set of APIs for building various types of applications. With decades of experience in distributed applications, Java EE is a promising platform for use with microservices. Enterprise features such as transactions, security, web sockets, persistence, messaging, asynchronous processing, Restful APIs, and an ever-growing set of open source tools and libraries, make it a compelling choice.

Here's what we will cover in this chapter:

- Fat JAR
- Skinny WAR
- Examples using Payara Micro
- MicroProfile:
    - Java EE already has support
    - WildFly Swarm
    - Spring Cloud
- Docker containers:
    - Working with distributed teams
    - Building custom images
    - Running multiple containers
    - Fat JAR or Skinny WAR with Docker

When building microservices, we have two packaging choices for deploying our service:

- **Fat JAR**: An Uber JAR approach which bundles the server runtime in it
- **Skinny WAR**: Traditional slim war which is deployed on a server

Fat JAR

The way we have been thinking about application servers is changing. The basics of developing a web application typically involves two steps:

1. Building a web project whose final output is a **web archive** (**WAR**) file. This WAR file will contain the application code and optionally third party libraries, which are not part of Java EE.

2. Deploying the artifact to an environment (local, test, prod) having the Java EE application server. The environment will have all the needed configurations applicable to it. There can be multiple WAR files deployed on a single JVM process.

Here's a logical view of a traditional WAR file deployment on a server:

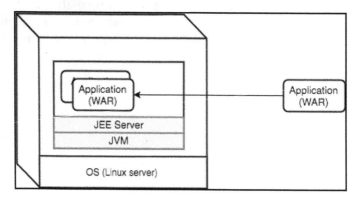

Fat JAR approach

The idea of creating a Fat JAR (all-inclusive JAR), is to allow us to have a single deployable unit that has all the application and runtime code in it. Thus, instead of deploying your application to an application server, you bundle everything needed to run your application into a JAR file, which includes an embedded server. This single artifact can then be promoted through your various environments, such as the test stage, till production.

Here's the logical view for a Fat JAR based deployment with bundled server runtime/libs:

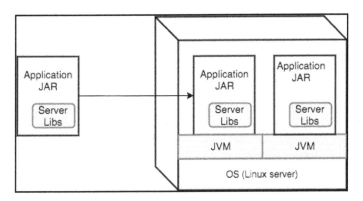

There already exist new frameworks that make it fairly easy to get started with microservices. We will look at two popular choices, WildFly Swarm and Spring Boot. WildFly Swarm is based on the WildFly application server, while Spring Boot is a popular choice among developers.

Both Spring Boot and WildFly Swarm allow us to build Uber JARs that are self-contained and have a small memory footprint, as they pack only the essentials of what the application needs. Both of these projects provide good support for developing microservices by means of third party library integrations such as Netflix OSS, which is a set of frameworks and libraries for building microservice applications.

Other noteworthy mentions include **DropWizard**, which also offers a similar approach to building an Uber JAR. We will see examples of WildFly Swarm and Spring Boot in the sections to follow.

Skinny WAR

The approach of having a single JAR with all its needed dependencies may sound nice to begin with, but this approach may not work for everyone. Fat JARs are easy to deploy and run, but they do bring some complexities along with them:

- Deployment size of the application JAR increases, as you would be bundling some parts of an application server within the deployment file
- Deployment time increases, considering the file size and the need to upload it to different environments

The traditional Skinny WAR, when built against Java EE standards, can be measured in a few **kilobytes** (**KB**). Moving this around over the network is much simpler than doing the same with a Fat JAR, which bundles shared libraries along with the application code.

A more familiar style of working with web applications is to create a WAR file. This is your unit of deployment, which gets placed in a Java EE application server such as WildFly, Payara, or any other JEE compliant server. The WAR file contains only the application code, but the runtime environment is provided to it by means of a Java EE server. In a microservice architecture, the server would contain a single microservice, which is deployed in it as a WAR file.

This approach provides for a clean separation of the infrastructure code from the application code.

Examples using Payara Micro

Payara Micro offers a new way to run Java EE or microservice applications. It is based on the Web profile of Glassfish and bundles few additional APIs. The distribution is designed keeping modern containerized environments in mind. Payara Micro is available to download as a standalone executable JAR, as well as a Docker image. It's an open source MicroProfile compatible runtime.

Here's a list of APIs that are supported in Payara Micro:

- Servlets, JSTL, EL, and JSPs
- WebSockets
- JSF
- JAX-RS

- EJB lite
- JTA
- JPA
- Bean Validation
- CDI
- Interceptors
- JBatch
- Concurrency
- JCache

We will be exploring how to build our services using Payara Micro in the next section.

Building our services

Let's start building parts of our **Issue Management System** (**IMS**), which is going to be a one-stop-destination for collaboration among teams. As the name implies, this system will be used for managing issues that are raised as **tickets** and get assigned to **users** for resolution. To begin the project, we will identify our microservice candidates based on the business model of IMS. Here, let's define three functional services, which will be hosted in their own independent Git repositories:

- `ims-micro-users`
- `ims-micro-tasks`
- `ims-micro-notify`

You might wonder, why these three and why separate repositories? We could create much more fine-grained services and perhaps it wouldn't be wrong to do so. The answer lies in understanding the following points:

- **Isolating what varies**: We need to be able to independently develop and deploy each unit. Changes to one business capability or domain shouldn't require changes in other services more often than desired.
- **Organisation or Team structure**: If you define teams by business capability, then they can work independent of others and release features with greater agility. The *tasks* team should be able to evolve independent of the teams that are handling *users* or *notifications.* The functional boundaries should allow independent version and release cycle management.

- **Transactional boundaries for consistency:** Distributed transactions are not easy, thus creating services for related features that are too fine grained, and lead to more complexity than desired. You would need to become familiar with concepts like eventual consistency, but these are not easy to achieve in practice.
- **Source repository per service**: Setting up a single repository that hosts all the services is ideal when it's the same team that works on these services and the project is relatively small. But we are building our fictional IMS, which is a large complex system with many moving parts. Separate teams would get tightly coupled by sharing a repository. Moreover, versioning and tagging of releases will be yet another problem to solve.

The projects are created as standard Java EE projects, which are Skinny WARs, that will be deployed using the *Payara Micro* server. Payara Micro allows us to delay the decision of using a Fat JAR or Skinny WAR. This gives us flexibility in picking the deployment choice at a later stage.

As Maven is a widely adopted build tool among developers, we will use the same to create our example projects, using the following steps:

```
mvn archetype:generate -DgroupId=org.jee8ng -DartifactId=ims-micro-users -
DarchetypeArtifactId=maven-archetype-webapp -DinteractiveMode=false

mvn archetype:generate -DgroupId=org.jee8ng -DartifactId=ims-micro-tasks -
DarchetypeArtifactId=maven-archetype-webapp -DinteractiveMode=false

mvn archetype:generate -DgroupId=org.jee8ng -DartifactId=ims-micro-notify -
DarchetypeArtifactId=maven-archetype-webapp -DinteractiveMode=false
```

Once the structure is generated, update the `properties` and `dependencies` section of `pom.xml` with the following contents, for all three projects:

```
<properties>
    <project.build.sourceEncoding>UTF-8</project.build.sourceEncoding>
    <maven.compiler.source>1.8</maven.compiler.source>
    <maven.compiler.target>1.8</maven.compiler.target>
    <failOnMissingWebXml>false</failOnMissingWebXml>
</properties>

<dependencies>
    <dependency>
        <groupId>javax</groupId>
        <artifactId>javaee-api</artifactId>
        <version>8.0</version>
        <scope>provided</scope>
    </dependency>
```

```
    <dependency>
        <groupId>junit</groupId>
        <artifactId>junit</artifactId>
        <version>4.12</version>
        <scope>test</scope>
    </dependency>
</dependencies>
```

Next, create a `beans.xml` file under WEB-INF folder for all three projects:

```
<?xml version="1.0" encoding="UTF-8"?>
<beans xmlns="http://xmlns.jcp.org/xml/ns/javaee"
        xmlns:xsi="http://www.w3.org/2001/XMLSchema-instance"
        xsi:schemaLocation="http://xmlns.jcp.org/xml/ns/javaee
http://xmlns.jcp.org/xml/ns/javaee/beans_2_0.xsd"
        bean-discovery-mode="all">
</beans>
```

You can delete the `index.jsp` and `web.xml` files, as we won't be needing them.

The following is the project structure of `ims-micro-users`. The same structure will be used for `ims-micro-tasks` and `ims-micro-notify`:

```
└── ims-micro-users
    ├── pom.xml
    └── src
        ├── main
        │   ├── java
        │   │   └── org
        │   │       └── jee8ng
        │   │           └── ims
        │   │               └── users
        │   │                   ├── JaxrsActivator.java
        │   │                   ├── boundary
        │   │                   ├── control
        │   │                   └── entity
        │   ├── resources
        │   └── webapp
        │       └── WEB-INF
        │           └── beans.xml
        └── test
            └── java
```

The package name for users, tasks, and notify service will be as shown as the following:

- `org.jee8ng.ims.users` (inside `ims-micro-users`)
- `org.jee8ng.ims.tasks` (inside `ims-micro-tasks`)
- `org.jee8ng.ims.notify` (inside `ims-micro-notify`)

Each of the above will in turn have sub-packages called **boundary**, **control**, and **entity**. The structure follows the **Boundary-Control-Entity (BCE)/Entity-Control-Boundary (ECB)** pattern.

The `JaxrsActivator` shown as follows is required to enable the JAX-RS API and thus needs to be placed in each of the projects:

```
import javax.ws.rs.ApplicationPath;
import javax.ws.rs.core.Application;

@ApplicationPath("resources")
public class JaxrsActivator extends Application {}
```

All three projects will have REST endpoints that we can invoke over HTTP. When doing RESTful API design, a popular convention is to use plural names for resources, especially if the resource could represent a collection. For example:

- `/users`
- `/tasks`

The resource class names in the projects use the plural form, as it's consistent with the resource URL naming used. This avoids confusions such as a resource URL being called a **users resource**, while the class is named `UserResource`. Given that this is an opinionated approach, feel free to use singular class names if desired.

Here's the relevant code for `ims-micro-users`, `ims-micro-tasks`, and `ims-micro-notify` projects respectively.

Under `ims-micro-users`, define the `UsersResource` endpoint:

```
package org.jee8ng.ims.users.boundary;

import javax.ws.rs.*;
import javax.ws.rs.core.*;

@Path("users")
public class UsersResource {
    @GET
```

```
@Produces(MediaType.APPLICATION_JSON)
public Response get() {
    return Response.ok("user works").build();
}
}
```

Under `ims-micro-tasks`, define the `TasksResource` endpoint:

```
package org.jee8ng.ims.tasks.boundary;

import javax.ws.rs.*;
import javax.ws.rs.core.*;

@Path("tasks")
public class TasksResource {

  @GET
  @Produces(MediaType.APPLICATION_JSON)
  public Response get() {
      return Response.ok("task works").build();
  }
}
```

Under `ims-micro-notify`, define the `NotificationsResource` endpoint:

```
package org.jee8ng.ims.notify.boundary;

import javax.ws.rs.*;
import javax.ws.rs.core.*;

@Path("notifications")
public class NotificationsResource {

  @GET
  @Produces(MediaType.APPLICATION_JSON)
  public Response get() {
      return Response.ok("notification works").build();
  }
}
```

Once you build all three projects using `mvn clean install`, you will get your Skinny WAR files generated in the `target` directory, which can be deployed on the Payara Micro server.

Running our services

Download the Payara Micro server if you haven't already, from this link: `https://www.payara.fish/downloads`.

The micro server will have the name `payara-micro-xxx.jar`, where `xxx` will be the version number, which might be different when you download the file.

Here's how you can start Payara Micro with our services deployed locally. When doing so, we need to ensure that the instances start on different ports, to avoid any port conflicts:

```
>java -jar payara-micro-xxx.jar --deploy ims-micro-users/target/ims-micro-
users.war --port 8081
>java -jar payara-micro-xxx.jar --deploy ims-micro-tasks/target/ims-micro-
tasks.war --port 8082
>java -jar payara-micro-xxx.jar --deploy ims-micro-notify/target/ims-micro-
notify.war --port 8083
```

This will start three instances of Payara Micro running on the specified ports. This makes our applications available under these URLs:

- `http://localhost:8081/ims-micro-users/resources/users/`
- `http://localhost:8082/ims-micro-tasks/resources/tasks/`
- `http://localhost:8083/ims-micro-notify/resources/notifications/`

Payar Micro can be started on a non-default port by using the `--port` parameter, as we did earlier. This is useful when running multiple instances on the same machine.

Another option is to use the `--autoBindHttp` parameter, which will attempt to connect on `8080` as the default port, and if that port is unavailable, it will try to bind on the next port up, repeating until it finds an available port.

Examples of starting Payra Micro:

`java -jar payara-micro.jar` `--port 8080`	Starts the server on port `8080`
`java -jar payara-micro.jar` `--autoBindHttp`	Starts the server on `8080` if available, else tries to use the next available port: `8081`, `8082`, and so on

`java -jar payara-micro.jar`
`--port 8080`
`--autoBindHttp`
`--autoBindRange 3`
	Tries to start using `8080`, if busy, tries `8081`, `8082`, `8083` respectively before giving up

Uber JAR option: Now, there's one more feature that Payara Micro provides. We can generate an Uber JAR as well, which would be the Fat JAR approach that we learnt in the Fat JAR section.

To package our `ims-micro-users` project as an Uber JAR, we can run the following command:

```
java -jar payara-micro-xxx.jar --deploy ims-micro-users/target/ims-micro-
users.war --outputUberJar users.jar
```

This will generate the `users.jar` file in the directory where you run this command. The size of this JAR will naturally be larger than our WAR file, since it will also bundle the Payara Micro runtime in it. Here's how you can start the application using the generated JAR:

```
java -jar users.jar
```

The server parameters that we used earlier can be passed to this runnable JAR file too. Apart from the two choices we saw for running our microservice projects, there's a third option as well. Payara Micro provides an API based approach, which can be used to programmatically start the embedded server.

We will expand upon these three services as we progress further into the realm of cloud-based Java EE.

MicroProfile

The **MicroProfile** project is an initiative to optimise Java EE for microservices. It was launched around mid 2016, as a collaborative effort between Java application server vendors and the enterprise Java community, with the intent of enabling fast innovation. Despite being a relatively new specification, there's already a large number of members participating in the project.

MicroProfile isn't limited to picking APIs from the Java EE specifications. It may also include third party libraries and APIs, which the community may need for building microservices. Since developers have great knowledge around the Java EE platform, they can leverage their existing skills and API knowledge for building microservices. The MicroProfile is a baseline standard, which defines APIs and their minimum version that all vendors must support. This makes the code portable across multiple MicroProfile runtimes, similar to standard Java EE portability.

The `http://microprofile.io` website has presentations and code samples that can help developers to get started. A reference application called **Conference Application** has been created for demonstrating MicroProfile capabilities, that can be run on the participating vendor provided servers.

Java EE already has support

Java EE already ships with various specifications that are part of its standards. MicroProfile is a specification, which groups together a subset of the existing APIs from Java EE and adds new ones that are focused towards microservices. The idea of a profile isn't new; since Java EE 6, there was a web profile defined which contained a subset of specifications that made it lighter than a full Java EE system. MicroProfile can be considered to be even smaller than the web profile. This is possible due to the modular design of Java EE.

The latest 1.1 MicroProfile specification contains support for:

- **JAX-RS 2.0**: To publish RESTful web services, as the standard API for building microservices
- **CDI 1.1**: The programming model for building microservices
- **JSON-P 1.0**: To enable working with the JSON format
- **Config 1.0**: Allows for the modification of application configurations from outside the application without needing the application to be repackaged

Payara is also part of the specification, and thus supports all APIs defined by the specification of MicroProfile.

WildFly Swarm

WildFly, formerly called JBoss, is an application server, and WildFly Swarm is a project that deconstructs the application server into modular parts. Swarm is aimed towards microservice applications, allowing the putting together of just enough subsets of the Java EE features that are required by the application.

An easy way to get started is to use the project generator page to select the features, or fractions, as they are called in Swarm terminology, and generate a maven project.

You can head over to the following link: `http://wildfly-swarm.io/generator/`:

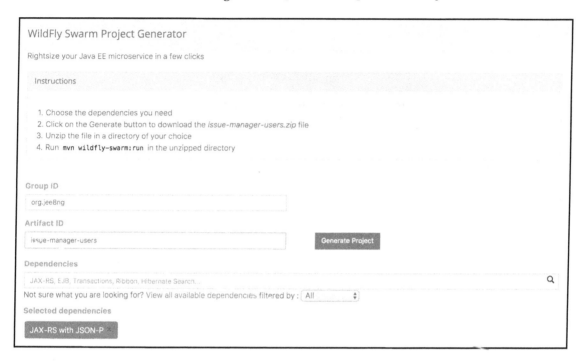

 The Wildfly Swarm link may change; it's best to use your favorite search engine, such as Google, to look this up.

The page presents a form where you can specify the maven projects **Group ID**, **Artifact ID**, and **Dependencies**. To create a microservice, let's use that page and fill in the following values:

- **Group ID**: org.jee8ng
- **Artifact ID**: issue-manager-users
- **Dependencies**: JAX-RS with JSON-P

Once done, you can click on the **Generate Project** button which will download the zipped project file to your machine. If you unzip the file, you will be presented with the following structure of the Maven project:

```
├── pom.xml
└── src
```

```
└── main
    └── java
        └── org
            └── jee8ng
                └── issuemanagerusers
                    └── rest
                        └── HelloWorldEndpoint.java
```

The generated project is a simple **Hello World** project, containing one REST endpoint. Now, let's create a `JaxrsBootup` class, which is required to activate JAXRS capabilities:

```java
package org.jee8ng.issuemanagerusers.rest;

import javax.ws.rs.ApplicationPath;
import javax.ws.rs.core.Application;

@ApplicationPath("rest")
public class JaxrsBootup extends Application { }
```

Next, update the `HelloWorldEndpoint.java` file with the code given as follows, which returns a JSON response when invoked. The code builds a `JsonObject` instance which contains a `name` key and a string value associated with it:

```java
package org.jee8ng.issuemanagerusers.rest;

import javax.json.Json;
import javax.json.JsonObject;
import javax.ws.rs.Path;
import javax.ws.rs.core.Response;
import javax.ws.rs.GET;
import javax.ws.rs.Produces;
import javax.ws.rs.core.MediaType;

@Path("/hello")
public class HelloWorldEndpoint {

    @GET
    @Produces(MediaType.APPLICATION_JSON)
    public Response doGet() {
        JsonObject json = Json.createObjectBuilder()
                .add("name", "hello microservice")
                .build();
        return Response.ok(json).build();
    }
}
```

Open the `pom.xml` and update the `finalName` tags value to match, as shown in the following code:

```
<finalName>issue-manager-users</finalName>
```

Also update the `dependencies` section, with the following single dependency of `microprofile`:

```
<dependencies>
  <!-- WildFly Swarm Fractions -->
  <dependency>
    <groupId>org.wildfly.swarm</groupId>
    <artifactId>micropofile</artifactId>
  </dependency>
</dependencies>
```

You will notice that there's just one dependency specified. We don't even a need Java EE dependency, as the `microprofile` dependency already includes JAXRS, CDI, and JSON-P transitively.

Apart from these, we have the `wildfly-swarm-plugin` declaration, which enables the Uber JAR generation.

Open a terminal, and from the project root directory, run the following command, which will build and start the application:

```
mvn wildfly-swarm:run
```

Once the application starts up, you can access the URL via a browser, or use the following `curl` command to fetch the response:

```
curl http://localhost:8080/rest/hello
```

Response: `{"name":"hello microservice"}`

Stopping the application is as simple as pressing *Ctrl* + *C* on the running terminal window.

If you look within the target directory of the project, you can see that the `wildfly-swarm-plugin` has generated two artifacts:

`issue-manager-users.war`	4 KB file containing just the application code.
`issue-manager-users-swarm.jar`	44 MB file. This is an Uber JAR which has application and server runtime.

Since the Uber JAR has the server runtime within it, we can execute it like any other standalone Java application JAR file:

```
java -jar issue-manager-users-swarm.jar
```

That will start up the WildFly swarm instance with the minimal dependencies that have been used. This allows our application footprint to be smaller, as we are packaging only a subset of WildFly fractions/modules.

The Java heap memory for this application can be as low as 17-22 MB, which would have been a dream stat when compared to running a full WildFly application server.

Spring Cloud

Spring framework needs no introduction for Java developers. Spring offers dependency injection as its core feature and provides many supporting modules such as Web MVC, persistence, AOP, and a huge number of integrations with popular projects.

Spring also integrates nicely with most IDEs and offers **Spring Tool Suite** (**STS**), which is an eclipse-based IDE for spring application development. In case of NetBeans, there's a NB Spring plugin, which enables support for spring-based development.

Spring Boot makes it very easy to get started with Spring-based projects. It sets up default configurations, and thus requires minimal to zero setup. It provides starter maven dependencies, which helps make the application production ready in a short amount of time. Similar to the WildFly Swarms generator approach, to get started with Spring Boot, you could use the link: https://start.spring.io/.

If you prefer to use an IDE, then you could use STS or any other IDE with Spring support to generate the project.

Here's how the **New project** wizard looks when using NetBeans, **File** | **New Project** | **Maven** | **Spring Boot Initialize Project** (this is provided by the NB Spring plugin):

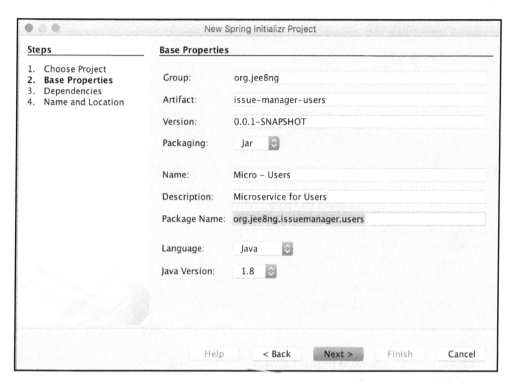

Having filled the fields as needed, you can select the Web dependency on the next step of the wizard. Once you finish the wizard, a Maven project is created with the following structure:

```
├── pom.xml
└── src
    └── main
        └── java
        │   └── org
        │       └── jee8ng
        │           └── issuemanager
        │               └── users
        │                   └── MicroUsersApplication.java
        └── resources
            ├── application.properties
            ├── static
            └── templates
```

Here's the relevant snippet of `MicroUsersApplication.java`:

```
@SpringBootApplication
public class MicroUsersApplication {

  public static void main(String[] args) {
    SpringApplication.run(MicroUsersApplication.class, args);
  }
}
```

This allows the application to be started using its `main` method. The next step would be to create the REST endpoint, the Spring way. Create a class called `HelloRestController.java` with the following code:

```
@RestController
@RequestMapping("/hello")
public class HelloRestController {
    @RequestMapping("")
    public String get() {
        return "hello microservice";
    }
}
```

It's a fairly simple code, which will publish a REST endpoint at the `/hello` path. When invoked, it should return the text `hello microservice`.

If you open the `pom.xml`, it will have these essential snippets:

```
<parent>
        <groupId>org.springframework.boot</groupId>
        <artifactId>spring-boot-starter-parent</artifactId>
        <version>1.5.6.RELEASE</version>
</parent>
<dependencies>
        <dependency>
            <groupId>org.springframework.boot</groupId>
            <artifactId>spring-boot-starter-web</artifactId>
        </dependency>
</dependencies>
```

The `spring-boot-starter-web` dependency is used to add support for full stack web development using the Tomcat web server and the Spring MVC framework.

Similar to `wildfly-swarm-plugin`, Spring provides a `spring-boot-maven-plugin` for Spring Boot projects. This enables the creation of an Uber JAR that can then be executed as a standalone application.

Open a terminal, and from the project root directory, run the following command, which will build and start the application:

```
mvn spring-boot:run
```

Once the application starts up, you can access the URL via a browser, or use the following `curl` command to fetch the response:

```
curl http://localhost:8080/hello
```

Response: `hello microservice`

Stopping the application is as simple as pressing *Ctrl* + *C* on the running terminal window.

After running `mvn clean install` to build the project, if you look within the `target` directory of the project, you can see the Uber JAR, which is approximately 14 MB in size:

`issue-manager-users-0.0.1-SNAPSHOT.jar.original`	4 KB JAR containing application code alone
`issue-manager-users-0.0.1-SNAPSHOT.jar`	14 MB executable runtime JAR file

Since the Uber JAR has the Spring runtime that contains an embedded Tomcat within it, we can execute it like any other standalone Java application:

```
java -jar issue-manager-users-0.0.1-SNAPSHOT.jar
```

This will start up the Tomcat instance and publish the REST endpoint. The **Java Heap Memory** (**JHM**) for this application can be as low as 18-25 MB (similar to WildFly Swarm).

Docker containers

Environment-specific issues have always plagued developers and operations teams. A developer may work locally on a Windows or Mac computer, while his code may end up running on a Linux server. When promoting builds from one environment to another (test, stage, production), yet again the environment changes and leads to more possibilities of failure.

Consider a few simple cases of what can go wrong with changes in the environment:

- The file path separator used in Windows is a back slash \, while Linux requires the forward slash /
- Java version mismatch issues between environments
- Environment variables or configurations, such as datasource name or other application server settings can differ
- The OS library versions may not be the same and any dependencies on these can break the code
- The database drivers are usually part of the application server and the versions may not be in sync across environments

To overcome the environment disparity or *it works on my machine* conversations, solutions such as **virtual machines** (**VM**) and containers have come up to provide a consistent and portable environment. Most Java architects and developers would have come across virtual machines.

It's useful to compare a container to a virtual machine; this helps us to understand some of the key differences. Virtualisation is used for creating multiple environments based on a single physical hardware system.

Docker isn't the same as traditional virtualisation, though there are similarities between the two, since they share some characteristics. Both provide isolation for your application and the ability to bundle the solution as a binary image. Docker provides an isolated environment called a container, which allows for packaging and running an application such as a microservice.

A VM houses not only the application, but an entire operating system with all its bells and whistles. The way you build a VM is by creating an OS image which has everything in it and can be stripped down later, based on your application needs. This is in contrast to how you work with containers. A Docker container is built by putting together the minimum software that is required for running the application.

Docker, unlike VM, is an application delivery solution which meets high scalability needs. Another aspect that is different from VMs is that your application data doesn't live within a container. Data is saved outside the container using defined volumes, which gets shared between multiple instances of a container. A container can save data to its filesystem as well; this will remain persisted until the container is deleted.

Deploying the actual container can be done on physical or virtual machines, on cloud, or on premise. Docker doesn't enforce any constraint regarding the underlying infrastructure, thus you can mix and match strategies as per your needs.

Technically, a VM requires a hypervisor which enables running multiple **Guest OS**'s on top of the host machine. Each virtual machine will have its own operating system, along with all the libraries and applications within it. Docker, on the other hand, doesn't require the additional hypervisor layer, as it directly utilizes the host machine's kernel, making it lightweight and incredibly fast to start and stop. VMs are usually gigabytes in size, while containers can be measured in a few megabytes.

The following table demonstrates the differences between the two:

Virtual Machine	Container
Measured in GB	Can be as small as 5MB
Requires a Hypervisor layer on top of OS	No hypervisor required, shares Host Kernel
Stateful as data lives inside it	Data lives outside container by using defined volumes
Backup of VMs is a must to avoid data loss	Container backups aren't required since no data is stored within the container
Slower than a container	Faster than a virtual machine
Virtualises the hardware	Virtualises the OS
Provides extreme isolation which can be useful for preventing any breakout by malicious applications	Operates at process level with isolation around process
Deployment unit is a machine	Deployment unit is an application

Here's a pictorial view of how the VM and Docker containers differ:

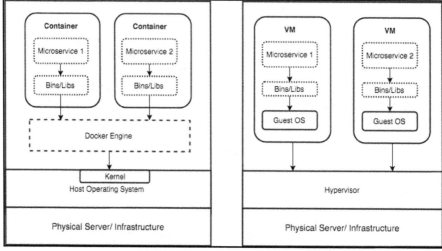

The Docker world can be considered to have these 3 parts:

- Docker Engine
- Client
- Registry

Here is the pictorial representation of the Docker world:

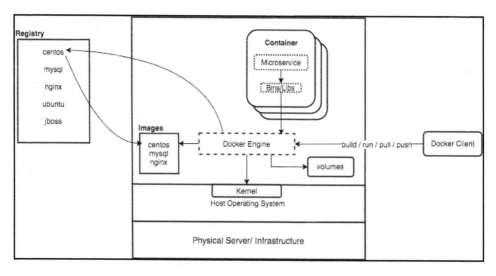

- **Docker Engine**: This is the server process that manages the runtime environment for containers. A host would have one daemon process running in the background, which provides a remote API for clients to talk to over network sockets.
- **Client**: Docker provides a command line tool, which is used for working with Docker. Client is used for passing the instructions to the Docker daemon which does the actual work of hosting the container applications. The client/server model allows the client to talk to any number of servers, where the server can be on a remote host.
- **Registry**: Used for the storage and transfer of container images. There are applications which allow you to run private registries, or you can even make use of cloud/public based ones. The installation process of Docker is well-documented here: `https://docs.docker.com/engine/installation/`.

Once the installation is done, you can start playing with Docker. As a example, running the following command will set a CentOS instance running locally and place you in its terminal:

```
docker run -t -i centos:latest
```

Working with distributed teams

With Docker, anyone can replicate an environment on their local machine. Docker provides a consistent development environment for the entire team. Team members need not struggle to set up their local machines with all the needed scripts and libraries needed to start working on a project. They can simply pull a Docker image and start working in a few seconds. Since Docker containers run as a process, most IDEs can be used to connect to the running instance for any debugging of applications as needed, without having to SSH into any remote system.

Docker features such as mounting Host machine volumes and exposing ports can be leveraged for local development. A developer working on a service can focus on just that and have other dependency services run as containers, without needing to know the details of how to run them.

In our example of *Issue Management System*, a team working on the `ims-micro-tasks` (tasks) microservice may need to run the `ims-micro-users` microservice as a dependency. Here, the users microservice team can build an image of its service and upload it to either a public or private registry. So, the tasks microservice team can simply download/pull the image and run it as a container. Thus, teams can share their application with all the required dependencies as Docker images.

This sharing becomes more convenient when the microservices are written using different languages, or cater to different needs. As an example, a team working on the UI in Angular need not know anything about the microservices written in Java. They can simply use Docker to run the Java-based microservices as a dependency.

Building custom images

You can build Docker images by creating a file called **Dockerfile,** which is used by Docker. This file can be considered to have executable instructions which are used to build the image. When building an image, it helps to recall that Docker is not a VM, but more of a process. So don't start bundling things that aren't really required for your application. Build an image based on the essentials that are required. There are many Docker images that rely on some OS, which influences the final image size as well.

A good base image selection can help to keep your image size in check. For example, an alpine Linux image is 5 MB versus a CentOS image, which can be close to 200 MB. Many of the official Docker images are moving to Alpine Linux as well. Consider using a JRE image rather than using a JDK if your project really needs just the Java runtime. The image size not only impacts the local storage but also the network latency while transferring it over the network. Smaller images help speed up build times and deployments.

Here's a simple Dockerfile for our `ims-micro-users` project. Create this file in the projects root directory next to the `pom.xml`.

The contents of `ims-micro-users/Dockerfile` are as follows:

```
FROM payara/micro:5-SNAPSHOT
COPY target/ims-micro-users.war $DEPLOY_DIR
```

The `FROM` instruction tells Docker to use a `payara/micro` image which is tagged as `5-SNAPSHOT`. This image is a public image hosted on Dockerhub that will be downloaded to your local machine when you run it for the first time. Think of it as a complete environment that is capable of running a Payara Micro server.

Next, run the following command, which will create an image for our application:

```
docker build -t jee8ng/ims-micro-users .
```

This builds an image on your local machine ready to be run or distributed to other members of your team. After you ran the preceding command, you should have a local image, which can be looked up by using the `docker image` commands:

Now, running the generated Docker image can be done like any other container:

```
docker run -p 8080:8080 jee8ng/ims-micro-users
```

This starts up the docker container and maps the local port 8080 to the container's port 8080.

Running multiple containers

It's possible to run multiple `docker` containers on any machine. Since they are lightweight processes, it is possible to run more containers locally than would have been possible with a virtual machine.

Just like we can run multiple application server instances on the same machine, we can run multiple `docker` containers too.

For example:

```
docker run -p 8080:8080 jee8ng/ims-micro-users
docker run -p 8081:8080 jee8ng/ims-micro-users
```

Notice that we specified different local binding ports for the **Host machine** (8080 and 8081), but the `docker` containers use port 8080. This is possible because each `docker` container has its own virtual Ethernet IP address.

Fat JAR or Skinny WAR with Docker

A `Dockerfile` can be used to describe the executable steps required to build an image, and this can be done for both Far JAR or Skinny WAR. When we built our custom image for the `ims-micro-users` project, we actually took our Skinny WAR and bundled it with the Payara Micro server. This resulted in a Docker image that we were able to run locally.

Similarly, a Fat JAR or Uber JAR is just an executable and can be used to build a Docker image; it has just enough runtime for it to run.

Since the Fat JAR already has the server bundled in it, all that's left as a requirement is to provide an environment, which has an appropriate Java runtime.

Let's build an Uber JAR for `ims-micro-tasks` (this can be any Fat JAR project you may have). To build an Uber JAR with Payara Micro, we can issue the following command:

```
java -jar payara-micro.jar --deploy ims-micro-tasks.war
--outputUberJar ims-micro-tasks.jar
```

If you check the size of the WAR and generated JAR, you will notice the Fat JAR is 66 MB as it bundles the server along with it (JAR has the server and application code):

```
66M ims-micro-tasks.jar
22K ims-micro-tasks.war
```

The `ims-micro-tasks.jar` is an executable JAR, which we can use to create our Docker image. This JAR would require a JRE to be run independently, so let's define a `Dockerfile` for our Fat JAR, kept here `ims-micro-tasks/Dockerfile`.

```
FROM openjdk:8-jre-alpine

COPY target/ims-micro-*.jar /app.jar

CMD ["/usr/bin/java", "-jar", "/app.jar"]
```

Observe the preceding code:

- The `openjdk` 8 acts as the base image, which is a JRE installed within **Alpine Linux**. This is the minimal runtime that is required for our Fat JAR.
- The `COPY` command will copy the specified file (JAR) and name it `app.jar`, which is placed at the root of the filesystem of the container.
- The `CMD` command is the line which executes the Java application.

To build the image and then run it, you can issue the following commands from the project root directory:

```
docker build -t jee8ng/ims-micro-tasks
```

Followed by:

```
docker run -p 8080:8080 jee8ng/ims-micro-tasks
```

That should run the application and make it available at the following URL:
`http://localhost:8080/ims-micro-tasks/resources/tasks/`.

There are going to be multiple containers running in a cluster and managing these requires specialized tools. A few popular container orchestration tools include:

- **Amazon EC2 Container services**: An Amazon offering
- **Docker Swarm**: Offered by Docker
- **Kubernetes**: An open source tool that has its origins tied to Google
- **Mesos**: An apache project for managing large scale clusters

The choice

Since we saw both ways of building a Docker image, which one should we pick? There are a couple of factors to consider.

Building a Fat JAR image is done by bundling all the libraries into a single file. This has an impact on the build time, which can be significant based on the number of libraries being bundled.

Skinny WAR, which depends on Java EE, specifies its dependencies as provided (maven scope). What this means is that the application doesn't contain the dependencies, but they will be provided to it by the application server. This results in the Skinny WAR, which leads to faster builds and deployments.

When creating a Docker image in Java EE, the base image contains an OS like CentOS or any other, along with another layer of an application server like Payara. Since these layers don't change, the image building process is faster, since it only deals with the rebuilding of the small WAR file. This rebuilding of the application is what developers keep doing all day, and getting the build times to be faster will help with developer productivity.

Sometimes, the difference may not be too much to worry about. But you need to consider how many times you will be building the project. How many microservices are you planning to deploy? Deployment time can become a bottleneck when the number of deployments and frequency increases. Overall, the choice is usually influenced by developer and team preference, but it's best to measure and decide.

Summary

While we have explored Payara Micro and MicroProfile, both of these have plenty to offer. It's best to get your hands dirty by following the sample applications offered by both. MicroProfile is relatively new and is gaining momentum in the Java community, so you can expect more specifications to get added to this soon.

Docker and microservices are becoming a perfect match and there is a growing number of tools being built around these. Fat JAR and Skinny WAR are both appealing choices and the teams can pick the one that meets their needs.

Building Docker images and running containers on select machines is one thing, but taking it to production with scalability needs is another matter.

5
Java EE Becomes JSON Friendly

JSON enhancements in Java EE allow for working with JSON in a much simpler way than before. The addition of JSON processing and binding has turned it into a first-class citizen of Java EE. Use APIs to serialize and deserialize Java objects, to and from JSON documents. JSON-B does for JSON, what JAXB did for XML. No longer do you have to rely upon third-party libraries to work with JSON. Most features will work out of the box, with sensible defaults.

We will cover the following topics in this chapter:

- REST prefers JSON
- JSON first-class citizen
- No more third-party libraries
- JSON processing:
    - JSON-P 1.1
    - JSON pointer and JSON patch
    - JSON merge patch
    - JSON collectors
- JSON binding:
    - Similar to JAXB with default mappings
    - Standardize current solutions (Jackson, Gson, and so on)
    - Mapping between classes and JSON
    - Customisation APIs
- A few tips in practice

REST prefers JSON

Web services are meant to be language-neutral which facilitate communication between disparate systems. REST APIs combined with JSON as the data interchange format is becoming the default choice for building web services. These APIs are published over the HTTP protocol and get invoked by passing some headers and a message body. Unlike SOAP which requires XML as its body, RESTful APIs don't enforce a constraint on the format. This flexible approach allows for the message body types to be Text, XML, HTML, binary data, or JSON, which is a text format easily readable by humans and machines. JSON doesn't have complex data types, but instead defines only a handful of them that are supported by almost every language. This makes JSON a very appealing choice as a data-interchange format for web services.

According to `http://json.org`:

JavaScript Object Notation (JSON) is a lightweight data-interchange format. It is easy for humans to read and write. It is easy for machines to parse and generate. It is based on a subset of the JavaScript.

Here's the relevant bits of the REST endpoint, that defines a method that is mapped to the HTTP GET request for `/tasks`. The annotation `javax.ws.rs.Produces` on the `get` method marks it as a producer of JSON content type. This method returns a JSON representation of a `Ticket` instance, when the request header `Accept` contains the value `application/json`:

```
@Path("tasks")
public class TasksResource {
    @GET
    @Produces(MediaType.APPLICATION_JSON)
    public Response get() {
        return Response.ok(
                new Ticket(1, "Fix slow loading")
                ).build();
    }
}
```

The `Ticket` class is shown as follows, which is used within the REST endpoint:

```
public class Ticket {
    private int id;
    private String name;
    // Assume the usual getters and setters here
}
```

To get a JSON representation of the resource, we can invoke it by passing the `Accept` header with value `application/json`:

```
curl -X GET -H 'Accept: application/json'
http://localhost:8080/ims-micro-tasks/resources/tasks/
```

The preceding call would return a JSON document as its response, which is shown as follows:

```
{
  "id":1,
  "name":"Fix slow loading"
}
```

Since, JSON is the default, we could have invoked the URL without passing any request headers and still got back the JSON response.

To get an XML representation of the `Ticket` data, we would invoke it by passing the `Accept` header with value `application/xml`. Here's an example using the `curl` command:

```
curl -X GET -H 'Accept: application/xml'
http://localhost:8080/ims-micro-tasks/resources/tasks/
```

But this call would fail, as the `TasksResource` only supports producing JSON responses. To enable XML support, we need to update `Ticket` class with JAXB annotations:

```
@XmlRootElement
@XmlAccessorType(XmlAccessType.FIELD)
public class Ticket {
... code omitted ...
}
```

Additionally, we need to update the `@Produces` annotation of the `get()` method to support producing both XML and JSON:

```
@GET
@Produces({MediaType.APPLICATION_JSON, MediaType.APPLICATION_XML})
public Response get() {
    return Response.ok(
            new Ticket(1, "Fix slow loading")
            ).build();
}
```

With these changes in place, now the earlier `curl` invocation for XML will work:

```
curl -X GET -H 'Accept: application/xml'
http://localhost:8080/ims-micro-tasks/resources/tasks/
```

The preceding call returns the XML representation of `Ticket`, shown as follows:

```
<ticket>;
  <id>1</id>
  <name>Fix slow loading</name>
</ticket>
```

With these updates, we can have the resource support both JSON as well as XML responses. It's worth noting that for JSON's response we didn't require any annotation to be applied to the `Ticket` class. This is facilitated by JSON-B, which is a new standard that handles object to JSON, and JSON to object conversions for us.

XML, the once dominant format for data exchange is being replaced with JSON as the preferred data interchange format in APIs. JSON is considered to be simpler and lighter, compared to the verbosity of XMLs. This does not mean developers should banish XMLs and crown JSON for all things. Developers must possess a wide range of tools to pick from for a given task. Which tool to pick is dependent on the task at hand rather than wielding one tool for every job. With the advent of JSON, XMLs may no longer be the best tool or choice for data transfer between systems. But XML has a lot more to offer, with established features such as namespaces, schema rules, and style sheets (XSLT) to transform its display, which makes it a viable choice for cases other than data exchange.

JSON, a first-class citizen

The simplicity of JSON has led to it gaining great support in various languages. If you ever considered XML to be simple, then you can think of JSON as being simpler. Have a look at the JSON site (`http://www.json.org/`), which has a list of programming languages that support JSON.

Many established businesses with an online solution publish their product capabilities as services. Companies such as Facebook, Twitter, Google, and Amazon all have web services that make use of JSON as the data-interchange format. It's no surprise that the new breed of architectural solutions such as microservices have chosen JSON as the preferred communication format. Similar to many of Google's products, Gmail has APIs published for accessing its features such as providing access to a user's inbox. The Amazon platform too provides REST APIs, which can be used to work with EC2 instances and many of its other offerings such as Simple DB or S3 storage. JSON has not only influenced the application stack but also other parts such as databases, making it a first-class citizen across the entire stack.

JSON in databases

JSON has made inroads not only over the web, but also in the database world. A relational database system is considered structured, which stores its data against a defined schema. On the other hand a NoSQL database is better equipped to store schema-less data. Document based databases such as MongoDB make use of JSON to store the documents as records, similar to rows of a table in the relational world. The support is not just for storage and retrieval, but also for operating over the data. Most relational databases have introduced JSON as a datatype for storage and allow for operating over this by means of functions, with some additionally providing operators as well. It's possible for JSON documents to be stored in a string based data type too, but this would not be an efficient way to work with this specialized format. Databases such as MySQL, PostgreSQL, Oracle, and others offer JSON support which can be leveraged by developers for their use case, rather than any makeshift approach. This allows for a hybrid solution, where a SQL based relational database can be used for storing non-structured information in the form of JSON documents.

While PostgreSQL did have JSON support for a while, MySQL only started providing native JSON support in version 5.7. Here's a short sample of how it looks:

```
//Using JSON type in MySQL 5.7
create table issue ( json_doc JSON)

insert into issue values ('{
  "id":1,
  "name":"Fix slow loading",
  "priority":"High"
}');

insert into issue values ('{
  "id":2,
```

```
    "name":"Increase JVM memory",
    "priority":"Low"
}');
```

Now, with our `issue` table having two records, we can perform JSON-based operations over this data. Here's how one could filter rows, based on the attribute/key of the stored JSON document:

```
//Selecting a record
select json_doc from issue where JSON_EXTRACT(`json_doc` , '$.id') = 2;

We get back:
{"id": 2, "name": "Increase JVM memory", "priority": "Low"}
```

Apart from the preceding code, it's also possible to use the provided functions for further processing over this data. As an example, we can use the following statements to update the `priority` from `Low` to `High`, for the 2nd entry having the JSON `id` value of 2:

```
update issue set json_doc =
JSON_REPLACE(
    `json_doc` ,
    '$.priority' ,
    'High'
)
where JSON_EXTRACT(`json_doc` , '$.id') = 2;
```

For more information on these kind of capabilities, it's best to reference your preferred databases documentation.

No more third-party libraries

XMLs are still widely used in many applications and have had great support in the Java language, but the same couldn't be said for JSON until recent times. Java didn't provide a convenient and portable way to work with JSON earlier, which resulted in developers having to rely upon third-party libraries for its support. Some of these libraries include:

- `Jackson`
- `Gson`
- `json-simple`

Developers using such libraries would have to learn specifics of each based on which one is being used in the project. The learning from one implementation can't be utilized fully for another implementation, since these are not based on a standard. This isn't necessarily bad; it's just not a part of the standard EE solution stack. Do you need a portable solution today? Well, maybe not. But will you need one in the future? That is an answer one cannot honestly predict. For Java EE, the much awaited JSON support has finally arrived as part of its standard. Specifications such as JSON-P and JSON-B makes Java a lot friendlier to JSON than it used to be before.

JSON-P offers mainly two approaches to work with the documents, one being an object model similar and the other a streaming solution for processing big JSON data. The streaming solution can be considered a low-level approach, which offers a memory efficient alternative to process data using tokens. JSON-P is also aligned with JSON-B and JAXRS. JSON-B is the binding layer for the conversion of a Java class to/from JSON.

JSON processing

JSON-P provides the ability for parsing, generating, querying, and transforming JSON documents in Java. The API allows producing and consuming JSON text in a streaming manner as well as a Java object model. Java EE 7 introduced the JSON-P specification for working with JSON documents. Java EE 8 is taking this a step further to keep it updated with the newer RFC standards by updating the version to JSON-P 1.1. With this, we have new features, such as:

- **JSON Pointer**: RFC 6901
- **JSON Patch**: RFC 6902
- **JSON Merge Patch**: RFC 7386/7396

To work with JSON, you can use any JEE 8 compliant server which provides the `json-api` `1.1`, a corresponding maven dependency specific to JSON API, shown as follows:

```
javax.json
javax.json-api
<version>1.1</version>
<scope>provided</scope>
</dependency>
```

With the API dependency set, you can write JSON processing code in either using the object model or the streaming fashion, shown as follows:

- **Object Model approach**: JSON Object model API for simpler ways of working with JSON documents in-memory:

```
JsonObject json = Json.createObjectBuilder()
        .add("name", "Raise alert on failure")
        .add("id", Long.valueOf(2003))
        .build();
String result = json.toString();
```

- **Streaming approach**: JSON Streaming API which parses a document and emits events without loading the entire document in memory. This is useful for large documents which can't be processed in-memory:

```
JsonParser parser = Json.createParser
    (Main.class.getResourceAsStream("/sample.json"));

while (parser.hasNext()) {
    JsonParser.Event e = parser.next();
    System.out.print(e.name());
    switch (e) {
        case KEY_NAME:
            System.out.print(" - " + parser.getString());
            break;
        case VALUE_STRING:
            System.out.print(" - " + parser.getString());
            break;
        case VALUE_NUMBER:
            System.out.print(" - " + parser.getString());
    }
    System.out.println();
}
```

JSON-P 1.1

JSON processing API 1.1 is an updated version which introduces some useful enhancements to the earlier JSON-P 1.0 version. The API changes include few additions to the Json class in the form of static methods, such as:

- `public static JsonString createValue(String value)`
- `public static JsonNumber createValue(int value)`

And similar methods for `long`, `double`, `BigDecimal`, and `BigInteger`, which also return a `JsonNumber`.

Additionally, we now have methods for creation of a JSON Pointer, Patch, or Merge Patch using the following static methods:

- `public static JsonPointer createPointer(String jsonPointer)`
- `public static JsonPatch createPatch(JsonArray array)`
- `public static JsonMergePatch createMergePatch(JsonValue patch)`

The API makes use of builder pattern to provide for a convenient and easy way to build a `JsonObject` or `JsonArray`. It is also possible to start building with an initial value based on an existing `JsonObject` or `JsonArray`. When instantiating a builder with the initial value, there are some editing methods provided for updating the underlying object. Once the builders `build` method is invoked, it returns an immutable `JsonObject` or `JsonArray` based on the builder type used.

Here's a sample usage:

```
JsonArray array =
Json.createArrayBuilder().add("java").add("ruby").build();

JsonArray transformedArray = Json.createArrayBuilder(array)
            .add(0,"python") //puts in first, shifting others
            .remove(2) // removes the 3rd element
            .build();
//Results in transformedArray having two values
[python, java]
```

Both `JsonReader` and `JsonWriter` have got new methods. These are backward compatible and doesn't break the API, which works because of the *default method* introduced in Java 8:

- **JsonReader**: `public default JsonValue readValue()`
- **JsonWriter**: `public default void write(JsonValue jv)`

We also have API updates that are used for low level operations on the JsonPatch class.

JSON Pointer and JSON Patch

JSON Pointer is a string syntax which acts as the pointer to a target location within a JSON document. The format is defined by RFC 6901 and contains reference tokens prefixed with a (/) character. The path used is an absolute path, so you can't use relative references.

Consider the following example `issues.json` document which holds a JSON array of issue objects:

```
[
    {
        "id": 1122,
        "name": "Fix slow loading"
    },
    {
        "id": 2003,
        "name": "Raise alert on failure"
    },
    {
        "id": 1903,
        "name": "Reponsive home page"
    }
]
```

The following table shows the pointer value used and the target value at the specified location that is referenced:

/1	{"id":2003,"name":"Raise alert on failure"}
/1/id	2003
/0/name	Fix slow loading

Consider the following code:

```
JsonArray issuesJson = ... // Assume the example JSON document is loaded
here

JsonPointer pointer = Json.createPointer("/1");
JsonValue value = pointer.getValue(issuesJson);

System.out.println(value.toString());
pointer = Json.createPointer("/0/name");
value = pointer.getValue(issuesJson);

System.out.println(value.toString());
```

```
// The output from the above code
{"id":2003,"name":"Raise alert on failure"}
"Fix slow loading"
```

JSON Patch is a standard described in RFC 6902 by **Internet Engineering Task Force (IETF)**. This is a format for describing partial updates to an existing JSON document. The idea is to send a JSON document which describes the patch operation to be performed on the resource. These operations that need to be performed can be specified within the document, which can have one of these values: add, remove, replace, move, copy, or test.

If any operation fails, then the whole patch fails. Here, we continue to reference our example JSON document, which has an array of JSON values (issues.json). So, going back to our issues.json document as defined previously, lets assume we wanted to update the name of the second object (id = 2003) and remove the third object (id = 1903). For doing this, we need to submit a JSON patch which looks like the following:

```
[{"op":"remove","path":"/2"},{"op":"replace","path":"/1/name","value":"Fix
alert not firing"}]
```

It's important to note that we are not sending just the key-value pair of changes, but instead we are sending a *set of changes* which describe how to apply these to the resource.

In the patch document, the path takes a JSON Pointer as its value, which references the location within the target document on which the operation will be applied. When programming, you need not create such patches by hand, as Java has a convenient way to build a patch in the form of the JsonPatch class, whose instance is obtained by using the Json.createPatchBuilder() static method. The JsonPatch class has an apply method which is used to perform the operation on the target entity passed as an argument to it.

Here's the complete code to create a JsonPatch and apply it to our example JSON document:

```
JsonArray issuesJson = ... // Assume the example JSON document is loaded
here

JsonPatch patch = Json.createPatchBuilder()
                .remove("/2")
                .replace("/1/name", "Fix alert not firing")
                .build();

JsonArray result = patch.apply(issuesJson);

//The resulting output with changes is stored in the variable result
[{"id":1122,"name":"Fix slow loading"},{"id":2003,"name":"Fix alert not
```

```
firing"}]
```

RESTful APIs use HTTP methods as verbs to describe the action on a resource. It's common to use the `POST`, `GET`, `UPDATE`, `DELETE` (CRUD) methods to work with a resource. The RFC 5789 adds a new HTTP method, PATCH, which is meant to modify an existing HTTP resource. An excerpt taken from the document states the following:

> *"The existing HTTP PUT method is meant to allow a complete replacement of a document and it does not have any notion of partial updates."*

JSON Patch offers a standardized way of a client who may not always be aware of the latest state of the resource that it's updating, so sending the entire JSON (state) for an update may not be a reliable approach. Consider a `Tickets` resource, where multiple clients may make modifications and send the updates over the `PUT` method. Each client would need to first perform a `GET` of the `Tickets` resource that it's modifying and then send the entire document, even though only a single field may have changed. This leads to an unnecessary exchange of large documents along with possible race conditions. Here, the JSON Patch combined with the `PATCH` method can be used to send only the changed data, along with the operation describing the change.

To make use of JSON Patch within REST APIs in a standard way, we should use it along with the `PATCH` method (`@PATCH` in JAXRS 2.1). The media type (Content-Type head) for this would be `application/json-patch+json`.

A REST endpoint method signature supporting the `patch` operation is shown as follows:

```
@PATCH
@Path("{id}")
@Consumes(MediaType.APPLICATION_JSON_PATCH_JSON)
public Response patch(@PathParam("id") Long id,
                                 JsonArray patchArray) {
    JsonPatch patch = Json.createPatch(patchArray);

    JsonObject jsonObject = ... // Code to load the Json entity
    JsonObject updatedJson = patch.apply(jsonObject);
    return Response.ok(updatedJson).build();
}
```

Here, we have made use of the `@PATCH` annotation along with the `Json.createPatch()` method usage, which takes a `JsonArray`. If we wanted to update the name of the stored entity, we could do so by using the following `curl` command:

```
curl -X PATCH -H 'Content-Type: application/json-patch+json' -d @patch.json
http://localhost:8080/ims-micro-tasks/resources/tasks/2003

{"id":"2003","name":"The new name goes here"}
```

Here, `-X` is used to specify the HTTP Method and `-d @patch.json` points to a file containing the actual JSON patch, which looks like the following:

```
[
    { "op": "replace", "path": "/name",
      "value": "The new name goes here" }
]
```

JSON merge patch

This is a standard described in RFC 7386/7396 by IETF. It can be considered to serve a similar purpose to JSON Patch, but takes a different approach. The syntax of the patch document is close to the target that is to be updated. It too uses the HTTP `PATCH` method for submitting the patch document with the content type as `application/json-patch+json`. When doing an update using the HTTP `PUT` method, we would send across the entire document, but with the HTTP `PATCH` we send only the partial change of the entity. A *null* value is used to denote a delete operation.

 Null has a special meaning, as it represents a delete operation. This can be a limitation for use cases where you may want to set a key's value as *null*.

Document	Patch	Result

`{`
  `"id": 1122,`
  `"name": "Fix slow loading",`
  `"priority": "Low"`
`}`
	`{"priority": null}`	`{`
		  `"id": 1122,`
		  `"name": "Fix slow loading"`
		`}`

To implement the preceding tabular sample, we need to create a `JsonObject` to represent the document. Next, we will create the actual `JsonMergePatch` instance which will hold the patch that needs to be applied. Once a patch JSON is created, the same can be passed to `Json.createMergePatch`, which builds the `JsonMergePatch` instance. This instance can then be utilized for applying the patch on a target document.

Here's the code showing that:

```
//Load JSON from a file called 'issues.json' which has our target JSON
JsonReader reader =
Json.createReader(Main.class.getResourceAsStream("/issues.json"));
JsonObject json = reader.readObject();

//Create the Patch
JsonObject removeName = Json.createObjectBuilder()
        .add("name", JsonValue.NULL)
        .build();

JsonMergePatch mergePatch = Json.createMergePatch(removeName);
JsonValue result = mergePatch.apply(json);

System.out.println("result: " + result);

//Output
result: {"id":1122,"priority":"Low"}
```

JSON Collectors

When working the JSON in Java 8, you would typically want to use them with streams sooner or later. `JsonObject` is a `Map`, while `JsonArray` is a `List`, which makes it possible to use them with lambda expressions and streams. While there are collectors for `List` and `Map`, we also would require similar collectors for `JsonObject` and `JsonArray`.

The class `JsonCollectors` provides static methods which can be used to return a Collector. These methods come in handy when working with streams, as it can be passed to the streams *collect* operation to transform the stream result into a `JsonArray` or `JsonObject`.

- `toJsonArray`: Collect the stream result into `JsonArray`
- `toJsonObject`: Collect the stream result into `JsonObject`

There's also a `groupingBy` method that provides us with functionality similar to an SQL group by clause. This can be used to group `JsonObjects` by passing a function classifier to the method as an argument.

Consider this sample JSON:

```
[
    {
        "id": 1122,
        "name": "Fix slow loading",
        "priority": "Low"
    },
    {
        "id": 1123,
        "name": "Implement feature X",
        "priority": "High"
    }
]
```

Now, we can write the following code to find all `JSONObjects` which have the priority set as `High` and collect them into an `JsonArray`:

```
JsonArray jsonarray = ...//This represents the above JSON
JsonArray result = jsonarray.getValuesAs(JsonObject.class)
            .stream()
            .filter(j ->; "High".equals(j.getString("priority")))
            .collect(JsonCollectors.toJsonArray());
```

Here's the `groupingBy` in action, which groups the `JsonObject` by priority:

```
JsonArray jsonarray = ...//Assume same as above JSON
JsonObject result = jsonarray.getValuesAs(JsonObject.class)
            .stream()
            .collect(JsonCollectors.groupingBy(
                    x -> ((JsonObject)x).getJsonString("priority")
                        .getString()
            ));
System.out.println("result: " + result);

//Output
result: {"High":[{"id":1123,"name":"Implement feature
X","priority":"High"}],"Low":[{"id":1122,"name":"Fix slow
loading","priority":"Low"}]}
```

Due to the Streams support, it's also possible to make use of operations that can run concurrently when processing big JSON data.

JSON binding

With JSON binding, it can be thought of as similar to JAXB. While we do have JSON-P, it's a specification that can be considered for parsing and writing JSON files. But when you need JSON to be mapped to Java objects, JSON-P falls short and thus we have JSON-B to fill this gap. The JSON-B, being a new addition to the Java EE 8 family of specifications, has the version 1.0. Yasson project is the reference implementation for JSON-B. For maven projects, the following dependency can be specified, which relies upon the server for providing the implementation:

```
<dependency>
    <groupId>javax.json.bind</groupId>
    <artifactId>javax.json.bind-api</artifactId>
    <version>1.0</version>
    <scope>provided</scope>
</dependency>
```

The `main` class to get started with JSON-B is the `Jsonb` class. To obtain an instance of this class, one would call the create method of `JsonbBuilder`, shown as follows:

```
Jsonb jsonb = JsonbBuilder.create();
```

The `Jsonb` class has two methods, which are overloaded:

- `toJson`: Writes the Java object tree to a string as a JSON document
- `fromJson`: Reads the JSON from a `InputStream` or `Reader` or `String`, and returns a Java object

Both of these methods also support working with collections. Consider the following `Issue` class, which we will be using for our examples to follow:

```java
public class Issue {

    private Long id;
    private String name;
    private String priority;
    //... Getters and Setters
}
```

Similar to JAXB with default mappings

This makes it possible to convert a Java class to a JSON representation and vice versa. There are defaults which get applied by a mapping algorithm when performing the conversion. These defaults can be customized by means of certain Java annotations on the class. JSON-B also supports mapping of collections which can be raw types or generic types.

The default mapping requires no configuration and no annotations. Here's a sample usage of how to obtain an `Issue` instance from a JSON string:

```
Jsonb jsonb = JsonbBuilder.create();
Issue newIssue = jsonb.fromJson(
    "{\"id\":1123,\"name\":\"Implement feature X\",\"priority\":\"High\"}",
    Issue.class
);
```

Similarly, to convert the object model `Issue` to a JSON string representation, one would use the `toJson` method:

```
Issue issue= now Issue();
issue.setId(200L);
issue.setName("Test");
Jsonb jsonb = JsonbBuilder.create();
String jsonString = jsonb.toJson(issue); // JSON String
```

There are overloaded version of `toJson`, which can be used to write the JSON string to an output stream. As an example, we could write the following liner to store the generated JSON text in a file:

```
JsonbBuilder.create().toJson(issue, new FileWriter("issue.json"));
```

The default mapping handles the *basic types* such as String, Character, Byte, Short, Integer, Long, Float, Double, Boolean, and additionally other *specific types* like `BigInteger`, `BigDecimal`, and so on. With default mapping, the static and transient fields are skipped, along with fields which have null values.

Standardizes current solutions (Jackson, Gson, and so on)

Both `Gson` and `Jackson` are open source projects and widely used in Java for working with JSON. These libraries not only provide basic mapping support, but also offer the ability to map objects without modifying their code. While these solutions are great to pick, there are discrepancies in the APIs and behavior. As an example, both of these handle Null values differently:

- `Gson`: Does NOT serialize null values by default
- `Jackson`: Does serialize null values by default

For ignoring of properties, both frameworks provide different annotations, making it difficult to swap one implementation for another if required.

JSON-B is an API to marshal and unmarshal Java objects to and from JSON. The API draws upon the best practices of existing libraries such as `Gson`, `Jackson`, and so on. Thus, it's not a competitor to any of these, but instead defines the common interface that each of the providers can adapt. Features such as ignoring properties, customization through adapters, and more are already established in some of these frameworks and JSON-B defines a standard way to utilize them all.

Mapping between classes and JSON

The default mapping rules would map the Java class's property name to a similarly named JSON property name. When the mapped name during serialization needs to be different than the one given to the Java property name, one can make use of the `@JsonbProperty` annotation.

The annotation `@JsonbProperty` can be placed on:

- **Field**: This will affect the custom change during both serialization and deserialization
- **Getter only**: This will affect serialization, but won't have any affect on deserialization
- **Setter only**: This will affect deserialization, but won't have any affect on serialization

We could place the `@JsonbProperty` annotation on the name field of the `Issue` class, which would look like the following:

```
@JsonbProperty("issue-label")
private String name;
```

Resulting in the following JSON object:

```
{
  "id": 200,
  "issue-label": "Test",
  "priority": "High"
}
```

There are times when use cases require ignoring of certain properties and this can be achieved by using the `@JsonbTransient` annotation. As mentioned in the `json-b` user guide, this annotations placement dictates changes to the processing behavior:

- **Field**: Property is ignored during serialization and deserialization
- **Getter only**: Property is ignored during serialization only
- **Setter only**: Property is ignored during deserialization only

Customisation APIs

JSON-B supports customization of the mapping rules by using compile time options such as annotations and runtime customization by using the `JsonbConfig` class. The `JsonbConfig` class can be configured by using its `withXXX` methods, where XXX will be replaced with a specific version of the method. Here's how one can format the JSON output when using `Jsonb`:

```
JsonbConfig config = new JsonbConfig().withFormatting(true);
Jsonb jsonb = JsonbBuilder.create(config);
```

Calling `toJson` on this `jsonb` instance would result in a formatted output. Apart from formatting, the customization allows for changes in the naming strategy for property names and change in the ordering of serialized properties.

Few tips in practice

Let's have a look at the following tips:

- **Dealing with null**: If you use the following code and try to obtain the JSON string, then you might be surprised by the output:

```
Issue issue= new Issue();
issue.setId(200L);
issue.setName("Test");
issue.setPriority(null);
Jsonb jsonb = JsonbBuilder.create();
String jsonString = jsonb.toJson(issue); // JSON String
```

Here, the output would ignore the `priority` field as it's having a null value. This is the default behavior, but it can be changed using multiple ways. A convenient option is to change it globally by using the `JsonbConfig` class:

```
JsonbConfig nillableConfig = new JsonbConfig()
        .withNullValues(true);
```

Other options include using the `@JsonbNillable` annotation on the class or using `@JsonbProperty(nillable=true)`.

- **Use Adapters for more control**: When annotations aren't an option, such as for cases where you may not be in control of the code of the class which is being serialized, then you can make use of Adapters. Using Adapters, it's possible to get better control over the serialize/deserialize process. What this requires is to create a class which implements `JsonbAdapter` and overrides its two methods: `adaptToJson` and `adaptFromJson`.

- **JsonObject in JAXRS**: When working with JAXRS, consider using the `JsonObject` itself in the domain model for your input and output needs, which can lead to eradication of the DTO requirement. `JsonObject` can itself serve as a DTO or value object.

Summary

We saw how JSON-P and JSON-B have turned JSON into a first-class citizen for Java EE 8, which is a welcome addition for developers working on REST APIs. The JSON Processing is a flexible API, as it offers an object model for working with in-memory JSON data and a streaming option for processing large JSON data. The JSON APIs are RFC compliant and have been updated according to the standards of JSON Patch, Merge, and Pointer. A JSON Pointer can be used to lookup a value within the target document, while a Patch or Merge is used along with HTTP PATCH for partial updates.

JSON-B does for JSON what JAXB did for XML. It offers a standard way of mapping Java classes to/from JSON. If you don't like the default JSON Binding mapping rules, which are useful for most use cases, you can still use the customisations available for both compile time and runtime.

While these APIs can be used on their own, the JAXRS alignment helps using JSON processing within the REST APIs as well. When delivering REST standard APIs, these offer the much needed flexibility to build a real world application, as we will see in the next few chapters.

6
Power Your APIs with JAXRS and CDI

Web service APIs are no longer kept hidden in the dark alleys of the internet. They have started surfacing more than ever, as businesses are using them a lot more than a decade ago. These businesses, building software solutions, need ways to broaden their reach in a simple yet effective manner. A company offering ticketing, e-commerce, insurance, or any other online solution, would want to make it easy for potential customers to reach them. The need to make the solution available over multiple channels such as desktop or mobile has led to the growth of web services. Web services can also be used by potential business partners with their own online presence.

Consider a simple example in which a company, AbcDroid, sells flight tickets and another company, EzTrips, sells hotel tickets. A customer who books a flight using the AbcDroid portal can be offered a hotel at their destination city. The hotel booking is offered by EzTrips as a web service; this makes it possible for AbcDroid to integrate this capability. The easier it becomes to integrate a business service, the greater its chances of higher adoption.

In this chapter, we will cover the following topics:

- Resources:
    - URI templates
    - Matching requests to resource methods
- Providers:
    - Entity providers
    - Exception mapping

- Client API:
    - Targets
    - Reactive clients
- Filters and interceptors
- Validation
- Asynchronous processing
- Server-Sent Events
- WebSockets
- Context
- Swagger:
    - API
    - Maven plugin

Resources

JAXRS allows developers to define REST APIs, which play a fundamental role in building microservices. JAXRS 2.1 is also one of the most important specifications in Java EE 8. But before we see all that in action, let's understand how a REST resource is represented over the web. A resource typically represents an entity and allows for operations on it (think domain entities such as `User`, `Address`, `City`, and so on). Typically, an entity will allow for create, read, update, and delete operations. In the RESTful world, a web resource is identified by its URI, and the actions to be performed are defined by HTTP methods such as `POST`, `GET`, `UPDATE`, and `DELETE`.

Here's an example of the `/users` URI, which is used to represent a web resource that is invoked over the HTTP protocol. The HTTP method used in the invocation signifies the operation to perform. Here are some samples of URI and HTTP method invocations in the following *URI request table*:

URI	Http Method	Request Body	Description
`/users`	`POST`	`{"name": "John"}`	Create a new user
`/users`	`GET`		Get all users
`/users/100`	`GET`		Get user identified by a value of 100
`/users/100`	`PUT`	`{"name": "Johnson"}`	Update the user identified by a value of 100 with given details

/users/101	DELETE		Remove user identified by a value of 101

The URI is the first aspect that a caller comes across for a REST resource and acts as the selector of the target resource. The specification itself doesn't define stringent rules concerning the URI format. But there are some basic principles that can be applied when defining a resource URI to keep it simple and intuitive:

- Keep URI naming convention consistent rather than mixed, so it's intuitive for others to make use of
- Use plural nouns for the resource URI such as `users`, `tasks`, `projects`, and so on
- To work with a specific item within the collection, use subresources such as `/tasks/12`, where `12` is the identifier for the item within the collection of tasks
- Attributes of the resource can be part of the query string, such as `/tasks?status=open&priority=high`
- Use HTTP status codes as part of the response to signal the invocation status
- Use JSON as the default format for the API request and response
- Use some form of version identifier for resources either in the request header or as part of the URI

In JAXRS, there are two kinds of resources that can be defined by the developer:

- A root resource is created by applying the `@Path` annotation on a Java class
- A subresource is a public method of the resource class which has `@Path` applied to it

To enable JAXRS features, we first define a class which will be used to define the base URI for all resources. This is done by creating a class which extends `javax.ws.rs.core.Application` and has an annotation of `@ApplicationPath` with the base URI value:

```
@ApplicationPath("resources")
public class JaxrsActivator extends Application { }
```

Then a resource class that defines operations such as read all entities, read single entity, add entity, update entity, delete entity, for the resource. The following code only highlights the relevant parts of a REST resource, which maps to the *URI request table* shown earlier:

```
@Path("users")
public class UsersResource {
    @Inject private UsersService service;

    @GET public Response getAll()...
    @GET @Path("{id}")
    public Response get(@PathParam("id") Long id)...
    @POST
    public Response add(User newUser,
                        @Context UriInfo uriInfo)...
    @PUT @Path("{id}")
    public Response update(@PathParam("id") Long id,
                           User existingUser)...

    @DELETE @Path("{id}")
    public Response delete(@PathParam("id") Long id)...
}
```

The requests will be handled by these resource methods. A new instance of a resource class will be created for each request made. As for the order of execution, first the public constructor will get executed followed by any dependency injections, and finally the resource method. If there are fields that have any of the following annotations, then the value is injected before the resource method is invoked:

- `@QueryParam`: Extracts the value of a URI query parameter
- `@MatrixParam`: Extracts the value of a URI matrix parameter
- `@PathParam`: Extracts the value of a URI template parameter
- `@CookieParam`: Extracts the value of a cookie
- `@HeaderParam`: Extracts the value of a header

You could make use of these for injecting parameters, and if you need defaults, then combine this with the `@DefaultValue` annotation. Here's a field declaration within a resource class, which injects the API version for the requested resource from the X-version request header:

```
@DefaultValue("v1") @HeaderParam("X-version")
private String apiVersion;
```

The value of the `apiVersion` field will be injected by extracting the `X-version` request header; if there is no such header then the default value of `v1` will be used.

The `UsersResource` class has resource methods returning the `javax.ws.rs.core.Response` type. It's also possible to return other types. Here are return types that you can make use of:

- `void`: This results in an empty response body with the HTTP status code `204`, meant for denoting no content.
- `Response`: This class allows for setting the entity which will be used as the response body along with the defined status. The default status, if nothing is specified explicitly, will be set to `200`. Use this class for more control over the response body and its metadata.
- `GenericEntity`: This class allows for wrapping an entity as the response body. When an entity is wrapped, this results in a `200` response code or else a `204` for no entity/content.

URI templates

A resource class URI is defined by the deployed application context followed by the value of `@ApplicationPath` and `@Path` annotations used. So, our application, with the context as `ims-micro-users` and the `UsersResource` class ,would result in the following URI:

```
/ims-micro-users/resources/users
```

The subresources, which are methods annotated with `@Path` annotations, are identified by a combination of the `@Path` value of the resource class followed by the method's own `@Path` annotation value. So, in the example used, we can invoke the `get` subresource method present on the `UsersResource` class by using the following URI:

```
/ims-micro-users/resources/users/10
```

The `@Path ("{id}")` annotation on the public `get` method exposes the subresource as `/users/xxx`, where `xxx` is replaced by the value `10`, based on the URI invocation. The method parameter makes use of another annotation called `@PathParam`, which is used to inject the passed value of `10` into the `id` method parameter.

Matching requests to resource methods

When a request is made to the resource, URI normalization is done as a first step. This is syntax-based normalization, which typically includes case normalization and percent encoding normalization, all of which is covered in the RFC Standard 3986. This resultant URI is also available from the `UriInfo` object.

Request matching is done in stages by implementation providers, using an algorithm suggested by the JAXRS specification. While vendors may tweak the internals of the algorithm, the basic gist is as follows:

- Normalize the request URI as per the IETF RFC 3986 standard, which simply does the case percent encoding that we often see in browser-based requests
- Identify the root resource classes; these are all classes with the `@Path` value matching the request
- Identify the potential resource methods from the obtained list of resources and, finally, select the one that matches based on a few tasks:
  - Checking the HTTP method supported, such as GET or POST; if none is found then a `404` response is returned
  - Checking for the media type of the input body; if none is found then a `415` response is returned
  - Checking for the media type of the output data format; if no suitable match is found then a `406` response is returned

The preceding is not a complete set of rules, but a short reference to keep in mind when mapping URIs to resource methods. These may also be useful when dealing with errors, such as a 415 or when a resource may return a 404 error.

Http request	Resource method mapped
`GET /users`	`@GET public Response getAll()`
`GET /users/10`	`@GET @Path("{id}")` `public Response get(@PathParam("id") Long id)`
`POST /users` `{"name": "sam"}`	`@POST` `public Response add(User u, @Context UriInfo uri)`

`PUT /users/10`
`{"name": "samson"}`
	`@PUT @Path("{id}")`
	`public Response update(@PathParam("id") Long id,`
	`User existing)`

| DELETE /users/10 | `@DELETE @Path("{id}")`
`public Response delete(@PathParam("id") Long id)` |

These are the general rules that should help when mapping the request to corresponding resource classes and methods. You can see how JAXRS makes it fairly simple to start building REST APIs with just a few lines of code.

Providers

When you start publishing services, you typically come across scenarios which require some additional layers of processing. You might need some special processing for mapping representations of entities and their Java types. Such cases are handled by supplying an entity provider to the JAXRS runtime. A provider class would implement JAXRS-specific interfaces and additionally use the `@Provider` annotation, which is used at runtime for auto-discovery of all providers. Apart from entity providers, there's context providers and exception mapping providers.

Entity providers

Entity providers can be used to do the marshaling and un-marshaling of Java objects to and from another representation. There are two options:

- `MessageBodyReader`: This class is used to provide a mapping service between an incoming request entity message body to the Java method parameter. Based on the media type used and the Java type of the method parameter, an appropriate `MessageBodyReader` provider is chosen at runtime. The `MessageBodyReader.isReadable` method is used to check if the provider supports the Java type, and if it returns true, then the `MessageBodyReader.readFrom` method is invoked. In the case of failure, no entity and a `NotSupportedException` of the `415` status code is generated.

- `MessageBodyWriter`: This class is used to provide mapping services for mapping the return value to the message entity body. When using the `Response` return value, the wrapped entity of the `Response` is considered for applying this provider. Based on the media type of the response and the Java type returned, an appropriate `MessageBodyWriter` provider is chosen at runtime. The `MessageBodyWriter.isWriteable` method is used to check if the provider supports the Java type, and if it returns true, then the `MessageBodyWriter.writeTo` method is invoked. In the case of failure, no entity and an `InternalServerErrorException` of the 500 status code is generated.

Exception mapping

Exceptions in the resource method or provider code can be handled by registering a provider to handle checked or runtime exceptions. This application-supplied provider implements the `ExceptionMapper<T>` interface. When multiple providers are used, then the runtime will choose the provider whose generic type is the nearest superclass of the exception thrown. Exception mapping providers can only be used with server-side code and are not supported in client APIs.

Similar to aspect-oriented programming, having an exception mapper allows for the separation of exception detection and processing code from the business logic. Let's assume a resource method throws an exception of `IllegalArgumentException` type, then the same can be mapped to a Response with status code of 400, for a bad request. Instead of using built-in exceptions such as `IllegalArgumentException`, we can map our own exception type too when needed.

```
@Provider
public class ResourceExceptionMapper
            implements ExceptionMapper<Throwable> {
    @Override
    public Response toResponse(Throwable exception) {
        if(exception instanceof IllegalArgumentException) {
            return Response.status(Response.Status.BAD_REQUEST)
                .build();
        }
        return Response.serverError().build();
    }
}
```

Client API

JAXRS has a Client API which is used for accessing web resources and also integrates with providers. When running microservices or writing tests, the Client API serves as a tool for invoking target web resources. To work with the API, we must first obtain an instance of `Client` using the `ClientBuilder.newClient` method. Using the fluent API, a request is created and submitted by chaining method invocations whose names should be self-descriptive:

```
Client client = ClientBuilder.newClient();
Response res = client.target("http://somewhere.org/hello")
                .queryParam("param","...");
                .request("application/json")
                .header("X-Header","...")
                .get();
```

Both `Client` and `WebTarget` provide for registering filters and interceptors on the client-side. The API can also be utilized for building complex URI paths, which makes it fairly handy when building targets, as shown in the next section.

Targets

When resource URIs have complex paths to be resolved, such as /users/xxx, where xxx is the identifier for a user such as /users/12, then creating a target can be achieved as shown here:

```
Client client = ClientBuilder.newClient();
WebTarget baseResource = client.target("http://ex.org/resources/");
WebTarget userResource = baseResource.path("users").path("{id}");

Response response = userResource.resolveTemplate("id", 12)
                                .request("application/json")
                                .get();
User user = response.readEntity(User.class);
```

The preceding code can be broken into steps that build `WebTarget` instances and then finally fires the request for getting the `User` entity Response:

- `baseResource`: This is a WebTarget instance which is immutable and points to the base path of the web resource.

- `userResource`: This is another `WebTarget` instance which is created by appending the path to the existing `baseResource`. The next `path("{id}")` sets the URI template parameter which will be resolved later.
- `response`: A response is obtained by using the `resovleTemplate` method to resolve the `id` URI template parameter to the value of 12, which is then sent over the network. The final `get()` method is a *synchronous* invocation which returns the `Response` object with the `User` entity.

Reactive clients

While synchronous and asynchronous calling was already supported in the Client API, now a new reactive style has been introduced with JAXRS 2.1. The Client API leverages the Java 8 `CompletableFuture` class (which implements `CompletionStage<T>`) and existing JAXRS 2.0 API to provide a reactive programming style:

```
Client client = ClientBuilder.newClient();
WebTarget base = client.target("http://ex.org/resources/planets");
CompletionStage<User> cs = base.request("application/json")
                                .rx().get(String.class);
cs.thenAccept(System.out::println);
```

The main difference is the addition of the `rx()` method call, which switches from the sync/async approach to a reactive one. This provides for greater flexibility in the computation of asynchronous responses. This addition now makes it easy to fetch data from multiple resources in parallel and then use the results to perform a task. Here's the code snippet showcasing that:

```
CompletionStage<Phone> csp = client.target("phones/{item}")
                .resolveTemplate("item", "android")
                .request().rx()
                .get(Phone.class);

CompletionStage<Number> csf = client.target("ratings/{item}")
                .resolveTemplate("item", "android")
                .request().rx()
                .get(Number.class);
csp.thenCombine(csf, (phone, rated)
                -> buyWhenAvailableAndRated(phone, rated));
```

The example fetches the phone and rating number in parallel to different resources, and then it combines the results to buy the phone if available and rated. The `thenCombine` method requires both the stages to be completed with their values, and only then will it invoke the passed `Consumer` code of `buyWhenAvailableAndRated(...)`.

Reactive programming with the Client API is a powerful addition to the developer's toolkit, and an approach that will only grow.

Filters and interceptors

Filters and interceptors are registered as providers. Filters are typically used for modifying the message headers. To understand filters, let's look at a practical use case. Cross-origin requests are requests that are made from one domain to another. It's not alien to have your web resources hosted on one domain while the requests may originate from another. For security reasons, browsers restrict such requests, which are made within scripts. The solution is **Cross-Origin Resource Sharing (CORS)**; this mechanism allows servers to publish the set of origins that are allowed for making web browser requests to it. This is done by adding the `Access-Control` headers to the response, and to do that we would need to define a provider which implements the `ContainerResponseFilter` interface:

```
@Provider
public class CorsRespFilter implements ContainerResponseFilter {
    @Override
    public void filter(ContainerRequestContext requestContext,
        ContainerResponseContext rspCtx) throws IOException {
      rspCtx.getHeaders().add("Access-Control-Allow-Origin", "*");
      ...
    }
}
```

- **Server-side:** For processing on the server, there are two filters that we can make use of:
    - `ContainerRequestFilter`
    - `ContainerResponseFilter`

    If you want to share data between the filters, then that can be achieved using an instance of `ContainerRequestContext` for the request and `ContainerResponseContext` for the response. Both of these provide a map-based structure to store a key-value pair. Thus, an item stored in one of the request filters can be later retrieved in the response filter.

- **Client-side:** Similar to server-side filters, there's also client-side filters:
    - ClientRequestFilter
    - ClientResponseFilter

    ClientRequestFilter can be used to intercept the request before it's sent to the network, while the ClientResponseFilter is invoked before the response is sent to the application code.

    Both Client and Container filters can stop any further chain execution by calling the abortWith(Response) method in their corresponding context object.

- **Controlling execution order with priority:** It's also possible to have multiple providers, and when such implementations are detected the order can be specified by making use of the @Priority annotation. This allows for controlling the order in which filters and interceptors are executed as part of their execution chain. The @Priority runtime annotation has been added to the JAXRS 2.1 specification. For request filters, the providers are sorted in ascending order by their priority numbers and executed from low to high. This is different to response filters, which are sorted in descending order by their priority numbers and executed from high to low. For example, if you had two response filter providers, *A* and *B*, with *A having @Priority(5)* and *B having @Priority(6)*, then the order of execution would be B then A. This would be reversed for request based filters, where the execution order would change to A followed by B.

- **Interceptors:** An interceptor is primarily used for manipulation of the message payload. The entity interceptor would implement either ReaderInterceptor or WriterInterceptor or both, based on what aspect it wants to intercept. It would also need to invoke the proceed method to continue the execution chain. ' Similar to filters, these are registered as providers. WriterInterceptor provides a method called aroundWriteTo, which wraps calls to MessageBodyWriter.writeTo. Similarly, the ReaderInterceptor provides a method called aroundReadFrom, which wraps calls to MessageBodyReader.readFrom. The API hasn't changed in JAXRS 2.1.

Validation

JAXRS 2.1 now enables declarative validation support by leveraging its integration with the Bean Validation API. This is done by using the *constraint annotations* for validating Beans, method parameters, and return values. These annotations can be placed on resource classes, fields and properties. For example, the following is a sample showing a User entity having a field level constraint of @NotNull. The same User class is then used as an argument to the resource method add which uses the @Valid annotation. A POST request would trigger the validation of the User entity field name to meet the @NotNull criteria:

```
class User {
    @NotNull
    private String name;
    ...
}

@Path("/")
class ResourceClass {
    @POST public void add(@Valid User newUser) { ... }
}
```

Similar to the method parameter, the response can also be validated by applying constraints on the return type, as shown:

```
@GET @Path("{id}") @Valid
public User get(@PathParam("id") String id) { ... }
```

There are features such as custom validators and more that can be explored by looking up the specification and Java EE 8 docs online for more details.

Asynchronous processing

JAXRS supports asynchronous processing in both server and client APIs:

- **Server API:** Asynchronous processing allows the resource method to inform the JAXRS runtime that a response is not ready yet and will be provided at a future time. This is done by temporarily *suspending* the connection and then *resuming* it once the response becomes available. For a resource method to utilize async processing it must inject an `AsyncResponse` instance using the special `@Suspended` annotation. The resource method code may perform a long-running operation as desired, and then finally publish the response using the `resume` method of the `AsyncResponse` instance. `AsyncResponse` also allows for specifying timeouts and callbacks:

```
@GET public void timeConsumingActivity(
    @Suspended final AsyncResponse ar) {
        executor.execute(() -> {
        //Executor to run job in background
        longRunningCode();
        ar.resume("async response here");
    });
}
```

We can also specify a timeout value by using the `setTimeout` method on the `AsyncResponse` instance. If the timeout does occur then the server will generate and return a `503` status. It's also possible to control the timeout behavior by supplying a timeout handler; this is done by setting an instance of `TimeoutHandler` and passing it to the `setTimeoutHandler` of the `AsyncResponse` instance.

Since JAXRS can be used along with EJBs, it's possible to use annotations such as **Singleton** and **Stateless** on root resource classes. This makes it possible to use the `@Asynchronous` annotation on the resource method, thus avoiding the need for any executor logic, since the EJB container will be responsible for the allocation of the needed resources for execution:

```
@GET @Asynchronous
public void timeConsumingActivity(
        @Suspended final AsyncResponse ar) {
    longRunningCode();
    ar.resume("async response here");
}
```

- **Client API:** While the server API allows for asynchronous processing, it's also possible to use async invocations on the client-side. Going back to our earlier code sample in the *Client API* section, let's see how we can convert the sync call to an async invocation. Here's the code:

```
Client client = ClientBuilder.newClient();
Future<Response> res = client.target("http://somewhere.org/hello")
            .request("application/json")
            .async() // doesn't block calling thread
            .get(new InvocationCallback<Response>() {
                @Override
                public void completed(Response response) {...}

                @Override
                public void failed(Throwable throwable) {...}
            });
```

The `async()` call returns immediately and the type used is `AsyncInvoker`. This provides the `get()` method which accepts an `InvocationCallback<T>` where the type parameter specifies the response type to be used. All async calls return a `Future<T>` instance where the type parameter matches that of the `InvocationCallback<T>` The Future instance allows for monitoring and canceling of the async call if required.

Server-Sent Events

Server-Sent Events (SSE) is a standard and part of HTML 5; it allows for one-way communication from the server to the client. So, a client can make one request and the server can keep sending multiple responses on the same connection. The client opens the connection with a server by passing the `Accept` header as *text/event-stream*. This connection is a long-running one between the client and server. The server can then publish events over the HTTP protocol. This allows for a better solution for pushing updates to clients than clients having to resort to inefficient means such as polling. JAXRS 2.1 has made API enhancements to support SSE. On the server-side, we can define a resource that produces *text/event-stream*, which clients can register with to receive events. Let's look at an example, where we combine CDI and JAXRS to push task updates to the interested clients. First, we need to understand the tools at our disposal to create this magic.

In order to listen to client requests, we need to publish a resource that produces the media type of *text/event-stream*. We also require a handle to two more APIs, the `Sse` and `SseEventSink` instances, which can be injected using `@Context`:

```
@Singleton
@Path("updates")
public class TaskUpdatesSSE {
    private SseBroadcaster broadcaster;
    private Sse sse;
    @GET @Produces(MediaType.SERVER_SENT_EVENTS)
    public void subscribe(@Context Sse sse,
                          @Context SseEventSink eventSink) {
        this.sse = sse;
        if(this.broadcaster == null) {
            this.broadcaster = sse.newBroadcaster();
        }
        this.broadcaster.register(eventSink);
    } ...
```

The `TaskUpdatesSSE` makes use of the following APIs from the `javax.ws.rs.sse` package:

- `Sse`: This is the entry point we need for creating `OutboundSseEvent` and `SseBroadcaster` instances
- `SseEventSink`: This can be used to send an individual `OutboundSseEvent`
- `SseBroadcaster`: This allows for managing multiple instances of `SseEventSink`

The code creates a single shared `SseBroadcaster` if not already created, and then registers the `SseEventSink` instance that was injected by the runtime. This `SseEventSink` is considered the return type, similar to async processing, thus the resource method itself has defined a `void` return type. Once we have a broadcaster created we can call the `braodcast(OutboundSseEvent)` method, which publishes an SSE event to all registered `SseEventSink` instances. Since we want to publish task updates, what better way to do it than using CDI observers? Observers are a perfect fit for code that needs to be triggered/informed of events to which it subscribes. We could define an observer in the same class that would look for task updates and then broadcast the information to everyone:

```
public void observeTaskUpdates(@Observes TaskUpdated updated){
    if(this.broadcaster == null) return;
    String stats = JsonbBuilder.create().toJson(updated);
    this.broadcaster.broadcast(this.sse.newEvent(stats));
}
```

The `TaskUpdated` class is just a Java class with some properties to publish the updated information about a task. Here, we also make use of `JsonbBuilder` to `create()` `Jsonb` instance and convert the `TaskUpdated` instance `toJson()`. Finally, the following line creates an `OutboundSseEvent` and passes it to the `broadcast` method:

```
this.sse.newEvent(String) - returns OutboundSseEvent
```

Any code within the project can fire the `TaskUpdated` event using the Event API. An instance of `Event<TaskUpdated>` would invoke the `fire(TaskUpdated)` method. This code should be enough to get an SSE feature running on the server-side.

WebSockets

As mentioned in `Chapter 1`, *What's in Java EE 8?*, while SSE is an HTTP-based standard for one-sided communication, **WebSockets** is a standard allowing for bidirectional communication between both client and server. WebSockets can be used in scenarios which require two-way communication, such as chat-based applications. WebSockets are published as endpoints using either a programmatic approach or an annotated one.

An endpoint would either extend the `javax.websocket.Endpoint` class for programmatic style or use the easier approach of using `@ServerEndpoint` annotation. An endpoint instance is created per connection:

```
@ServerEndpoint("/chat")
public class ChatEndpoint {
    @OnMessage
    public void onMessage(final Session session, String msg) {
        try {
            session.getBasicRemote().sendText(msg);
        } catch (IOException e) { ... }
    }
}
```

While this is a simple way to send messages to one connected peer, there's also the possibility of sending a message to all connected peers. This can be done by saving the opened sessions in a collection from within the @OnOpen method and then using the @OnMessage code to broadcast the message to all such sessions that are still open. Here's how it can be done:

```
savedSessionsSet.stream().filter(Session::isOpen).forEach(s -> {
    try {
        s.getBasicRemote().sendObject(msg);
    }catch(Exception e) {... }
});
```

There are also other annotations that can be made use of, as shown in the following table:

Annotation	Sample usage	Purpose
@OnOpen	`@OnOpen` `public void open(Session session)`	Open a new connection

@OnMessage	`@OnMessage`
	`public void message(Session session,`
	`String msg)`
		One new message received

@OnClose	`@OnClose` `public void close(Session session)`	The connection is closed

WebSockets can also make use of encoders and decoders to handle the message payload processing. An instance of Encoder.Text<T> would override the encode method to convert a Java type to string, and a Decoder.Text<T> instance would override the decode method for converting a string to desired Java type. These can be configured on the server endpoint itself as argument to the @ServerEndpoint annotation.

Context

JAXRS applications typically need context-based information to be obtained; this is made available by use of the @Context annotation. This information is available for all root resource classes and providers. Instances of an Application subclass can be used to store central configuration, and the same instance can then be accessed via @Context injection in resources or provider classes. We looked at UsersResource.add earlier, making use of , which was injected as a parameter. This instance can be injected into class fields or method parameters using @Context annotation. Similarly, there are other types that can be injected using this annotation, such as:

- Application
- UriInfo
- HttpHeaders
- Request
- SecurityContext
- Providers
- ResourceContext
- Configuration

It's also important to understand that the context is specific to a request.

Swagger

Java EE 8 standards don't define any documentation standards, but this gap is filled by a popular choice called **Swagger**. As described on the swagger.io home page, it is an API tooling solution.

> Swagger is the world's largest framework of API developer tools for the **OpenAPI Specification (OAS)**, enabling development across the entire API lifecycle, from design and documentation, to testing and deployment.

This API tool allows for REST API documentation that stays closer to the code and evolves along with it. As an API framework, Swagger allows us to use annotations on the resource classes and its resource methods. Swagger has a lot to offer, and many features that are beyond the scope of this short brief. Developers should explore it further on its site.

The basic idea is to document the code with enough metadata in the form of annotations and then use build tools such as Maven to generate a JSON or YAML document that describes the API. This generated file (`swagger.yaml`) can then be used in other swagger tools to browse and explore the APIs. There's also support for bundling `swagger-ui` with the project, which can be very handy.

The Swagger website allows for two approaches, one called top down that allows for defining the details via a Swagger editor and then using code generation tools to create the code conforming to the specification. The bottom up approach, on the other hand, is used to create a Swagger definition from an existing REST API. The varying range of tools and support in build tools makes this a popular choice to leverage when documenting or generating code for JAXRS.

API

You can make use of Swagger annotations by adding the Maven dependency to it. This allows us to use metadata on the resource class and methods that are then used by the code generation tools to generate the Swagger format from it.

The following Maven dependency is required:

```
<dependency>
    <groupId>io.swagger</groupId>
    <artifactId>swagger-annotations</artifactId>
    <version>1.5.16</version>
</dependency>
```

Then the resource class can have annotations such as the few listed as follows:

- `Api`: To mark a resource as a Swagger resource
- `ApiOperation`: Describes an operation or typically an HTTP method against a specific path
- `ApiResponse`: To describe the response of a method
- `ApiParam`: Additional metadata for operational parameters of a method

Maven plugin

A Maven plugin can be used to generate the `swagger.yaml` file based on the metadata placed on the code:

```
<build>
...
<plugin>
    <groupId>com.github.kongchen</groupId>
    <artifactId>swagger-maven-plugin</artifactId>
    <version>3.1.5</version>
    <configuration>
        <apiSources>
            <apiSource>
                <springmvc>false</springmvc>
                <locations>org.jee8ng.users.boundary</locations>
                <schemes>http</schemes>
                <host>localhost:8081</host>
                <basePath>/${project.build.finalName}/resources
                </basePath>
                <info>
                    <title>Users API</title>
                    <version>v1</version>
                    <description>Users rest endpoints</description>
                </info>
                <outputFormats>yaml</outputFormats>
                <swaggerDirectory>${basedir}/src/main/webapp
                </swaggerDirectory>
            </apiSource>
        </apiSources>
    </configuration>
    <executions>
        <execution>
            <phase>compile</phase>
            <goals>
                <goal>generate</goal>
            </goals>
        </execution>
    </executions>
</plugin>
...
</build>
```

The `swaggerDirectory` is where the `swagger.yaml` file gets generated. This way, it's possible to use a combination of plugins and annotations to create the **Swagger Spec** format with the desired output, such as JSON, configured here. The plugin and API details can be explored further on the Swagger website and on the GitHub pages of the plugin.

Summary

REST APIs are the standard for building web services that publish business capabilities. The Java EE 8 release has enhanced the underlying JAXRS specification to version 2.1, and has brought in additions that help programmers efficiently work with the APIs. The enhancements are not restricted to server-side, but there are changes such as reactive-style programming for Client APIs. Integration with CDI and Bean Validation APIs have made declarative programming a breeze. The validation of API input and output, along with container-based dependency injection of resources and support for JSON, makes this a powerful model to use for microservices.

While standards aid in building services, external tools such as Swagger fill the gap of documentation support. SSE, as part of JAXRS, along with WebSockets, bring in different capabilities that can be leveraged when building solutions that meet modern day demands.

In the next chapter, we will put this knowledge into action by building a real-world application that publishes business capabilities as microservices.

7
Putting It All Together with Payara

We have covered enough ground in the Java EE 8 realm; now, we can start building an end-to-end application. Our application, which serves the purpose of building an understanding of the concepts learned so far, is by no means a trivial one. It brings together real-world practices when working with Java EE 8 and microservice architecture.

In this chapter, we will cover the following topics:

- Building an Issue Management System backend
- Using Java EE 8 technologies:
    - Defining the data model
    - Building microservices using REST
    - Swagger documentation
    - Using JPA for persistence
    - Deploying on Payara
    - Uber JAR and Skinny WARs
- Running multiple microservices in Docker
- Learning to use the new features of Payara Micro
- Extras:
    - CDI event bus
    - Tips and tricks

Building an Issue Management System (IMS) backend

We will be building an **Issue Management System** (IMS), which serves the purpose of creating tickets as issues, and allows a team to track and close them. The concept is fairly simple and one that most developers and teams should be familiar with. The system will facilitate a user to access the list of issues and view its details. A *user* should also be able to create and update the *issue*. It will also be helpful for getting *updates* about various *issues* in the system. The activities done for an issue can be tracked by means of *comments* added to it. It would also be nice to be able to *chat* with other users.

We will develop the backend for this system using a microservice architecture leveraging Java EE 8 technologies. Our domain model will consist of *user, issue, chat message, chat thread*, and *comment*. We will also need to model the notifications for updates around an issue. To keep things simple, the chat can be considered a group chat with all. When defining the number of services required, the idea is to keep it fine-grained enough for it to be efficiently worked upon. We will develop the following microservices for the IMS backend, which can be managed by separate teams with an independent workflow:

- `ims-users`: Services for user-specific features
- `ims-issues`: Services for task-related features which are represented as issues
- `ims-chat`: Chat for bidirectional communication using WebSockets
- `ims-comments`: Services for comments on issues within the system

You can explore the completed project by simply cloning the Git repository. To keep things simple to refer, the project has been put in a single repository, but if greater separation is desired, then each project can be placed within its own repository:

```
git clone https://github.com/PacktPublishing/Java-EE-8-and-Angular
```

As a prerequisite, apart from JDK 8, you need to have Git, Maven, and Docker installed.

Each project directory contains a `buildAndRun.sh` script, which has the Maven and Docker commands to build and run the project. Just navigate to each of the project folders and run the script in a terminal. The script performs three steps for a project:

1. Builds the Maven project
2. Builds the Docker image containing the generated WAR file
3. Runs a container using the Docker image

Having run the script for all the four projects, we should now have Docker containers started locally with port bindings, shown as the following:

```
→ ims-chat git:(master) ✗ docker ps --format "{{.Image}}\t{{.Names}}\t{{.Ports}}"
org.jee8ng/ims-chat      ims-chat        4848/tcp, 8009/tcp, 8181/tcp, 0.0.0.0:8084->8080/tcp
org.jee8ng/ims-comments ims-comments    4848/tcp, 8009/tcp, 8181/tcp, 0.0.0.0:8083->8080/tcp
org.jee8ng/ims-users     ims-users       4848/tcp, 8009/tcp, 8181/tcp, 0.0.0.0:8081->8080/tcp
org.jee8ng/ims-issues    ims-issues      4848/tcp, 8009/tcp, 8181/tcp, 0.0.0.0:8082->8080/tcp
→ ims-chat git:(master) ✗ ▮
```

The preceding image shows Docker containers started for ims-chat, ims-comments, ims-users, and ims-issues.

The first column is the image name, followed by the container name and port binding information. Each container runs on port 8080, but for the host (local machine), we have different port bindings to make it available locally without conflict.

Using Java EE 8 technologies

The backend system will comprise of REST APIs delivered as microservices. We will be using JAXRS for creating the web resources in each project and CDI as a dependency injection solution. While not strictly required, it is a popular choice of pattern. The project structure will make use of the **Boundary-Control-Entity** (BCE) or the **Entity-Control-Boundary** (ECB) pattern. The persistence layer will be written using the **Java Persistence API** (**JPA**) and the services will be stateless EJBs, which helps bolster scalability needs.

Defining the data model

Given the requirements, we can identify the following list of entities:

- ims-issues: Issue is the work item that needs to be resolved by a user
- ims-users: User represents the user of the IMS system
- ims-comments: Comment will represent the comments made on an issue
- ims-chat: Chat is a single chat message that a user sends and gets
- ims-chat: ChatThread groups the chat messages into a chain of messages

When developing each of these services, we will create our domain entities with just enough information that's relevant for the microservice, following the bounded context approach. Thus, an `Issue` entity within `ims-issues` would have a reference to a `User` entity, which will have only the minimal attributes, such as the user's `id` and `username`. This is enough to assign an issue to the user. But the `User` entity defined within the `ims-users` microservice will have more attributes in addition to these:

ims-issues	Entity: User	ims-users	Entity User
| ```
public class User {
    Long id;
    String name;
    Issue issue;
}
public class Issue {
    Long id;
    String label;
    User assignedTo;
}
``` | ```
public class User {
    Long id;
    String name;
    String email;
    Credential credential;
}
public class Credential {
    String username;
    String password;
}
``` |

So, our issues REST endpoint will have a JSON with issue information along with the basic user information to whom the issue is assigned:

```
{
    "assignedTo":{
        "id":23,
        "name":"marcus"
    },
    "created":"2017-12-04T14:38:47.654Z",
    "description":"Bug A is critical for product",
    "id":7564,
    "label":"Fix Bug A"
}
```

We continue following the bounded context principle and define the `Comment` entity within `ims-comments` to have only the IDs of an issue and user and nothing more. We avoid polluting the `comments` microservice with `user` and `issue` details; it isn't concerned with that. When the comments resource displays the comments, we enrich the comment by user data by querying the `users` microservice for the `username`. We will look at more details about this approach in later sections, when we explore intercommunication within microservices.

Building microservices using REST

Our microservices are Java EE 8 web projects, built using maven and published as separate Payara Micro instances, running within docker containers. The separation allows them to scale individually, as well as have independent operational activities. Given the BCE pattern used, we have the business component split into boundary, control, and entity, where the boundary comprises of the web resource (REST endpoint) and business service (EJB). The web resource will publish the CRUD operations and the EJB will in turn provide the transactional support for each of it along with making external calls to other resources.

Here's a logical view for the boundary consisting of the web resource and business service:

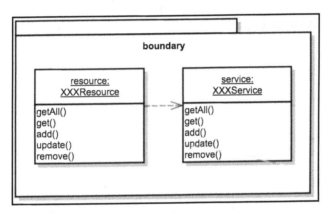

The microservices will have the following REST endpoints published for the projects shown, along with the boundary classes `XXXResource` and `XXXService`:

ims-users	ims-issues	ims-comments
• `GET /users` • `POST /users` • `DELETE /users/{id}` • `GET /users/{id}` • `PUT /users/{id}`	• `GET /issues` • `POST /issues` • `DELETE /issues/{id}` • `GET /issues/{id}` • `PUT /issues/{id}`	• `GET /comments/{issueid}` • `POST /comments/{issueid}` • `DELETE /comments/{issueid}/{id}`
Endpoint: `UsersResource`	**Endpoint:** `IssuesResource`	**Endpoint:** `CommentsResource`
Service: `UsersService`	**Service:** `IssuesService`	**Service:** `CommentsService`

The `ims-issues` project also leverages the code we looked at in Chapter 6, *Power Your APIs with JAXRS and CDI*, for Server-Sent Events. In IMS, we publish task/issue updates to the browser using an SSE endpoint. The code observes for the events using the CDI event notification model and triggers the broadcast.

The `ims-users` and `ims-issues` endpoints are similar in API format and behavior. While one deals with creating, reading, updating, and deleting a `User`, the other does the same for an `Issue`. Let's look at this in action. After you have the containers running, we can start firing requests to the `/users` web resource.

The following `curl` command maps the URI `/users` to the `@GET` resource method named `getAll()` and returns a collection (JSON array) of users. The Java code will simply return a `Set<User>`, which gets converted to `JsonArray` due to the JSON binding support of JSON-B.

The method invoked is as follows:

```
@GET
public Response getAll() {... }
```

```
curl -v -H 'Accept: application/json'
http://localhost:8081/ims-users/resources/users
...
HTTP/1.1 200 OK
...
[{ "id":1,"name":"Marcus","email":"marcus_jee8@testem.com"
  "credential":{"password":"1234","username":"marcus"}
},
{ "id":2,"name":"Bob","email":"bob@testem.com"
  "credential":{"password":"1234","username":"bob"}
}]
```

Next, for selecting one of the users, such as `Marcus`, we will issue the following `curl` command, which uses the `/users/xxx` path. This will map the URI to the `@GET` method which has the additional `@Path("{id}")` annotation as well. The value of the `id` is captured using the `@PathParam("id")` annotation placed before the field. The response is a `User` entity wrapped in the `Response` object returned.

The method invoked is as follows:

```
@GET @Path("{id}")
 public Response get(@PathParam("id") Long id) { ... }
```

```
curl -v -H 'Accept: application/json'
http://localhost:8081/ims-users/resources/users/1
...
HTTP/1.1 200 OK
...
{
    "id":1,"name":"Marcus","email":"marcus_jee8@testem.com"
    "credential":{"password":"1234","username":"marcus"}
}
```

In both the preceding methods, we saw the response returned as 200 OK. This is achieved by using a `Response` builder. Here's the snippet for the method:

```
return Response.ok( ..entity here..).build();
```

Next, for submitting data to the resource method, we use the `@POST` annotation. You might have noticed earlier that the signature of the method also made use of a `UriInfo` object. This is injected at runtime for us via the `@Context` annotation. A curl command can be used to submit the JSON data of a `user` entity.

The method invoked is as follows:

```
@POST
public Response add(User newUser, @Context UriInfo uriInfo)
```

We make use of the `-d` flag to send the JSON body in the request. The `POST` request is implied:

```
curl -v -H 'Content-Type: application/json'
http://localhost:8081/ims-users/resources/users -d '{"name": "james",
"email":"james@testem.io",
"credential": {"username":"james","password":"test123"}}'
...
HTTP/1.1 201 Created
...
Location: http://localhost:8081/ims-users/resources/users/3
```

The `201` status code is sent by the API to signal that an entity has been created, and it also returns the location for the newly created entity. Here's the relevant snippet to do this:

```
...
//uriInfo is injected via @Context parameter to this method
URI location = uriInfo.getAbsolutePathBuilder()
               .path(newUserId) // This is the new entity ID
               .build();
// To send 201 status with new Location
return Response.created(location).build();
```

Similarly, we can also send an update request using the `PUT` method.

The method invoked is as follows:

```
@PUT @Path("{id}")
public Response update(@PathParam("id") Long id, User existingUser)
```

```
curl -v -X PUT -H 'Content-Type: application/json'
http://localhost:8081/ims-users/resources/users/3 -d '{"name": "jameson",
"email":"james@testem.io"}'
...
HTTP/1.1 200 Ok
```

The last method we need to map is the `DELETE` method, which is similar to the `GET` operation, with the only difference being the HTTP method used.

The method invoked is as follows:

```
@DELETE @Path("{id}")
public Response delete(@PathParam("id") Long id)
```

```
curl -v -X DELETE http://localhost:8081/ims-users/resources/users/3
...
HTTP/1.1 200 Ok
```

You can try out the `Issues` endpoint in a similar manner.

For the GET requests of /users or /issues, the code simply fetches and returns a set of entity objects. But when requesting an item within this collection, the resource method has to look up the entity by the passed in id value, captured by @PathParam("id"), and if found, return the entity, or else a 404 Not Found is returned. Here's a snippet showing just that:

```
final Optional<Issue> issueFound = service.get(id); //id obtained
if (issueFound.isPresent()) {
    return Response.ok(issueFound.get()).build();
}
return Response.status(Response.Status.NOT_FOUND).build();
```

The issue instance can be fetched from a database of issues, which the service object interacts with. The persistence layer can return a JPA entity object which gets converted to JSON for the calling code. We will look at persistence using JPA in a later section.

For the update request which is sent as an HTTP PUT, the code captures the identifier ID using @PathParam("id"), similar to the previous GET operation, and then uses that to update the entity. The entity itself is submitted as a JSON input and gets converted to the entity instance along with the passed in message body of the payload.

Here's the code snippet for that:

```
@PUT @Path("{id}")
public Response update(@PathParam("id") Long id, Issue updated) {
    updated.setId(id);
    boolean done = service.update(updated);
    return done ?
            Response.ok(updated).build() :
            Response.status(Response.Status.NOT_FOUND).build();
}
```

The code is simple to read and does one thing—it updates the identified entity and returns the response containing the updated entity or a 404 for a non-existing entity.

The service references that we have looked at so far are @Stateless beans which are injected into the resource class as fields:

```
// Project: ims-comments
@Stateless
public class CommentsService {... }

// Project: ims-issues
@Stateless
public class IssuesService {... }
```

```
// Project: ims-users
@Stateless
public class UsersService {... }
```

These will in turn have the `EntityManager` injected via `@PersistenceContext`.
Combined with the resource and service, our components have made the boundary ready
for clients to use.

Similar to the *WebSockets* section in `Chapter 6`, *Power Your APIs with JAXRS and CDI*, in IMS,
we use a `@ServerEndpoint` which maintains the list of active sessions and then uses that to
broadcast a message to all users who are connected. A `ChatThread` keeps track of the
messages being exchanged through the `@ServerEndpoint` class. For the message to be
sent, we use the stream of sessions and filter it by open sessions, then send the message for
each of the sessions:

```
chatSessions.getSessions().stream().filter(Session::isOpen)
.forEach(s -> {
    try {
        s.getBasicRemote().sendObject(chatMessage);
    }catch(Exception e) {...}
});
```

Swagger documentation

We annotate the resource class with additional metadata, which makes it a Swagger
resource. These annotations are then processed by the Maven plugin and a `swagger.yaml`
gets generated in the `src/main/webapp` folder, which becomes available in the project's
root URL. To achieve this, here's an example of `UsersResource` with Swagger annotations:

```
@Path("users") @Api(value = "users")
public class UsersResource {
...
    @GET
    @ApiOperation(value = "Get all users")
    public Response getAll() { ... }

    @GET @Path("{id}")
    @ApiOperation(value = "Get user by id", response = User.class)
    @ApiResponses({
      @ApiResponse(code = 400, message = "Invalid input"),
      @ApiResponse(code = 404, message = "User not found")
    })
    public Response get(@ApiParam(
        value = "ID of user that's to be fetched", required = true)
```

```
        @PathParam("id") Long id) { .... }

    @POST
    @ApiOperation(value = "Create user",
            notes = "This can only be done by the logged in user.")
    public Response add(User newUser, @Context UriInfo uriInfo)
    { .... }
```

The APIs are part of the artifact `swagger-annotations` library, which we add to our project as a dependency. We then use `swagger-maven-plugin` as part of the build to generate the Swagger Spec file (`swagger.yaml`):

```
<plugin>
    <artifactId>swagger-maven-plugin</artifactId>
    ...
            <apiSource>
                ...
                <locations>org.jee8ng.users.boundary</locations>
                <schemes>http</schemes>
                <host>localhost:8081</host>
                <basePath>
                    /${project.build.finalName}/resources
                </basePath>
                <info>
                    <title>Users API</title>
                    <version>v1</version>
                    <description>Users rest endpoints</description>
                </info>
                <outputFormats>yaml</outputFormats>
                <swaggerDirectory>
                    ${basedir}/src/main/webapp
                </swaggerDirectory>
            </apiSource>
    ....
</plugin>
```

That's it for getting `swagger.yaml` file generation done. The same can be loaded in the online editor provided at: `https://editor.swagger.io/`.

Another option is to bundle the Swagger UI along with the WAR file; this can be done by simply copying the UI dist directory to the `src/main/webapp` folder. Next, we need to edit the `index.html` file to the updated `swagger.yaml` file location reference.

The Swagger UI git location is: `https://github.com/swagger-api/swagger-ui/tree/master/dist`.

If you did checkout/clone the `putting-together-ims` project, then these changes are ready for you to explore. From a running container, you can simply browse to `swagger-ui`, as shown here, for the two projects: `http://localhost:8081/ims-users/swagger-ui`.

In the IMS backend, Swagger, as an example, has been set up for the `ims-users` project, while the other projects have not used this. Just like in a microservices architecture, each team can make their own decision about how to present the APIs to other parties. But, needless to say, using Swagger does have its advantages.

Using JPA for persistence

Our service needs to interact with a database for working with the entities. As an example, we have set up H2 as an in-memory database for our microservices. We need to have a datasource configured, which will be used by JPA. This can be done by using the `<datasource>` tag in the `web.xml` file:

```xml
<data-source>
    <name>java:global/datasource</name>
    <class-name>org.h2.jdbcx.JdbcDataSource</class-name>
    <url>jdbc:h2:mem:users;DB_CLOSE_DELAY=-1</url>
</data-source>
```

The `<url>` value defines the H2 in-memory database called `users`, and the `DB_CLOSE_DELAY` flag is used to ensure the database is retained in memory, even if connections are closed to it.

Then the datasource/name is referred to in `src/main/resources/META-INF/persistence.xml`:

```xml
...
<persistence-unit name="UsersDS" transaction-type="JTA">
  <jta-data-source>java:global/datasource</jta-data-source>
  <exclude-unlisted-classes>false</exclude-unlisted-classes>
  <properties>
    <property
      name="javax.persistence.schema-generation.database.action"
      value="drop-and-create"/>
  </properties>
</persistence-unit>
...
```

Each project is configured with a JPA and H2 database, but we can easily swap the underlying persistence solution with any external database such as MySQL or PostgreSQL.

Our entities, such as `User`, `Issue`, `ChatThread`, `Chat`, and `Comment`, would accordingly be mapped as a JPA `@Entity` with an `@Id` property. Here's how the `User` entity is used:

```
@Stateless
public class UsersService {
    @PersistenceContext private EntityManager em;
...

    public void add(@Valid User newUser) {
        em.persist(newUser);
    }

    public Optional<User> get(Long id) {
        User found = em.find(User.class, id);
        return found != null ?
                    Optional.of(found) :
                    Optional.empty();
    }
...
@Entity
public class User {
    @Id @GeneratedValue(strategy = GenerationType.IDENTITY)
    private Long id;

    @NotNull @Size(min=2, max=20)
    private String name;
...
```

The validation constraints are not only updated for improved runtime behavior, but the same will also reflect in the `swagger.yaml` file. You can apply a `@Valid` constraint on a service or on resource methods. By doing this, an invalid entity message payload (failing to meet the constraint added to the `name` property) would get rejected with a `400 Bad Request`.

While we have the `UsersResource` and `IssuesResource` providing similar CRUD operations, the `CommentsResource` always works with an `Issue`, thus its endpoint accepts an issue ID for its operations:

```
@Path("comments/{issueid}")
public class CommentsResource {
    @PathParam("issueid")
    private Long issueId;
...
    @GET
```

```
public Response getAll() {
    return Response.ok(service.getAll(issueId)).build();
}
...
```

The service for comments works with a `Comment` entity for three operations: get all comments, add comment, and delete comment. While fetching comments for an issue ID, we also request the `ims-users` microservice for additional user details. Following the bounded context approach, the comments service doesn't store a user's name, but instead it references the ID of the user who made the comment. The code first obtains a list of comments from its database, then for each comment retrieves the user's name from the `users` endpoint, as shown here:

```
return commentsList.stream()
        .map(CommentInfo::new) // Map Comment to CommentInfo
        .map(CommentsService::updateName) //Update UserName
        .collect(Collectors.toSet());
....
class CommentInfo {
    Comment comment;
    String byUserName;
    CommentInfo(Comment c) { ... }
    ...
}

public static CommentInfo updateName(CommentInfo info) {
    Client client = ClientBuilder.newBuilder()
                .connectTimeout(500, TimeUnit.MICROSECONDS)
                .readTimeout(700, TimeUnit.MICROSECONDS).build();

    JsonObject userJson = client.target(
      "http://ims-users:8080/ims-users/resources/users/{id}")
            .resolveTemplate("id",info.getComment().getByUser())
            .request().get(JsonObject.class);
    info.setByUserName(userJson.getString("name"));
    return info;
}
```

For the `ims-users` microservice, we are using the `http://ims-users..` hostname, which is resolved in the docker container IP for the `ims-users` container name. When running the comments container, we link it with the `ims-users` container, thus allowing for this lookup:

```
docker run -d -p 8083:8080 --name ims-comments --link ims-users
org.jee8ng/ims-comments
```

Deploying on Payara

While there are other manual ways to run a local Payara Micro instance, the Docker way is more flexible and allows for disparate developer teams to work together quicker. Docker images of Java runtimes can be shared to the UI team, who may not really have Java installed. Docker makes it easy to share infrastructure and applications with other developers. Each of the IMS projects contain a single `Dockerfile`, which defines the custom image for the application. This file extends the `payara/micro` image and adds an application WAR file to the deployable directory, identified by the `{DEPLOY_DIR}` variable. The `payara/micro` image uses OpenJDK 8 images with an Alpine Linux base, which helps keep image size fairly small. Here's the `Dockerfile` contents:

```
FROM payara/micro:5-SNAPSHOT
COPY ./target/ims-*.war ${DEPLOY_DIR}
```

Building an image involves running the `mvn build` command and then creating the Docker image containing the latest code:

```
mvn clean package && docker build -t org.jee8ng/ims-users .
```

After having got the image, we can run this image as a container using the following Docker command:

```
docker run --rm -d -p 8081:8080 --name users org.jee8ng/ims-users
```

Uber JAR and Skinny WARs

We touched upon this in the `Chapter 4`, *Building and Deploying Microservices*, where we looked at both options. For the IMS backend, we are using the *Skinny WARs* approach.

Docker builds can be created extremely fast, given we are using the standards and have very little external dependency. This keeps our WAR file size small, which helps in building the Docker image quicker. On decent machines, you may get images built in less than a second. Your result may vary, but this still shows the promising world of Docker. Here's the general output you would see when building the image:

```
docker build -t org.jee8ng/ims-users . Sending
build context to Docker daemon 8.318MB Step
1/2 : FROM payara/micro:5-SNAPSHOT
 ---> 44c7a1b4d858
Step 2/2 : COPY ./target/ims-*.war ${DEPLOY_DIR}
 ---> 6e992011086c
Successfully built 6e992011086c
Successfully tagged org.jee8ng/ims-users:latest
```

If the WAR file doesn't change and you issue the docker command again, then *Step 2* will print a line stating Using cache, due to no real changes being present in the COPY instruction.

Alternatively, it's easy to switch to Uber JAR if desired—instead of using the Docker-based images, we use the payara-micro JAR to create our JAR and run it as an executable. This will bundle the server within the application, making it self-contained:

```
java -jar payara-micro.jar --deploy ims-users.war --outputUberJar users-
payara.jar

java -jar users-payara.jar
```

Running multiple microservices in Docker

We can have multiple instances of the same service or just different services altogether running on a single machine. Docker containers are self-contained and isolated. Since each Docker container has its own virtual Ethernet IP address, there are no port conflicts. When running containers, it's often desired to have more than one container deployed for load balancing needs. There are full-scale solutions, such as Docker Swarm or Kubernetes, for the production of grade container orchestration, which greatly help. Multiple containers can also help when one of the services/containers is not responding or needs to be replaced. The speed by which you spawn new containers and add them to the cluster of containers will matter.

If you are running containers on a single machine and want to spawn another instance of ims-issues, then you need to invoke the docker run command using the ims-issues image we built earlier, and specify a different local port binding:

```
docker run --rm -d -p 8085:8080 --name ims-issues-2 org.jee8ng/ims-issues
```

Here are the containers. You can see ims-issues and ims-issues-2 are running:

```
→ ims-users git:(master) ✗ docker ps --format "{{.Image}}\t{{.Names}}\t{{.Ports}}"
org.jee8ng/ims-issues    ims-issues-2    4848/tcp, 8009/tcp, 8181/tcp, 0.0.0.0:8085->8080/tcp
org.jee8ng/ims-chat      ims-chat        4848/tcp, 8009/tcp, 8181/tcp, 0.0.0.0:8084->8080/tcp
org.jee8ng/ims-comments  ims-comments    4848/tcp, 8009/tcp, 8181/tcp, 0.0.0.0:8083->8080/tcp
org.jee8ng/ims-issues    ims-issues      4848/tcp, 8009/tcp, 8181/tcp, 0.0.0.0:8082->8080/tcp
```

This makes the service available on both these URLs locally:

- http://localhost:8082/ims-issues/resources/issues
- http://localhost:8085/ims-issues/resources/issues

Learning to use the new features of Payara Micro

Payara Micro takes a new approach to deploying and running Java applications. It also comes with automatic and elastic clustering and takes into consideration modern day approaches, such as Docker containers. The Payara Micro executable itself is less than 70 MB and is a self-contained JAR. This JAR can be used to generate an Uber JAR or start a micro instance with the application deployed to it. Some of the capabilities that Payara offers are:

- Embedded servers
- Uber JAR approach
- Deploying and running an application using the Payara JAR executable
- Automatic clustering

This capabilities can be briefly explained as follows:

- **Embedding server**: This can be done by using the `fish.payar.micro` package, which offers APIs for bootstrapping a micro instance programmatically with a single line:

    ```
    PayaraMicro.bootstrap();
    ```

- **Uber JAR approach**: An Uber JAR is generated by passing arguments to the Payara executable for outputting the executable JAR along with the application WAR file. The WAR file is placed separately in `META-INF/deploy`, within the JAR.

- **Deploying and running**: The application is deployed and run by issuing the following simple command:

    ```
    java -jar payara-micro.jar --deploy application.war
    ```

    It's also possible to deploy multiple applications in a single micro instance, using the `--deploy` option twice.

- **Automatic clustering**: Clustering features are provided by Hazlecast. When you run multiple micro instances, they can automatically discover each other, and members form a group. When instances join or leave the cluster, this is all managed by Hazlecast internally. If you look at the server logs, you will see a similar output for the members discovered and listed:

    ```
    Members [3] {
       Member [172.17.0.2]:5900 - cdaa2b2a-3bc1-4097-a299-ac39d1e05467
       Member [172.17.0.3]:5900 - ffb58095-fde7-4c7d-a571-e1cafbd9e308
       Member [172.17.0.4]:5900 - 27870c1d-b80d-4f68-9270-2cc2a84b5ae3
    }
    ```
    this

Extras

- **MicroProfile:** Since Payara Micro supports this profile, it has support for Microprofile Configuration API to inject configuration properties. You can define a property file, such as `resources/META-INF/microprofile-config.properties`, with the following contents:

    ```
    file.location=/tmp
    ```

Then, in the code, you can inject the property using the `@ConfigProperty`, which is provided by the `microprofile-config-api` library dependency:

```
@Inject @ConfigProperty(name = "file.location")
String fileProperty;
```

- **Maven plugin:** Payara also has Maven plugin support which can be used for generating the Uber JAR, as shown here:

```
<plugin>
    <groupId>fish.payara.maven.plugins</groupId>
    <artifactId>payara-micro-maven-plugin</artifactId>
    <version>1.0.0</version>
    <executions>
        <execution>
            <goals>
                <goal>bundle</goal>
            </goals>
        </execution>
    </executions>
    <configuration>
        <payaraVersion>5.0.0.173-SNAPSHOT</payaraVersion>
        <useUberJar>true</useUberJar>
    </configuration>
</plugin>
```

When running the `maven build` command, this will generate a WAR and an Uber JAR. The JAR name will have a suffix of `-microbundle.jar` and will be an executable JAR.

The Maven goals, such as `payara-micro:bundle`, `payara-micro:start`, and `payara-micro:stop`, can then be used as part of the Maven commands.

CDI event bus

We have looked at the CDI Event bus. Payara takes this a step further by introducing a Clustered CDI Event Bus. This makes it possible to use lightweight distributed messaging using CDI, rather than a heavy weight JMS solution. It allows code to send data from one instance of Payara to another. Since this is non-standard feature, we depend on `payara-api` for it.

This allows for using the annotation `fish.payara.micro.cdi.Outbound` on the `Event<T>` instance. We can then send the Java object as the payload, which is *serializable*. On the receiving side, the code will have an observer which uses the annotation `fish.payara.micro.cdi.Inbound` in combination with `@Observes`. This makes it possible to send events to other instances that are part of the Payara cluster.

Tips and tricks

- **Docker**: When running the Docker containers, we use the `--rm` flag which removes the container on exit. This is helpful for repeat builds, so consider using it. To check the logs of a running container, you can issue the `docker logs nameofcontainer` command.

  You can use the `docker-compose` command to have the Docker containers spin up quickly rather than having to individually use docker run with various commands. Here's a sample `docker-compose.yml` file for the IMS backend:

  ```yaml
  version: "2"
  services:
      ims-users:
          image: org.jee8ng/ims-users
          ports:
              - "8081:8080"
      ims-issues:
          image: org.jee8ng/ims-issues
          ports:
              - "8082:8080"
      ims-comments:
          image: org.jee8ng/ims-comments
          ports:
              - "8083:8080"
          links:
              - ims-users
      ims-chat:
          image: org.jee8ng/ims-chat
          ports:
              - "8084:8080"
  ```

  Run `docker-compose up -d` to start the containers and `docker-compose down` to shut them down.

- **JSON support**: Consider using `JsonObject` or `JsonArray` as the resource method input or output. You don't always need a Java class to represent data. If JSON is what you want, then use JSON types provided out of the box by Java EE 8.
- **Postman:** While unit tests are essential, you can consider using a tool such as **Postman**, which offers the saving of requests, creating a consolidated group, and even having a mock server for the APIs. This can be a quick and handy way of testing your APIs during development.
- **Shared library:** When building microservices, there are times when you need to reuse some code such as a generic base resource class or a base class for your service code. You can create a library with the essentials and add that as a maven dependency to the projects.

Summary

Our APIs are developed with standard Java EE 8 features using modern day solutions such as Docker and Payara Micro. The solution built is flexible in terms of the deployment strategy, as it can be distributed as a standard **web application archive** (**WAR**), as an Uber JAR, or as a Docker image. We learned how Payara features such as Payara API, Clustered CDI Events, and maven plugins can ease development when working with Payara Micro.

Our REST API endpoints use a standard JSON format for data exchange and conform to HTTP standards. By using standards, we improve our code portability. Also, the web services approach allows other developers to consume our API without having to know the implementation details. JSON is an industry leader when it comes to data exchange and provides a very simple structure, which we have utilized in this IMS backend project. The project was built using microservices, with each having its own database for the entities used. The WebSockets API allowed for building bidirectional communication support, while SSE allowed us to push issue updates to the client's browser. With these capabilities, we now know how a functional backend for the Issue Management System.

In the chapters to follow, we will learn how to use TypeScript and Angular for building a real-world application connected to these microservices.

8
Basic TypeScript

Developers who love the comfort of strongly typed languages such as Java are rarely impressed with JavaScript. But nonetheless, it's a language that almost every developer comes across sooner or later. The goal of writing cleaner and concise code seems like a distant dream in the scripting world. But JavaScript is not to be ignored, as modern day browsers are providing very capable JavaScript engines, making it possible to deliver complex client-side applications. As client-side code grows, so does the need for better programming features for writing code that scales. Browser vendors have implemented JavaScript engines which are compliant to different ECMAScript standards. Thus, when running JavaScript code on different engines or browsers, there are differences to deal with, as code that works in one browser may fail in another. TypeScript, developed by Microsoft, seems to solve some of these challenges by strengthening JavaScript with features that are missing from it. It serves as a bridge for developers to cross to reach their goal of writing better code for the frontend.

Here's what we will cover in this chapter:

- Getting Started with TypeScript:
    - Why use it?
    - Features
    - Visual Studio code
    - Hello World example
- Using variables, types and functions
- Working with classes and interfaces
- Working with arrays

Getting started with TypeScript

TypeScript is an open source solution which has entered the spotlight in recent times. With frameworks such as Angular promoting its use, it has gained popularity among web developers. But before we explore TypeScript, let's get familiar with some of the terms you may often come across:

- ES5
- ES6/ES2015
- TypeScript

ECMAScript (ES) is a standard specification that JavaScript implements, similar to Java EE standards that vendors implement. ES5, being older, is what most browsers support, and then there's the newer ES6/ES2015, the sixth edition. The good old JavaScript that most developers have learnt is most likely the ES5 standard, which was never intended for writing large complex applications. ES6 tries to transform JavaScript into a mature language by addressing its predecessors' shortcomings. It brings some much needed features that developers coming from a Java or other high-level language should be familiar with. This helps by reducing the learning curve for ES6. But since these features may not be fully supported by all browsers, developers cannot use it today without risking browser compatibility.

TypeScript (TS) is a language that helps write **JavaScript (JS)** that scales. As defined on its website (`https://www.typescriptlang.org/`):

> *"TypeScript is a typed superset of JavaScript that compiles to plain JavaScript."*

It uses a transpiler to transform the TS code into a target JS version or standard such as ES5 or ES6/ES2015. A transpiler is a source to source compiler used to convert code from one language to another. The TypeScript transpiler uses the source code written in TypeScript to transform it into JS. Since TypeScript is a superset of JavaScript, plus adds more features to it, any JavaScript code is valid in TypeScript code and any TypeScript code can be transpiled to valid JavaScript.

Why use it?

TypeScript is supported by Microsoft and even promoted by Google for Angular. When considering any large scale JavaScript development, it's recommended to use TypeScript. Angular, as a framework, has become a popular choice for frontend development and was itself written using TypeScript. The language syntax has some similarities to Java, which makes it easy for Java developers to work with.

Developers coming from a strongly typed language such as Java might consider JavaScript evil for not having any type safety. This is an aspect that TypeScript primarily solves by providing some much needed, but optional, type safety, along with classes and interfaces. Developers writing JavaScript get very little help from their IDEs to catch bugs at development time. Errors, such as passing a Boolean where a number was expected, or invoking a method with the wrong number of arguments, can all be caught during development when using TypeScript. Needless to say, it's crucial to catch errors early rather than finding it fail on production.

When developers pick any language to learn, they would hope to learn the latest standard or version. ES6 features, such as block scopes and classes, are great to use, but going back to the previous point, ES6 may not be supported today by all browsers. This puts a dent in this wish of learning the latest JavaScript standard. TypeScript solves this dilemma, as it offers the features of future ES versions plus a few extras which can be used today. Think of TypeScript as a language that allows for using the latest JavaScript standards and produces code, which is still compatible with today's versions such as ES5.

Features

TypeScript brings type safety to JavaScript, similar to other strongly typed high-level languages support. JavaScript is known as a weakly typed language, but with TypeScript, we get the huge benefit of static code analysis, which helps in validating code during development.

TypeScript code, once compiled, is output as JavaScript, which is what runs on the browser. The TypeScript compiler can pass flags to signal the target ES version to be used for code generation. Here's a TypeScript code:

```
class Person {
    name: string;
    age: number;
    constructor (name: string, age: number) {
        this.name = name;
        this.age = age;
```

```
        }
        show() {
            console.log(`Hello ${this.name} is ${this.age} years old`);
        }
    }
    let p = new Person('bob',35);
    p.show();
```

The code uses ES6 features along with the optional type safety. Once the transpiler is passed in this code, it will transpile it to a specified target ECMAScript version. Here's what the transpiled code looks like for ES6/ES2015:

```
class Person {
    constructor(name, age) {
        this.name = name;
        this.age = age;
    }
    show() {
        console.log(`Hello ${this.name} is ${this.age} years old`);
    }
}
let p = new Person('bob', 35);
p.show();
```

Most of the TypeScript code remains unchanged, as ES6 features include classes and template literals. The static types disappear at runtime and thus don't show in the generated ES6 code. The template literals used are strings enclosed in back-ticks (` `). Instead of using quotes, this allows the usage of embedded expressions similar to EL expressions in Java using the dollar sign and curly braces. It even supports multiline strings which otherwise could only be written using the plus (+) sign for string concatenation.

Consider this code snippet, which is typically written in ES5 and earlier versions:

```
var msg = "Hello " + this.name + ", how are you doing " + "today.";
```

With ES6/ES2015, it is possible to use back-ticks for expression and multi-line support, allowing the same code to be rewritten, as shown next:

```
var msg = `Hello ${this.name}, how are you doing today.`;
```

While the transpiled code didn't change much when using ES6 as target, it's a different case for ES5. Given the `Person` class, here's what the transpiled code in ES5 looks like:

```
var Person = /** @class */ (function () {
    function Person(name, age) {
        this.name = name;
        this.age = age;
    }
    Person.prototype.show = function () {
        console.log("Hello " + this.name + " is " + this.age + " years
old");
    };
    return Person;
}());
var p = new Person('bob', 35);
p.show();
```

TypeScript thus makes it possible to use ES6 features, even if the browser doesn't support it today. The TypeScript compiler transpiles the code into the target ES version, which is compatible with browsers and does not sacrifice type safety and ES6 features.

Visual Studio Code

Visual Studio Code (VS Code) is a free open source editor which runs on all major platforms, such as Windows, macOS, and Linux. It may not be as feature rich as Java IDEs, but it serves the purpose of a lightweight and feature rich editor. Similar to Java IDEs such as Eclipse and NetBeans, VS Code offers plugins called **extensions**, which can enhance the features of the base installation. Writing a large application requires good tooling support for developers to be productive. If the existing features out of the box aren't enough, then extensions can be installed to enhance the editor further.

Here's the editor in action, showing TypeScript code next to ES5 transpiled code:

IntelliSense

The VS Code editor has **IntelliSense**, which provides code completion support as you type for JavaScript and TypeScript out of the box. This also provides a quick reference to the documentation as well, as part of IntelliSense.

Debugging

Another key feature is the built-in debugger, which aids in the debugging of any language that gets transpiled to JavaScript. An integrated debugging feature, that makes it possible to inspect a variables value, check the call stack, step through code execution and more.

SCM support

With out of the box Git integration, it's possible to stage changes and commit code as part of the workflow from within the editor itself. The changes made can also be compared to previous versions side by side. Using extensions, it's possible to add more SCM support as well.

Terminal

Having an integrated terminal in the comfort of the editor helps in providing a complete environment for development. This allows for the executing of shell commands quickly and comes in handy when working with CLI tools, such as Angular CLI.

Hello World example

To see TypeScript in action, the first thing you want to do is install **Node.js**.

The installation of Node.js is fairly simple and can be done in multiple ways:

- Using the official website (`http://nodejs.org`), to get the binaries, and following the instructions
- On Linux, you can install `node` and `npm` from Debian/Ubuntu packages
- On Mac, you can use **Homebrew**, a package manager for macOS, which can be used to install the node with the one command, `brew install node`

Whichever approach you pick, at the end you should have `node` and `npm` installed. To verify the installation you can run the following commands (your versions may vary, just ensure you use the latest available version):

```
node -v
v8.7.0
npm -v
5.5.1
```

You can think of npm as a tool to install software and dependencies for your project, similar to Maven. Now we need TypeScript to be installed, and to do that, we can issue the following command on macOS or Linux:

- **Installing TypeScript**: npm install -g typescript

  After using the install command, you have TypeScript globally installed and ready to compile TypeScript code. Let's take a look at our hello-world.ts file, which has the following code:

  ```
  let priority: string = "high";
  priority = "low";
  console.log(priority);
  ```

- **Compiling TypeScript to JavaScript**: tsc hello-world.ts --target ES5

  This results in the creation of a JavaScript file, hello-world.js, placed in the same directory. That's it for getting up and running with TypeScript. The JS file can now be executed using node as follows:

- **Run JS**: node hello-world.js

  Additionally, we can use tsconfig.json, a configuration file, for various configuration options when running tsc. This file can be created by using tsc --init, which generates the tsconfig.json file in the same directory.

Using variables, types, and functions

Declaring a variable can be done using the traditional var keyword, which has some gotchas. A variable declared using var becomes available not only inside the block in which it's defined, but also outside the block scope in the containing module, namespace, or global scope. This can lead to programming errors that are hard to catch. A better way to declare variable types is by using the two relatively new keywords like let and const. These are used similar to the var keyword, but the outcome is very different. Using let is the same as using block-scope, and unlike var these variables aren't leaked outside their containing blocks. The keyword const just augments let and prevents any reassignment to its variables.

When declaring a variable, the variable name is followed by a colon and then its type. It may also contain an optional initial value that can be assigned during the variable initialization. The types are annotated by using the `:Type` syntax, such as `:boolean` or `:number`, and so on. You can also use `:any` to specify any type in the type system. But the type itself is optional, so you can declare a variable without any `:Type` added to it and the type would be inferred by TypeScript.

Type inference

Consider this example:

```
var percent = 100;
```

Here, since the variable name `percent` is declared using the `var` keyword and set to an initial value of `100`, TypeScript will determine that `percent` is going to be of `number` type and will do the type checking for it. Later in the code, we can assign `percent` a type other than `number`, such as the following:

```
percent = 'test';
```

The compiler will throw an error, since the inferred `percent` type is of `number` type.

 Java developers are used to declaring the types for variables, while TypeScript makes it a relaxed choice. So, in Java, `int percent = 100;` can be `var percent = 100;` in TypeScript.

Using const

Let's consider this example:

```
const flag: boolean = false;
flag = true;
```

The preceding reassignment won't be allowed if we try to compile the code. **TypeScript Compiler (TSC)** would complain with the following message: `[ts] Cannot assign to 'flag' because it is a constant or a read-only property.`

Using let

Let's consider the following example:

```
for (var i = 0; i <= 9; i++) {
    console.log(i);
}
console.log(i); //prints 10 as 'i' is accessible outside the loop

// Below let ensures x is accessible only within the for loop
for (let x = 0; x <= 9; x++) {
    console.log(x);
}
console.log(x); //TypeScript compiler error: Cannot find name 'x'.
```

Since `let` is stricter it helps prevent the programmer from making unknowing mistakes. TypeScript also introduces enums, which allow for defining set of named constants:

```
enum Priority { High, Low};
let priorityEnum: Priority = Priority.High;
priorityEnum = Priority.Low;

function show(id: number, priority: Priority): void {
    // ...
}
```

Here, `High` will be assigned a value of 0, followed by `Low` with value of 1. The variable of an enum type can only be passed named constants belonging to the enum type. So, the `show` function, which returns nothing (void), can take the first argument as a number and the second as either `Priority.High` or `Priority.Low`.

Here's how you can declare variables and their types:

```
let isDone: boolean = true;
let author: string = "Prashant";
let age: number = 35;
let environments: string[] = ['dev', 'qa','prod'];
let something: any = "any value";
something = 99;

let random; //inferred as type any
let x: number;
let y: number = 2;
let z = 98 + y; //inferred as type number
```

When declaring variables, consider:

- Using the `let` keyword over `var`
- Specifying the type annotation `:Type` when the type is known
- Combining the `:Type` with initialization when you want to declare and set a value

Using functions

In JavaScript, when you declare parameters to a function, all are by default considered optional and users can invoke them as needed. So, you can invoke a function which takes one or more parameters without any parameters and it will still work. Consider the code shown here, which works in JavaScript:

```
function dumb(a,b) {
    console.log('a ' + a + ',b ' +b);
}
dumb();
dumb(1);
dumb(1,2);
dumb(1,null);

//output of the above calls in plain JavaScript
a undefined,b undefined
a 1,b undefined
a 1,b 2
a 1,b null
```

All four invocations of the `dumb` function will work, but with parameters initialized with passed in values, or undefined if not specified explicitly. Here, `null` is also considered a value. This is different in TypeScript, as all parameters declared are by default required and invocations that do not match the method parameters won't compile. Thus, the first and second calls of `dumb` would not compile. It's possible to get similar behavior to JavaScript in TypeScript code by adding a `?` at the end of the parameter name. This would result in the same output as seen in JavaScript. Here's the function with optional parameters:

```
function dumb(a?,b?)
```

Within the function, we could check if a value was passed for the optional parameter by comparing it with `undefined`, as shown here:

```
if(a === undefined) { ... }
```

A function can also be declared and captured in a variable:

```
var work = function() { return true; }
var isComplete = work();
```

Here, the type of `work` would be of `Function` type and could be invoked like any normal function. The variable `isComplete` would be inferred as Boolean type, based on the `work()` functions return value.

We could also declare an object as the parameter type when declaring the function, as shown here:

```
function addUp( addition: { x: number, y: number}) {
    return addition.x + addition.y;
}
var result: number = addUp( { x: 2, y: 5});
```

Here, the call to `addUp` will pass the value of x as 2 and y as 5, which matches the object literal argument for `addUp`, called `addition`. While literals can be used, a cleaner approach would be to use interfaces, which we will explore in the next section.

Here's a comparison of a Java method versus a TypeScript function (in TypeScript, the `:number` before the opening curly brace for the return type is optional):

Java	TypeScript

`public int squareIt(int a) {`
`    return a * a;`
`}`
	`function squareIt(a: number): number {`
	`    return a * a;`
	`}`

Arrow functions

These are like lambda expressions, which allow us to skip the `function` keyword when declaring a function and to omit the `return` statement. They also allow for creating anonymous functions which can be easily passed around. So, consider the `squareIt` function example in TypeScript, which we can rewrite as follows:

```
var squareItFunc = (a: number) => a * a;
```

Working with classes and interfaces

Those familiar with working in object-oriented world, would feel at home with these of classes and interfaces. TypeScript adds support for both classes and interfaces, the former being also part of ES6 / 2015. If you think of some structured data with behavior, then you would typically represent that as a class. A common use of interface is to enforce that a class conforms to a particular contract. With TypeScript its now possible to use both these features of classes and interfaces in JavaScript applications that make use of TypeScript.

Interface

TypeScript has the concept of an `interface`. An `interface` is an abstract type and does not contain behavior. It can be used to define a structure containing data members, some of which can even be marked as optional. Let's look at an `Author` type defined as an interface:

```
interface Author {
    name: string;
    age?: number;
}
function showInfo(author: Author):string {
    if(author.age) {
        return 'Author ' + author.name + ' with age ' + author.age;
    }
    return 'Author ' + author.name;
}
showInfo({name: 'bob',age: 35}); // Valid
showInfo({name: 'tom'});          // Valid
```

The following syntax is an object literal:

```
{name: 'bob',age: 35}
```

The `showInfo` function will accept an object literal that matches the required interface type. The second call doesn't pass the `age` parameter and the code will still work, due to `age` being marked as optional.

Classes

This is similar to classes defined in languages such as Java. It's just a container and will encapsulate functions and variables. ES5 and earlier doesn't support the concept of classes, but TypeScript has this built in. A class is defined by using the `class` keyword and comprises of:

- Fields
- Constructors
- Properties
- Functions

Here's a class `Project` which has a constructor and a function in addition to the fields:

```
class Project {
    static numberOfTasks: number = 0;
    id: number;
    constructor(id: number) {
        this.id = id;
    }
    add(taskId: number) {
        Project.numberOfTasks++;
    }
}
```

The `numberOfTasks` is a static member that is shared by all instances of this class. The `id` field is of `number` type and has the default access of `public`, and the constructor of the class takes a `number` value which is then set as its `id`. A constructor is optional and can be left out if not required. Another way a constructor can be used is to declare the fields using a shorthand:

```
class Project {
    constructor(private id: number) { }
    show() { console.log(this.id); }
}
```

Here, TypeScript would look at the constructor, and on seeing the `private` (or `public`) keyword, create the `id` field for the class `Project`. This is a shorthand approach rather than explicitly declaring the `id` field as a member. The `this` keyword, based on the context in which it's used, gives us access to the current instance fields or members.

TypeScript supports three access modifiers: `public`, `protected`, and `private`. The default is `public` when nothing is specified. The access rules are similar to those found in Java, where `public` is accessible anywhere, while `private` is restricted to only within the class. Similarly, `protected` is for access restriction to the class and its children classes.

In Java, developers are used to creating getters and setters for the properties of a class. A similar feature, known as accessors, is available, and here's how it's done in TypeScript:

```
class Person {
    private _name: string;
    get name() {
        return this._name;
    }
    set name(n: string) {
        this._name = n;
    }
}
let john = new Person();
john.name = 'John';
```

These accessors can act as filters to restrict or validate the input, before applying it to the property of the class. The `get` keyword is used to denote the getter and `set` for the setter. The `this.` is required to reference the `_name` field, since `_name` won't be available in the context of the function. The naming convention of an underscore prefixed to the variable name is just a popular convention used in the scripting world. It's worth noting that accessors are only available when targeting ES5 and higher.

Inheritance

While JavaScript (ECMAScript 5 and earlier) doesn't support the traditional inheritance feature available in other object-oriented languages, we can use TypeScript, which supports inheritance. This is achieved by using the keyword `extends`, so if we have a child class which needs to extend the base class functionality, we can do this as follows:

```
class Parent {}
class Child extends Parent {}
```

The Child class can invoke the Parent class constructor by simply calling the super() function from the Child class constructor, similar to Java. In TypeScript, an interface can also extend from another interface.

Working with arrays

There are multiple ways to work with an array and this works similar to how an array works in JavaScript. You can also declare an array using generics:

```
let a: number[] = [1,2,3];
let b: Array<number> = [1,2,3];
let c: Array<any> = ['Hello',10];
```

Here we make use of the for of loop to iterate over the elements in the array, and print each element. Next, we loop again, but using the forEach function:

```
var numArray = [1, 2, 3];
for (let item of numArray) {
 console.log(item); //Produces: 1,2,3
}

//Using forEach to get same output as above
numArray.forEach(element => {
 console.log(element);
});
```

Similar to using a stream() and map() in Java, we can use the map function available to produce a new result which processes each element within the array:

```
let priorities = ['low', 'medium', 'high'];
let priorityUpperCase = priorities.map(p => p.toUpperCase());
```

Each string element of the array is converted to upper case and the entire result is returned as a new array. The array also provides other methods such as push, pop, sort, and so on, which makes it a very flexible container to use.

Summary

For developers with a Java background, picking up TypeScript as an additional language would be arguably easier than learning Ruby or Python. The ability to use the latest standards even before they are fully supported, and good tooling support along with type safety, makes it a compelling choice for development. VS Code is a great tool which has built-in features and many extensions, making developers very productive. VS Code is not the only choice as there are other IDEs which also provide good support for using TypeScript, such as Eclipse, NetBeans, Sublime Text, Webstorm, and so on.

Type inference is a very powerful mechanism, through which TypeScript offers static type checking. The need to write large scale client-side applications is not easy using traditional JavaScript, but TypeScript helps bridge this gap by bringing high-level language features to it. We have covered enough TypeScript concepts to put them into practice when working with any client-side framework such as Angular.

In the next chapter, we will explore the world of Angular, which uses TypeScript as the language of choice for building frontend applications.

9
Angular in a Nutshell

Web-based development typically involves creating pages using HTML and CSS. While HTML describes the page structure and content, CSS is responsible for the looks. If you want these pages to be interactive, then you will undoubtedly require JavaScript. Needless to say, once the scripting code grows, effective maintenance becomes an uphill task. Angular is a JavaScript framework that helps in building non-trivial client side applications. The road to learning Angular can be taken with an understanding of HTML and some basic JavaScript. If you know TypeScript fundamentals, which we covered in the previous chapter, you already have a head start! You may not become an expert on Angular with this chapter, but it should help cover enough ground for us to start building Angular applications.

The topics we will cover in this chapter are as follows:

- Understanding Angular:
  - Anatomy of a component
  - Pipes
  - Modules
  - Boostrapping process
- Angular 2 and beyond:
  - Angular CLI
  - Managing packages
  - Bootstrap dependency

- A better Hello World:
    - Modules
    - Components
    - Handling events
- Data binding:
    - One way
    - Two way
- Services
- Routes
- Building a project:
    - Setup and run sample
    - Introduction to PrimeNG

Understanding Angular

As a JavaScript framework, Angular runs in the browser (client side). It is used to build **Single Page Applications** (**SPA**) that offer an app-like experience as opposed to traditional web pages. SPAs are web applications that loads a single page at first, and further UI updates are handled by dynamic DOM/page updates rather than page reloads. Angular is not a library and should not be compared with jQuery or any other utility library. The framework consists of core modules and optional ones that are put together to build an application. Angular comes with great tooling support in the form of Angular CLI, which is a code generation tool that we will explore further in the CLI section.

Angular is a component-based model and thus you can break the sections of a page or user interface into various components. Let's look at the anatomy of a sample page shown here, with its various sections represented as components:

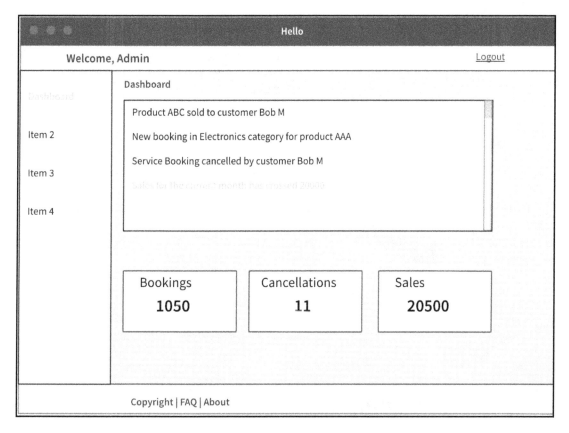

Anatomy of an sample Angular page

We can break this page into sections such as a top header, bottom footer, and the content area, which is the middle section. The middle section can be considered as a two-column layout with the left column as the navigation area and the right as the content area. The content area is dynamic and keeps getting updated by different components based on the link or item selected from the left side navigation. If we are to build this page in Angular, then we would require a root container or root component that represents the entire page, followed by a hierarchy of components that form the component tree.

Here's a table showing the container or layout components for this sample page:

User interface	Components
	AppComponent (Root Component) for the page, having: • **HeaderComponent** • **NavComponent** • **DashboardComponent** • **FooterComponent**

These layout components can themselves contain other components that are part of the page. As an example, the **DashboardComponent** could consist of a feed component which shows the latest updates, followed by a list of items below it displaying some statistics. An item with statistical data could be represented by an `ItemComponent`.

Rendered ItemComponent UI	Description
Bookings **1050**	A child component of `DashboardComponent`. Represented by class `ItemComponent` with a header and a value.

Anatomy of a component

We have been using the word *component* for a while now, so let us look at it in more detail. In Angular, a component is just a class that has an annotation on it, with some additional metadata, along with the required HTML template for the view. This component would be responsible for controlling the part of the view that it represents. The component class interacts with the view with its API consisting of methods and properties. The view in turn will use the component class's properties to display data and its methods for any event based interaction.

Ingredients of a component = HTML template + Styling in CSS or SCSS + Class with logic

Components live and die

Components in Angular have a lifecycle that is managed internally by the framework. One can listen into these phases of the lifecycle by defining methods that get invoked by the framework, the most basic being when a component gets initialized and when it's about to be destroyed or removed. You can implement the `OnInit` and `OnDestroy` interfaces and their corresponding `ngOnInit` and `ngOnDestroy` methods to hook into these lifecycle moments:

```
import { Component, OnInit, OnDestroy } from '@angular/core';

class SomeComponent implements OnInit, OnDestroy {
  constructor() { } // when using, new SomeComponent
  ngOnInit()    { } // when component is considered initialised
  ngOnDestroy() { } // when component is about to be destroyed
}
```

The constructor always runs first before any lifecyle hook. Apart from `ngOnInit` and `ngOnDestory`, there are other lifecycle hooks as well. Here's all the hooks for a component:

- `ngOnChanges()`: Gets called every time any input property of component changes. Additionally, we get a map containing the change from a previous to a new value.
- `ngOnInit()`: Called only once and immediately after the first `ngOnChanges()` runs. Invocations of `ngOnChanges()` later does not trigger this hook again.
- `ngDoCheck()`: Invoked as part of the change detection process, it allows us to write our own change detection logic.
- `ngAfterContentInit()`: Invoked after any external content is projected in the components view.
- `ngAfterContentChecked()`: Invoked after checking the external content that got projected in the components view, even if no change has occurred.
- `ngAfterViewInit()`: Invoked after a component's views (including child views) have been fully initialized.
- `ngAfterViewChecked()`: Invoked after every check of a component's view.
- `ngOnDestroy()`: Invoked just before the component is removed. This allows for writing cleanup code such as resource release.

Interfaces are part of TypeScript but JavaScript doesn't have them, so the transpiled code from TypeScript to JavaScript will not have any interface. Technically, this means that the framework cannot rely upon an interface to invoke lifecycle methods. Thus, Angular simply checks if any lifecycle hook methods are defined on the component and invokes them based on the lifecycle phase. While it's alright to leave out the interface, it's still best to use them so IDEs can catch incorrectly implemented cases early.

Component in code

Here's the `ItemComponent` class and its corresponding template coded in Angular; this is saved in a file named `item.component.ts`, a naming convention from the Angular style guide:

```
import { Component, OnInit } from '@angular/core';

@Component({
  selector: 'app-item',
  template: `
    <div>
        <h2>Bookings</h2>
        <h1>1050</h1>
    </div>
  `
})
export class ItemComponent implements OnInit {
  constructor() { }
  ngOnInit() {  }
}
```

Here, the `import` statement at the top allows the importing of other modules' components/features into this module. The `@Component` annotation marks this class as an Angular component with some metadata:

- `selector`: It is called **app-item** which can be referenced in other component templates using the HTML tag—`<app-item></app-item>`.
- `template`: Within this class back ticks (`` ` ``) are used to define the template. This allows it to span over multiple lines and contains the HTML code used to render this component.

With this way of building, a component can work for smaller templates. The moment the HTML code grows, you are better off using the `templateUrl` property, which can point to an external HTML file, allowing for cleaner separation of view and component code. Similar to templates, you can also define the CSS within the same class using the styles property or reference an external style sheet using the `styleUrls` property. Here's how the `ItemComponent` class code would look with external HTML and CSS references:

```
@Component({
   selector: 'app-item',
   templateUrl: './item.component.html',
   styleUrls: ['./item.component.css']
})
export class ItemComponent implements OnInit { ... }
```

Needless to say, the external reference approach is cleaner, and it is also the default approach when using the CLI for generating a component.

Angular supports data binding, which facilitates interaction between the template and component class. Here's a simple form of data binding syntax that reads a variable `title`, defined on the component class, within the HTML template:

```
<li>{{ title }}</li>
```

The double curly braces syntax is known as **interpolation**, which allows for reading and displaying the `title` variable data. We will see more details on binding in the sections to follow.

Pipes

Angular has a concept called pipes, which can be thought of as filters that can transform the data before displaying. There's a pipe (|) operator that can be used within an interpolation expression as follows:

```
{{ title | uppercase }}
```

Here, the uppercase pipe is a **built-in** pipe. It's also possible to chain multiple pipes to get the desired output and its behavior is similar to the Unix pipe in this regard. We can also create our own pipes by defining a class with the `@Pipe` decorator and implementing the `PipeTransform` interface. Here's a custom pipe that takes a number array and transforms it into a filtered array of positive numbers:

```
import { Pipe, PipeTransform } from '@angular/core';

@Pipe({ name: 'positiveNumbers' })
export class PositivePipe implements PipeTransform {
  transform(value: number[]): number[] {
    return value.filter( v => v > 0);
  }
}
```

A component that uses this pipe in its template would then reference it as shown here, where `numbers` is an array of the numbers declared in the `Component` class:

```
{{ numbers | positiveNumbers }}
```

Modules

Most developers understand that writing large applications leads to complexity. Most of the complexity arises due to the code having been written in one or more large files, without any separation of concern. Modularity is a strategy that groups together related functionality and exposes well-defined interfaces for other code to interact with. Angular applications are built using libraries that are part of Angular itself and third party libraries that are represented as modules. Similar to how we may use external modules in the application, we can also build our own modules. Modularity offers a good way to organise code, especially when structuring large applications.

Every Angular application has one root module, which is conventionally called the `AppModule`. As code grows, it's desirable to create *feature modules* which group together related code. The *Components*, *Pipes*, and so on can all be grouped within a module by creating a class which has the `@NgModule` decorator/annotation on it and describing the module using metadata.

Bootstrapping process

When launching an Angular application, the code within `main.ts` gets executed, which bootstraps the root module (`AppModule`). Here's the excerpt from `main.ts`:

```
import { platformBrowserDynamic }
                        from '@angular/platform-browser-dynamic';
import { AppModule } from './app/app.module';
...
platformBrowserDynamic().bootstrapModule(AppModule)
```

The `AppModule` is a root module with the `@NgModule` decorator that's used for defining a module:

```
@NgModule({
    declarations: [ AppComponent, PositivePipe ],
    exports:      [ AppComponent ],
    imports:      [ BrowserModule, AppRoutingModule ],
    providers:    [ DashboardService ],
    bootstrap:    [ AppComponent]
})
export class AppModule { }
```

Let us discuss the significance of the properties in the earlier code:

- `declarations[]`: This holds components, directives, and pipes belonging to the module. The declaration of a component here allows the referencing of it in the template of another component. For example, `PositivePipe`—if not declared here, then `app.component.html` that belongs to this module cannot use it in its template.
- `exports[]`: A feature module would use this to publish its classes (part of its declarations) for other modules who import it. The root module need not export anything, as it's not imported by any other module.
- `imports[]`: Used for importing other modules whose declarations are required within this module's code.
- `providers[]`: Configure providers for the dependency injection mechanism. This is used to declare services that are part of the global collection of services.
- `bootstrap[]`: Only used by the root module to reference the root component, which holds the entire component tree.

While Angular is a popular choice of web framework, it's also positioned as a platform for building mobile and desktop applications. Check out the resources section for more details.

Reference: https://angular.io/resources.

Angular 2 and beyond

Angular, which is created and maintained by Google, was first released as AngularJS, which later got rewritten and named Angular. Both of these are different frameworks with conceptual differences. For Angular, since version 2, it is possible to build cross-platform applications as well. Here's how the versions differ:

- **1.x versions**: AngularJS (Angular 1.0, 1.1, 1.2, and so on)
- **2 and above**: Angular (Angular 2, 4, 5, and so on)

Version 2 has been written using TypeScript for delivering applications for the web. The Angular team follows a time-based cycle where they have a release every six months. These are not necessarily breaking changes and can be considered maintenance updates. A deprecation policy is used for notifying of API changes, which allows for developers to be prepared for an upcoming release.

Angular CLI

There are probably many good libraries and frameworks out there that have never gained much popularity, owing to the friction in getting started with them. Angular CLI is a tool that makes it incredibly easy to get started and build an Angular application which is ready for production. It is a command line interface for building Angular (version 2 and above) applications, but not for AngularJS. When building a project, the tooling can help with setting up the environment, running tests, the build and deploy cycle, and finally, moving it to production. Even for a developer who knows Angular inside and out, using the tooling can greatly boost productivity. The CLI, apart from helping with the initial setup, is also handy for code generation, which aids in day-to-day development. While the CLI generates code, it's not to be mistaken for an end to end code generation solution.

Using the CLI requires having Node and NPM installed, the installation of which is best covered on the `https://nodejs.org` website. The CLI tooling should be installed globally, so it becomes available throughout the system. This can be done by running the following command:

```
npm install -g @angular/cli
```

The next step would be to create a new project and then try to run it. This can be done by using the `ng new <project name>` command, which sets up the basic structure that is ready to be built upon. The `ng` command is the CLI tool, which we just installed. Without writing a single line of code, you can use the `ng serve --open` command to spin a local development server, which runs the project locally and launches the web browser. Let's see how a project can be created using the CLI tool:

```
ng new hello-angular
cd hello-angular
ng serve --open
```

After the `ng serve` command, the application can be accessed via a URL such as `http://localhost:4200` with support for live reloads. Now, that's a fairly fast way to get started with Angular.

To kill the running server, you can use the keyboard shortcut *Ctrl* + *C*.

These are the basic commands that would typically be used when working with the CLI. The `ng` command can also be passed in a few parameters to control its behavior:

CLI command	Purpose
`ng new`	Creates a new angular project and puts it under version control, such as Git. Yes, you get that too.
`ng test`	Run unit tests after the build.
`ng build --prod`	Compile and build the project. The `--prod` flag will optimize the build for production.
`ng serve`	Builds the project and launches a web server.
`ng serve --host 0.0.0.0 --port 4300`	Builds the project and additionally changes the default host and port used by web server.

Project structure

The generated project directory structure has an `src` folder that contains all the application code along with the environment configuration files. The root directory also contains a `package.json` file, which holds the dependencies of the project. Here's the structure for the `hello-angular` project, showing only the important files for reference:

```
.
├── e2e/                      //folder with end-to-end tests
├── karma.conf.js             //Config file for unit tests
├── node_modules/             //npm folder of dependencies
├── package.json              //package dependencies go here
├── dist/                     //Post build generated static content
├── src                       //source code for application
│   ├── app
│   │   ├── app.component.css      //CSS of component
│   │   ├── app.component.html     //HTML template of component
│   │   ├── app.component.spec.ts
│   │   ├── app.component.ts       //AppComponent a Component
│   │   └── app.module.ts
│   ├── assets                //static content holder
│   ├── environments          //config file for local, prod env
│   │   ├── environment.prod.ts
│   │   └── environment.ts
│   ├── favicon.ico
│   ├── index.html            //first html that user loads
│   ├── main.ts               //Like java main method but in JS
│   ├── polyfills.ts
│   ├── styles.css            //global stylesheet
│   └── typings.d.ts
└── tsconfig.json             //TypeScript config
```

The structure is generated by the CLI in conformance with the best practices outlined in the style guide, which includes a recommended app structure.

Reference: https://angular.io/guide/styleguide.

Rapid development

CLI makes it easy to create an application that already works, right out of the box. When working with an application, we need to create the components that make up the UI along with any supporting classes. There are certain guidelines or suggested rules that should be followed when defining components, modules, and the other pieces that make up the app. These can become cumbersome to remember and even code by hand. CLI not only generates components, but also registers them as part of a module, which if missed can leave you wondering about the issue. Generating code using CLI is mostly done by running the `ng` command and passing it some arguments, as shown here, for some code:

- **Class:** `ng generate class class-name`
- **Components:** `ng generate component component-name`
- **Directives:** `ng generate directive directive-name`
- **Pipes:** `ng generate pipe pipe-name`
- **Services:** `ng generate service service-name`

It's also possible to use shortcuts for commands—`ng g c component-name` has the same effect as generating a component. Similar shortcuts can be used for others, as referenced here:

Reference: `https://github.com/angular/angular-cli`.

The CLI tool uses a configuration file `.angular-cli.json`, which is present in the root directory of the project. You would usually not edit this file, unless you wish to change some defaults.

Managing packages

NPM makes it possible for JavaScript developers to bundle or package reusable code. The users of this package would then be able to check for updates and download it as it's made available. A package is defined by having an directory that contains the needed scripts or code along with a `package.json` file. The `package.json` file contains metadata about the package, which leads to a module-like approach. This can be considered similar to a library which gets distributed and shipped as part of a larger application that depends on it. A `package.json` file allows for:

1. Defining the dependencies required by the project

2. Declaring the version information for the project as well as its dependencies
3. The build becomes reproducible given that the dependencies are documented and thus easy to download (via npm) by other developers

This file gets generated as part of using the CLI to create a project, but we could very well create it from scratch or by using the `npm init` command. The `npm init` command acts as a utility that provides an interactive prompt for creating the `package.json` file.

Most Java developers are familiar with build tools such as Maven that capture the dependencies in a `POM.xml` file. The `package.json` can be considered to serve a similar purpose for JavaScript developers.

Dependencies

These can be specified using `dependencies` or `devDependencies`. Both allow for listing the packages the project depends on.

1. `dependencies`: Runtime packages required in production code
2. `devDependencies`: Required packages during development and testing only

Here's an excerpt from our generated `package.json` showing angular core and forms as dependencies (runtime), while `typescript` and `cli` are under `devDependencies`:

```
"name": "hello-angular",
"version": "1.0.0",
. . .
"dependencies": {
  "@angular/core": "^4.2.4",
  "@angular/forms": "^4.2.4",
  . . .
},
"devDependencies": {
  "@angular/cli": "1.4.9",
  "typescript": "~2.3.3",
  . . .
  }
}
```

node_modules </strong>**is a folder that holds all the packages or modules that are downloaded locally to the project folder as result of running the** `npm install` **command.**

Bootstrap dependency

Bootstrap is a popular choice among web developers for designing websites. One of its core feature is the grid system, which is used for building responsive layouts. Angular applications can add *bootstrap* by specifying it as a dependency for the project. While dependencies can be added manually, by editing the `package.json` file, an easier option is to use the npm command. Since there are two sections, `dependencies` and `devDependencies`, we need to pass a flag to the `npm install` command to specify which section to update.

Adding any dependency to the `dependencies` section:

```
npm install <package_name> --save
```

Adding any dependency to the `devDependencies` section:

```
npm install <package_name> --save-dev
```

For installing bootstrap, we can use the *install* command and specify the version we want to save as a dependency. When you run the `npm install` command, it will inspect the `package.json` file for dependencies and accordingly download the versions specified:

```
# Latest bootstrap version (Such as version 3.x)
npm install bootstrap@3 --save
# Or
# Upcoming bootstrap version (Such as version 4.x)
npm install bootstrap@next --save
```

Once *bootstrap* is installed, we need to configure the Angular project to use this framework.

1. Open the `.angular-cli.json` file that is present in the projects root directory.
2. Find the `styles` array, which holds the external CSS that gets applied to the app.
3. Add the `bootstrap.min.css` file to this array as an entry. The result should look like this:

```
"styles": [
  "../node_modules/bootstrap/dist/css/bootstrap.min.css",
  "styles.css"
],
```

If you don't like the idea of touching the `.angular-cli.json` file, then you can import the bootstrap CSS by referencing it in the `styles.css` file as well, as shown here:

```
@import '~bootstrap/dist/css/bootstrap.min.css';
```

Start or restart the application by using the `ng serve` command. This will get the `hello-angular` project up and running with bootstrap support added.

A better Hello World

With an understanding of Angular basics and the CLI, let us go through an app building experience. We will build a basic project and then see how it gets enhanced as we add more components and some routing to the application. The completed code for this project is available for download under `Chapter 9`, *Angular in a Nutshell*. Here's the set of commands that will set up a `hello-ng-dashboard` project with our components:

```
ng new hello-ng-dashboard --routing
cd hello-ng-dashboard
ng generate component header
ng generate component footer
ng generate component nav
ng g c dashboard
```

Here, the `g c` argument used for dashboard component creation is the same as `generate component` as used for others. For each component, the CLI will create a folder by the name of the component, containing the TypeScript file along with HTML and CSS files. These components will need to be declared as part of a module. This is done for us by the CLI, which updates the `AppModule` (`app.module.ts`) with declarations for these.

The `app.component.html` can then reference our newly created components to form the page:

```html
<header>
    <app-header></app-header>
</header>
<main>
    <nav>
        <app-nav></app-nav>
    </nav>
    <article>
        <app-dashboard></app-dashboard>
    </article>
</main>
<footer>
    <app-footer></app-footer>
</footer>
```

The *header* and *footer* components can serve as plain HTML for display purposes. We can now work on the DashboardComponent class for displaying feed and statistical data for bookings, cancellations, and sales, as we saw in figure of *sample angular page*. To hold the statistics data, we can use a domain class by creating the file statistics.ts under the src/app/domain folder:

```
export class Statistics {
    bookings: number;
    cancellations: number;
    sales: number;
}
```

The DashboardComponent class will then reference an instance of this class and use it to display data. The feed can be string[] holding our feeds. Here's the dashboard.component.ts class file written in TypeScript, shown with the relevant bits that initialise the feed and stats data:

```
...
export class DashboardComponent {
  feeds: string[];
  stats: Statistics;

  constructor() {
    this.feeds = [
      'Product ABC sold to customer Bob M',
      'New booking in Electronics category for product AAA'
    ];
    this.stats = {
      bookings: 100,
      cancellations: 11,
      sales: 5000
    }
  }
  show(feed: string) {...}
}
```

The dashboard.component.html references properties and events using bindings, as follows:

```
...
  <ul>
    <li *ngFor="let feed of feeds; let index = index"
      (click)="show(feed)"
      [class.even]="index % 2 !== 0"
      [class.odd]="index % 2 === 0">
      {{ feed }}
```

```
      </li>
    </ul>
    <div class="row">
      <div class="item">
        <h2>Bookings</h2>
        <h1>{{stats.bookings}}</h1>
      </div>
      ...
    </div>
  ...
```

The template uses the directive `*ngFor`, which will repeat the element to which it is applied. Here, we use it to loop over the *feeds* array and display each using the string interpolation `{{ feed }}`. We can also bind to the DOM `click` event which triggers the `show` function defined on the component class. We have made use of `class` bindings here, which we will check out shortly, along with other forms of bindings.

Modules

Angular style guide suggests the following rules when creating a module:

- Do append the symbol name with the suffix *Module*
- Do give the file name the `.module.ts` extension
- Do name the module after the feature and folder it resides in

The CLI already incorporates these rules when generating a module, thus promoting a consistent convention across the application. So far, we have created our project with just one root module `AppModule` and multiple components. Now, we will create a feature module called `dash-feature` by using the `ng g module dash-feature` command. We can then move the dashboard component folder along with its files (HTML, CSS, TS) under this newly generated module. Additionally, we need to update our `app.module.ts` file by removing all references to `DashboardComponent` from it. The `DashboardFeatureModule` will look as follows:

```
...
import {DashboardComponent} from './dashboard/dashboard.component';

@NgModule({
  imports: [ CommonModule ],
  declarations: [DashboardComponent],
  exports: [ DashboardComponent ]
})
export class DashFeatureModule { }
```

Our folder structure for the dash-feature module should look as follows:

```
src/app/dash-feature
├──── dash-feature.module.ts
├──── dashboard
    ├──── dashboard.component.css
    ├──── dashboard.component.html
    └──── dashboard.component.ts
```

The AppModule will now need to import this feature module in its import[]. Since the feature module exports the DashboardComponent class, it can be referenced in the app.component.html file as <app-dashboard>.

Components

Our hello world project so far has the *App*, *Header*, *Footer*, and *Nav* components, along with a feature module that contains the dashboard component. The items shown within the dashboard for statistical data are another candidate for a component. So, let us do that by creating an item component. From the hello-ng-dashboard folder, run the following commands:

```
$ ng g c dash-feature/item
create src/app/dash-feature/item/item.component.css (0 bytes)
create src/app/dash-feature/item/item.component.html (23 bytes)
create src/app/dash-feature/item/item.component.ts (261 bytes)
update src/app/dash-feature/dash-feature.module.ts (475 bytes)
```

This creates a ItemComponent class and also updates the feature module with its declaration. This child component would take two inputs of header and value, which it displays as shown:

```
import { Component, OnInit, Input } from '@angular/core';
...
export class ItemComponent implements OnInit {
  @Input() header: string;
  @Input() value: string;
...

/* Data is passed to these from dashboard.component.html */
<app-item [header]="'Sales'" [value]="stats.sales"></app-item>
```

We used property bindings here, of [header] and [value], to pass data to the child component. This allows us to use multiple app-item or ItemComponent instances within the dashboard component.

Handling events

In this application, we will need to capture the `click` event when the user clicks on a `feed`. We can use this to intercept the click and perform some processing on the selected feed. The example here is a simplistic one that displays the chosen feed on the dashboard. Here's the event binding in action:

```
<li *ngFor="let feed of feeds" (click)="show(feed)">
  <button (click)="remove(feed)">X</button> <span>{{ feed }}</span>
</li>
```

The `click` event, captured in parenthesis on the `li` element, is used to show the selected feed, while the button **Click** is used to remove the chosen feed. Here's what it's done in the component code:

```
show(feed: string) {
  this.selected = feed;
}
remove(feed: string) {
  this.feeds = this.feeds.filter( f => f !== feed);
}
```

The `filter` method used above is for updating the feeds array with all feeds other than the chosen one, in effect removing the chosen feed. With these features, we now have a fully working dashboard page, which displays and updates information.

Data binding

The simplest form of binding is string interpolation, which uses double curly braces `{{ expression }}`. This template expression is evaluated and then converted to string by Angular. It can take expressions such as `{{ 'Hell' + 'o' }}` which outputs `Hello`, or `{{ 100 === 100 }}` which returns a Boolean of true. It can even contain functions such as `{{ 1 + getAge() }}`.

Here's another case where we use a template expression that references a template input variable `{{ feed }}`:

```
<li *ngFor="let feed of feeds" (click)="show(feed)">{{ feed }}</li>
```

When the user interacts with a view, it's often required to intercept these events and perform some activity. The events such as `click` can be intercepted by surrounding the event name in parentheses and assigning it to a handler of the event, such as `show(...)`. You can have other types of binding, such as property binding, which is used for binding to the property of an element or component. The syntax is of the form `[property]="..."`:

- **Property binding**: Data is sent from component to the view
- **Event binding**: View sends an event to the component

Components can react to the events that are raised in its view. Events can be default events, such as those found in DOM events, and also custom events that a component may publish.

One way

Binding of data can be done from component to view or from view to component. We saw how event binding can take the DOM event from the view to the component using the `(...)` syntax. Similarly, we can also use the square brackets `[...]` property binding to get and set the value from our component to the view. Both cases are still unidirectional, where data flows in one direction. This doesn't imply a one time update, as the change from the component would reflect on the view as and when it keeps occurring. Here's an example, where the `userName` is read from the component and output in view:

```
/* Somewhere in the view template */
<input [value]="userName" [class.red]="1 === 1">
...

/* Below is in a corresponding Component */
class MyComponent {
    userName: string = 'John';
}
```

While event binding has just one form `(event)="..."`, the component to view bindings include:

- **Interpolation**: `{{ expression here }}`
- **Property binding**: `[...]="expression here"`
- **Class binding**: `[class.red]="1 === 1"`
- **Style binding**: `[style.color]="isError ? 'red': 'black'"`

Both the `class` and `style` bindings follow a form of attribute binding that can toggle the class or inline style of a element using the binding. The syntax starts with the prefix of class followed by a period and then the name of the CSS class. The same syntax rules apply for the style binding, but instead of class, it uses the prefix of style.

Two way

To keep bi-directional binding where the data is synced in both directions, we can use two-way binding. This is achieved by combining the property binding [. . .] and event binding (. . .) syntax like this—[(. . .)]. Another way to think of this is, (. . .) allowed us to push events from view -> component, while [. . .] allowed for binding data from component -> view. So, both are combined with the special syntax of [(. . .)]. Here's an example:

```
/* Somewhere in the view template */
<input [(ngModel)]="userName">
...
/* Below is in a corresponding Component */
class MyComponent {
    userName: string = 'John';
}
```

We have used the `ngModel` here, which is Angular-provided feature that enables two-way binding. It can be considered a combination of event and property binding. This is useful for binding to form elements. To use `ngModel` the `FormsModule` will be required, so that needs to be imported into the root module or a feature module.

Services

Another fundamental aspect of Angular is a **service**. These can be thought of as a class that is responsible for some processing or data fetching logic. A component uses a service class to delegate the responsibility of fetching data over HTTP or other processing, which keeps the component code clean. Components can be injected with the services they need using dependency injection. The injection is done using the components constructor which references the service class. Angular obtains the service from an *injector,* which maintains the already created service instances and returns a new one if it doesn't exist. Here's the constructor of `DashboardComponent` class, which can be rewritten to use `DashboardService`:

```
constructor(private service: DashboardService) { }
```

```
//Use lifecyle-hook ngOnInit to perform complex fetch operation
ngOnInit(): void {
    this.stats = this.service.getStats();
}
```

The service needs to be registered in a module or component for it to be available. This is typically done by adding it to the `providers[]` within the `app.module.ts` file or a feature module such as our dash-feature module. It can also be placed in the `@Component` decorators `providers[]`. When declared within `@Component`, a new instance of the service is obtained for each newly created component. But when declared in the root module, such as `app.module.ts`, the service instance is shared. The service itself would simply contain a method for fetching a `Statistics` instance:

```
...
@Injectable()
export class DashboardService {
  private dummy: Statistics;
  constructor() {
    this.dummy = {bookings: 10, cancellations: 2, sales: 500 }
  }
  /* This in real world would be fetched over HTTP service */
  getStats(): Statistics {
    return this.dummy;
  }
}
```

Services are the workers that components heavily use. Given that a service instance can be shared globally, it's also possible to use it to share data between components.

Routes

Routing from one view to another is facilitated in Angular by use of a **router**. The links of a view component can be bound to the router, which will then trigger the configured routes. Route configuration is done by creating and exporting routes. For our sample application, we can create a routing module and then import this module into the root module (AppModule). Here's how a routing module `app-routing.module.ts` for the dashboard sample looks:

```
import { NgModule } from '@angular/core';
import { Routes, RouterModule } from '@angular/router';

const routes: Routes = [];
```

```
@NgModule({
    imports: [RouterModule.forRoot(routes)],
    exports: [RouterModule]
})
export class AppRoutingModule { }
```

In order to start defining routes, we need to populate the routes with mappings. When the route or URL changes, a component mapped to the route can be rendered on the page. We will make use of a `<router-outlet>` HTML tag that acts as the placeholder for displaying dynamic components based on the selected route. Since we don't want the `<app-dashboard>` to be hard coded but instead displayed based on the `/dashboard` route, we need to make two changes:

1. Update the `app.component.html` file, replacing `<app-dashboard>` with `<router-outlet>`.
2. Update the `app-routing.module.ts` file, which contains the routes as shown in the following code:

```
const routes: Routes = [
    { path: '', pathMatch: 'full', redirectTo: '/dashboard' },
    { path: 'dashboard', component: DashboardComponent }
];
```

The empty `path: ''` is used to redirect the user to `/dashboard`, thereby triggering the `DashboardComponent` to load at the `<router-outlet></router-outlet>` placeholder.

The `nav.component.html` file will contain links that map to these routes. When a route such as `/about` or `/dashboard` is selected, then the corresponding component is rendered dynamically at the `<router-outlet>` placeholder. Here's a route in the `nav.component.html` file:

```
<a routerLink="/dashboard"
    routerLinkActive="active-link">Dashboard</a>
```

routerLinkActive

This simply references a CSS class that will be applied dynamically by updating the DOM when the link is active. The router module also provides us with ways to programmatically change routes. These URL routes can even take parameters, which can then be used for any additional checks for displaying or hiding components. Angular routes have a mechanism called **guards** that protect the routes that can be blocked based on certain business logic. We will see how to protect routes in later chapters, when putting together the Angular frontend for our project.

Building a project

When doing local development, we can use the `ng serve` command for quick build and deploy cycles on a local development server. But for creating a development build that needs to be *deployed* somewhere else, we can simply create it using the `ng build` command. Here, the build will output the generated files to a `/dist` folder whose content can be copied to a web server for deployment. While this is the simplest way to create a build, the output is not production optimized. To create a production quality output, we must create the build with few additional parameters. Here's how you can create a better quality build:

```
ng build --prod
```

The `--prod` option is actually a meta flag, which encapsulates a few other flags that get activated when creating the `build`. The overall effect is we get a lean and optimized output that can then be copied to our web server as static content. When creating a `build` with `--prod`, you may also want to include the source maps, which are useful to debug if things fail on production environment. Here's the command to add source maps:

```
ng build --prod --sourcemaps
```

The Angular CLI reference ahead has more details on the available build options at `https://github.com/angular/angular-cli/wiki/build`

Setup and run sample

Here's a Docker file setup that can be placed at the root of the project:

```
FROM nginx
EXPOSE 80

COPY ./dist /usr/share/nginx/html
```

If we run the `ng build` command, it will generate the static content in the `dist` folder, and then we can issue the `docker build` command:

```
docker build -t hello-ng-dashboard
```

This generates a Docker image that we can then execute:

```
docker run --rm -p 80:80 --name hello-ng hello-ng-dashboard:latest
```

Finally, the URL to access the application would be http://localhost, which points to an NGINX web server that is running our application.

Introduction to PrimeNG

PrimeNG serves as a UI library for Angular, similar to what PrimeFaces does for **Java Server Faces (JSF)**. PrimeNG comes with a large collection of UI components - 70+ at the time of this writing - that can meet most UI requirements. All the widgets are open source and free to use, which makes it a compelling choice to boost productivity. Similar to how JSF is complemented by RichFaces, PrimeFaces, and other component libraries, Angular developers can leverage PrimeNG, a third party library for their component needs.

For an existing project, adding PrimeNG can be done using npm, as follows:

```
npm install primeng --save
```

Some of the components offered do have third party dependencies which would also be required for setup. You may want to refer the PrimeNG website for details on the setup and dependencies, as these may change over time.

Reference: https://www.primefaces.org/primeng/#/setup.

PrimeNG components are represented as modules, thus before using it, you need to import the relevant module and then refer the component in code. Here's how we can use a PrimeNG component called **InputText** in the application.

First, we will add `InputTextModule` to the app by importing it in the `app.module.ts` file:

```
import { InputTextModule } from 'primeng/primeng';
@NgModule({
  declarations: [ ... ],
  imports: [
    InputTextModule,
    ...
  ]...
})
export class AppModule { }
```

It's now possible to reference the **InputText** component from components linked to the `AppModule`:

```
<input type="text" pInputText />
```

While PrimeNG is a good option to evaluate, there's also Angular Material, which offers components that conform to Google's Material Design. Angular Material has been built by the Angular team to integrate seamlessly with Angular. While this library doesn't offer a large number of components like PrimeNG docs today, it certainly shouldn't be ignored as it is bound to grow in time. As a developer, these choices allow you to evaluate both libraries and pick the one that meets your needs. It is also possible to use both in the same application, if you really need to.

Reference: `https://material.angular.io/`.

Summary

We have covered some good ground in the Angular world. The fundamental pieces include modules, components with views, services, and routes. The template syntax offers event and property bindings along with two-way bindings, making it easy to create interactive components. Angular's dependency injection makes it easy to tie together the various parts of the application. The component and its template focus on view logic, while the heavy lifting of processing logic is moved to services. The modularity features that use `NgModule` make it possible to organize a large application to separate feature modules along with the root `AppModule`.

Angular CLI offers a powerful tool for project setup and code generation that makes it easy to get started with Angular quickly. When working with modules and their components, it's helpful to use the CLI for generating these components, services, and so on. The CLI not only makes it easy to generate code, but it also helps in having a consistent convention and ensures relevant configurations for the generated code is updated. The Maven, such as `package.json`, makes it possible to declare third party dependencies along with the dependency on Angular core framework and its supporting libraries.

With an understanding of these parts, it's time to take our knowledge to the next level by diving into Angular Forms, and more.

10
Angular Forms

Here we dive further into Angular, and especially how forms are used in single page applications. There comes a time when you must submit your form data to some backend server, and Angular offers two approaches to meet this need. You will be learning the Angular way of dealing with data submission, validation, capturing submitted values, and some powerful features of Angular forms over the course of this chapter. We will cover:

- Two approaches to forms:
  - Template-driven forms
  - Reactive forms
- Understanding forms with an example
- Building custom forms with validations
- Checking the state of a form
- Forms with `NgModel`
- Reactive forms:
  - Setting up forms with `FormBuilder`
  - Adding validations
  - Creating a custom validator
  - Grouping controls
  - Setting and patching values
- Handling forms in Angular
- Gaining more control with Reactive Forms

Two approaches to forms

Angular offers developers the ability to build feature-rich forms. Form capabilities alone can make using Angular a compelling choice. In the HTML world, a form is represented by the <form> tag placed somewhere in the HTML code of a page. Here's a simple form, which uses bootstrap CSS for styling and captures the user input, such as email and phone:

```
<form class="form-inline">
    <div class="form-group">
        <input type="text" class="form-control" id="email"
        name="email" placeholder="Email">
    </div>
    <div class="form-group">
        <input type="text" class="form-control" id="phone"
        name="phone" placeholder="Phone">
    </div>
    <button type="submit" class="btn btn-primary">Save</button>
</form>
```

The form doesn't have the action attribute defined, since it won't directly POST to a server. The two form inputs, email and phone, are submitted by clicking the Save button. We could ignore the form and work with each input directly by binding to the click button and keyboard-based events for the fields, but that would get ugly as our form grows. We now define a User model that our form will bind to:

```
export class User {
    constructor(public email: string, public phone: number) {}
}
```

Let's look at the transition of this form to **template-driven** and later to the **model-driven** approach. But before we begin, we need to import the two modules that enable the form capabilities:

```
...
imports: [ BrowserModule, FormsModule, ReactiveFormsModule ]
...
export class AppModule { }
```

Template-driven forms

To handle form submission, we need to bind to the ngSubmit event, which is placed on the form tag. Here, the onSave method gets triggered upon form submission. Additionally, we export the ngForm directive into a local variable, #userForm, which gives us the aggregate value and validation status of the form. The ngForm directive gets activated on all form tags because of the FormsModule import. Just think of #userForm as your reference to the form data and validation state:

```
<form (ngSubmit)="onSave(userForm)" #userForm="ngForm">...</form>
```

All children from controls (read inputs) can use ngModel along with the name attribute to register themselves with the form. We have used the [(ngModel)] syntax, which allows for two-way data binding. This allows for the changes to be read from and written to our User model:

```
<input type="text" class="form-control" id="email"
       name="email" placeholder="Email" [(ngModel)]="user.email">
<input type="text" class="form-control" id="phone"
       name="phone" placeholder="Phone" [(ngModel)]="user.phone">
```

The model is defined as a user property in the component code. The onSave method takes the details submitted and populates the users array represented by Array<User>:

```
export class BasicFormComponent {
  users: Array<User>;
  user: User;
  constructor() {
    this.users = new Array<User>();
    this.user = new User(null, null); //Initialise the model
  }

  onSave(userForm: NgForm) {
    console.log(userForm.valid);
    let newUser = new User(this.user.email, this.user.phone);
    this.users.push(newUser);
  }
}
```

We are printing the form's validation state by referencing the passed-in form instance. This would return true even if you just clicked the **Submit** button, since we haven't added any validations to the form so far. We will learn about validations in the sections ahead. In terms of the updated array, it's possible to display the `users` in our template as shown in the following code:

```
<li *ngFor="let u of users">
    Email: {{u.email}}, Phone: {{u.phone}}
</li>
```

Reactive forms

While the template-driven approach makes it easy to set up a form and submit data, it isn't the most flexible approach. The `ReactiveFormsModule` has more options, bringing in more flexibility to our form-based applications. Unlike template-driven forms, reactive forms don't use the ngModel directive on form elements, but instead use a programmatic approach. There are three classes that you will come across while using reactive style forms: `FormControl`, `FormGroup`, and `FormArray`, all of which extend from `AbstractControl`.

Form input is represented by a `FormControl` class, while `FormGroup` and `FormArray` act as containers for `FormControl` instances:

- `FormGroup`: Map that holds the control name as the key and the control itself as a value
- `FormArray`: It is an aggregator of the `FormControl` instances that are kept in an array

Before we cover the theory any further, let's see what the code looks like for a reactive form:

```
import { FormGroup, FormControl } from '@angular/forms';
...
export class ReactiveFormComponent {
    public userForm: FormGroup;
    constructor() {
        this.userForm = new FormGroup({
            email: new FormControl(),
            phone: new FormControl()
        });
    }
    onSave() { console.log(this.userForm.value); }
}
```

With that, we have our `userForm`, which is a `FormGroup` with `email` and `phone` values in `FormControl` instances. The template then uses `[formGroup]` property binding on the `<form>` tag to map the component's `userForm` instance. Additionally, each field is mapped with the `formControlName` directive, which takes the name of the key used within the `FormGroup`:

```
<form [formGroup]="userForm" (ngSubmit)="onSave()">
    <input type="text" class="form-control" id="email"
           formControlName="email">
    <input type="text" class="form-control" id="phone"
           formControlName="phone">

    <button type="submit">Save</button>
</form>
```

Unlike our template approach, we don't need to pass the `form` to the `onSave()` function, as the component already holds the `userForm` reference and can save details as needed. We will learn more about reactive forms in the upcoming sections.

Understanding forms with an example

Let us explore the world of angular forms by creating one. We will create a page that lists the tasks in a table and allows for adding new ones. While we can do all of this in a single component, it's best to strive for the separation of concern. Thus, we split the logic between two components, one for listing the tasks and another for adding tasks by means of a form:

Task listing		
Title	Assigned	Created
Learn Angular	Me	12-Nov-17
Build Awesome UI	Bootstrap	12-Nov-17
Share with friends	Me	12-Nov-17
Add some validations	You	12-Nov-17

The task page for the form

We use a template-driven approach here, so we rely on `FormsModule`, which needs to be imported. Here's how we can build our project:

```
ng new forms-demo
cd forms-demo
npm install bootstrap@3 --save
ng serve
```

We added a `bootstrap` dependency to our project. Bootstrap, though not really required, does help with building good form layouts.

Update the `AppModule` import array with a reference to the `FormsModule` added:

```
imports: [ BrowserModule,  FormsModule ]
```

Let's add the two components to our project, one for listing tasks and the other for adding them. We require `TaskListComponent` and `TaskAddComponent`, along with a domain class for holding the `Task` detail:

```
ng g c task-list
ng g c task-add
ng g class task
```

The `task.ts` file contains the `Task` details such as `title`, `created` and the name of the employee to whom the task is assigned. The ? after the variable name is used to indicate it's an optional argument:

```
export class Task {
    constructor(public title: string,
        public created: Date, public assigned?: string) { }
}
```

The `task-list.component.ts` file (`TaskListComponent`) holds an array of tasks that it will render on the UI. Its template also has a child component, `TaskAddComponent`, which it uses for adding new tasks to the listing. The parent `TaskListComponent` listens to the (`created`) event, that is, the event emitted from the child component, when a new task is added:

```
<div class="action-bar">
    <app-task-add (created)="addTask($event)"></app-task-add>
</div>
<table class="table table-hover table-striped">
  <thead>...</thead>
  <tbody>
    <tr *ngFor="let task of tasks">
      <td>{{task.title}}</td>
```

```
        <td>{{task.assigned}}</td>
        <td>{{task.created | date: 'dd-MMM-yy'}}</td>
      </tr>
    </tbody>
  </table>
```

We have used the `date` pipe to format the output of `task.created`. Our `addTask` function on the parent component simply accepts the new task and updates the `tasks` array:

```
addTask(task: Task) { this.tasks.push(task); }
```

Our child component (`TaskAddComponent`) provides a form for adding the task. The form takes two inputs, one for the `title` and another for the assignment. This form has an `Add` button that uses an `EventEmitter` to output the `created` event, which holds the new `Task` instance that the parent is listening for. Here's the `task-add.component.html` contents with only the relevant portions:

```
<form class="form-inline" (ngSubmit)="onSave(taskForm)"
        #taskForm="ngForm">
  ...
    <input type="text" class="form-control" id="title"
        name="title" ngModel>
    <input type="text" class="form-control" id="assigned"
        name="assigned" ngModel>
  ...
    <button type="submit">Add</button>
</form>
```

We used the ngModel syntax of one-way binding (only write), without the [(...)] syntax. The corresponding `task-add.component.ts` contents with the relevant bits is as follows:

```
export class TaskAddComponent {
  @Output() created: EventEmitter<Task> = new EventEmitter<Task>();
  onSave(taskForm : NgForm) {
    let newTask: Task = taskForm.value;
    newTask.created = new Date();
    /* Fire the event which emits the Task instance */
    this.created.emit(newTask);
    /* Reset clears the form */
    taskForm.reset();
  }
}
```

The child component is responsible for the form and emitting new tasks on submission. It doesn't know anything about its parent component. In this example, we have achieved the separation of concerns between the `TaskListComponent` and `TaskAddComponent`. Additionally, we have loosely coupled components, as we use events for parent-child communication.

Building custom forms with validations

No matter how well you present a form with instructions to users, there's always the need to check the correctness of the data submitted. In template-driven forms, the `ngForm` holds the form's value and state, which can be queried for correctness. Each input that is mapped to `ngModel` is part of the form and has its own value and validity status. Angular creates a `FormControl` for this mapped input behind the scenes in the template-driven approach. The form's status and validity is a result of the collective status and validity of its child form controls. Even if one form control is invalid then the entire form is marked as invalid:

```
<form class="form-inline" (ngSubmit)="onSave(userForm)"
                                            #userForm="ngForm">
    <input type="text" class="form-control" id="email"
        name="email"
        required pattern="[^ @]*@[^ @]*"
        [(ngModel)]="user.email" #email="ngModel">

    <input type="text" class="form-control" id="assigned"
        name="phone" required minlength="9" minlength="9"
        [(ngModel)]="user.phone" #phone="ngModel">

    <button type="submit" [disabled]="!userForm.valid">
        Add
    </button>
</form>
```

We have used standard HTML 5 validations, which Angular detects for us when used on the inputs. We have also exported the email and phone ngModel references into #email and #phone local variables. The userForm.valid is checking for the validity of the form, based on which disabled property of the button is set. Angular dynamically updates the CSS classes on the form, and its inputs, which can be used to present visual validation feedback to the user. Here's an example for showing a validation error for invalid email input, when the input has been touched (focused on) or dirty (modified):

```
<div class="form-group" [ngClass]="{
  'has-error': email.invalid && (email.dirty || email.touched),
  'has-success': email.valid && (email.dirty || email.touched)
}">
```

The ngClass directive will dynamically add or remove the CSS class based on the condition passed.

Checking the state of a form

When debugging angular forms, it's useful to get some diagnostics for the form state. Since a form can contain multiple form controls, it would be cumbersome to find the state of a form by going through each of its child form controls. Instead, Angular makes it possible to get the state of the form from the form group itself. The FormGroup instance tracks the aggregate form value and validation status. A valid control is one where it passes all validation checks and thus has its status set as VALID. A control failing one of its validation checks will be invalid with its status set as INVALID:

```
{{someForm.valid}}
//Above can return boolean of true or false

{{someForm.status}}
//Above can return string of "VALID" or "INVALID"
```

The previous snippet shown here will return true or false based on the validity status of the overall form:

```
{{someForm.value | json}}
//Above would return JSON representation of the form
// Example: {"email": "test@test.co","phone": 91000 }
```

Forms with NgModel

Understanding what happens behind the scenes when we use `ngModel` will helps us grasp the concept of template-driven forms. When an `ngModel` directive is placed on an element of the form, such as a text input, Angular creates a form control for us.

NgModel facilitates two-way data binding, which is very useful for reading and writing data to a model that is linked with the form. We saw an example of this in our user form when we took the email and phone inputs. The template-driven form uses an `ngForm` instance, which we can reference to get the form details; let's look at its internals. If you print the passed form, the `ngForm`, you will get the following output:

```
NgForm {_submitted: true, ngSubmit: EventEmitter, form: FormGroup}
```

The `ngSubmit` event is what we were binding to, which is of `EventEmitter` type. There's a `FormGroup` representing the actual form containing a value `Object`, which can be passed to a backend. A `FormGroup` has many properties for holding the form's state and its controls:

```
controls:{email: FormControl, phone: FormControl}
```

The `FormControl` instances are held in the `controls` property of a `FormGroup`, which contains our `email` and `phone` inputs that were bound by `ngModel`. When we use the `ngModel` directive on the form elements, Angular creates a `FormControl` instance from a domain model and binds them. When `ngModel` is used without the `[(...)]` syntax, it implies one-way binding for writing data back, while the `[(ngModel)]` syntax implies two-way data binding. Two-way binding helps with loading an initial value from the domain model and writing it back as needed.

Reactive forms

We briefly touched on reactive forms earlier; now let's take a deeper look at these. For complex cases that demand more control over the form, the reactive style comes in handy.

In the template-driven example, we explored building forms with validations to capture email and phone inputs. This was mostly done by using directives such as `ngForm` and `ngModel` in the template. In the reactive style, we take a programmatic approach when working with forms.

Setting up forms with FormBuilder

In the earlier reactive example seen, we built the `FormGroup` and `FormControl` instances without using a `FormBuilder`. A more convenient option is to make use of the `FormBuilder` which leads to setup code like the following, which is simpler to read:

```
constructor(fb: FormBuilder) {
    this.formGroup = fb.group({
        email: null,
        phone: null
    });
}
```

Arguably, the benefits of a builder aren't evident if you have only one or two controls. A builder adds syntactical convenience, which you do require for readability. There are more options for setup when adding validations and initial values, as we will see in the next section.

Adding validations

In reactive style, when using validators we can use either built-in validators or build our own. The `Validators` class provides a set of validators for form controls. A validator takes one or more form controls and returns a map of errors, if any. If no error map is returned, then the validation has passed. Our form can be updated to validate the fields, like so:

```
constructor(fb: FormBuilder) {
    this.formGroup = fb.group({
        email: [null, [Validators.required, Validators.minLength(3)]],
        phone: [null, Validators.required]
    });
}
```

Both fields will have null values to begin with and are flagged as required. The `phone` field has one more constraint of min length. Even if we mark our input field as required in the template, Angular will add the validation implicitly. Finally, to display the validation messages, we can update our template with conditions based on the `FormControls` state:

```
<form [formGroup]="userForm">
...
    <input type="number" class="form-control" id="phone"
          formControlName="phone" required>
    <span *ngIf="userForm.get('phone').touched &&
                  userForm.get('phone').invalid">
          Invalid Phone
    </span>
...
</form>
```

The `*ngIf` directive is used for checking the `form control` class's `phone` validity. By using the form group's `get` method, the `FormControl` instance is retrieved to check its `touched` and `invalid` states. Additionally, Angular also updates the form control element by dynamically updating the CSS class names on it. So, an `Invalid Phone` input state would result in the following CSS class additions on the input element, which we can then style as needed for feedback:

```
class="form-control ng-pristine ng-invalid ng-touched"
```

Creating a custom validator

When creating a custom validator, we need to create a static method accepting an `AbstractControl` (our `FormControl` instance) and return either null for valid input or an error map for invalid cases. Here's a custom validator that validates if the input phone number begins with `91`:

```
export class Phonenumber {
    static indiaPhone(control: AbstractControl) {
        const phone = control.value as number;
        if(phone === null || !phone.toString().startsWith("91")) {
            return { india : false};
        }
        return null;
    }
}
```

To use this validator in our reactive user form, which captured email and phone inputs, we would update the `formGroup` initialization code as follows:

```
this.formGroup = fb.group({
    email: [null, Validators.email ],
    phone: [null, Phonenumber.indiaPhone ]
});
```

While the `Phonenumber.indiaPhone` validator didn't have any expensive computation to be performed, there could be cases where you need to use a service to fetch remote data for validating the input. Such operations are best handled by async validators. Let's consider that we need to check for unique emails in the system by validating them against a database. To do that, we need to return a `Promise` instance from our static validation method as shown here:

```
export class Email {
    static unique(control: AbstractControl) {
        /* USERS could have been loaded from a service call */
        return new Promise(resolve => {
            if (USERS.indexOf(control.value) !== -1) {
                console.log('err', control.value);
                resolve({ unique: 'false' });
            }
            resolve(null);
        });
    }
}
```

Instead of returning the result, we use the `resolve()` method to publish the outcome. During the check, the status of the control and parent becomes PENDING. We need to assign this async validator as the third argument, which is meant for the async validator array as shown here:

```
this.formGroup = fb.group({
    email: [null, Validators.email, Email.unique ],
    phone: [null, Phonenumber.indiaPhone]
});
```

Grouping controls

We have learned how to build a form group along with form controls for simpler use cases. When your form uses a domain model, which has a nested structure, the same can also be expressed by nesting form groups. Consider we want the user's name, which itself is made up of first and last names. Here, we would nest the name form group under a parent form group:

```
this.userForm = fb.group({
     email: [null, Validators.email, Email.unique],
     phone: [null, Phonenumber.indiaPhone],
     name: fb.group({
       first: '', last: ''
     })
});
```

In the template code, we need to wrap the form control under a `formGroupName` directive:

```
<div class="form-group" formGroupName="name">
  <input ... formControlName="first">
</div>
<div class="form-group" formGroupName="name">
  <input ... formControlName="last">
</div>
```

The grouped controls can have validators and other settings similar to parent form groups.

Setting and patching values

When using `FormControl` in reactive style, we often need to update form values as well. To do this, we can use the `FormGroup` and refer to its controls property which holds the key value pair of form control instances:

```
(property) FormGroup.controls: {
  [key: string]: AbstractControl;
}
```

To update a particular control, we need to pass its name as a key and then call `setValue` to update its value. To update the form model, we can also pass in the object mapped for the form:

```
//Single form control update
(<FormControl>this.userForm.controls['phone'])
      .setValue('91');
```

```
// Update form model
let theUser = new User('a@a.com',919999999);
this.userForm.setValue(theUser);
```

The `setValue` is strict and fails if you have any typos or the data doesn't match the `FormGroup` structure. This is useful to catch any errors when developing the application.

The `patchValue` object allows for updating sections or parts of the form data, without having to set the entire value. Unlike `setValue`, this is not strict and doesn't provide any errors upon failure:

```
this.userForm.patchValue( {
    email: 'a@a.com'
})
```

Handling forms in Angular

Having looked at adding validations to the forms, let us see how we can go about reacting to specific validation errors. Consider the simple case of the registration of a user using their email. The form control for the email can have validations for email format and additionally a validation for checking if the email already exists in the system. The form building can be similar to what we did in the custom validator section earlier.

```
email: [null, Validators.email, Email.unique ]
```

In the template code, we could then check for the failure reason by using the `hasError` method, which is present on both `FormGroup` and `FormControl`. We also used the `touched` condition, so the check is made only if input has been touched by the user:

```
<div *ngIf="userForm.get('email').touched &&
    userForm.get('email').hasError('unique')">
        Email already exists
</div>
```

The `hasError` method returns true, if the `'unique'` check returns a JSON having `{ unique: 'true' }` which is provided by our `Email.unique` validator.

Gaining more control with reactive forms

Form handling can become a complex piece of code in any application. Angular's form model allows us to split the form handling and rendering into independent code. This separation allows for testing the form processing code without rendering the UI. This method of building forms is synchronous, giving you better control over the logic and validation aspects involved in processing a form. You typically come across two kinds of model with this approach—one is the UI form model and the other is the domain model. This separation of the data model from the UI also ensures that it isn't written to directly by the UI, providing for more control to revert changes and preserve the initial state if required.

After having initialized a form, it's also possible to subscribe to it for any changes:

```
this.userForm.valueChanges.subscribe(val => {
        console.log('changes', val);
});
```

We just added an observer to the form, which can then process the data as needed. Now it's possible to save the form updates as the user makes them, without having to click **Submit**.

Summary

Since Angular's `ReactiveFormsModule` makes it possible to build feature-rich forms that can handle complex dynamic and static forms, it's best to use this module for most large forms. In the `ReactiveFormsModule`, we create the model using code, and in the template-driven approach, it gets created for us by use of NgModel and NgForm directives. Whichever approach is chosen, a form model does get created consisting of `FormGroup`, `FormArray`, and `FormControl`.

Angular offers validations that can be processed in a synchronous and asynchronous manner. At first, the Angular forms can seem daunting given the architectural choices to be dealt with. But it's this very set of choices offered that makes working with complex forms possible. In the next chapter, we will begin building a frontend Angular application using the knowledge gained thus far.

11
Building a Real-World Application

Armed with the knowledge of Angular, you will learn what it's like to build an end-to-end application. You will build an **Issue Management System**. We earlier developed the backend services, and now we will expand upon the idea by building a modern single page application frontend. You will develop the UI with some styling and forms, allowing for the capturing of the issues and activity done by users of your awesome system. While building this project, you will work independently from the backend team, and later begin to integrate with the backend services as we progress. We will cover:

- Building an Issue Management System frontend
- Setup:
    - Structuring the project
    - Working independently of the backend
    - Data models
- Securing the application
- Issue list and details:
    - Rendering data with templates
    - Injectable service
- Issue creation and updates:
    - Reactive forms
    - Validation
- Issue comments
- Chatting on an issue
- Production-ready builds

Building an Issue Management System frontend

Before we begin building the Angular frontend app, let's go over the goal of the project once again.

The system will facilitate a user to access the list of issues and view its details. A user should also be able to create and update the issue. It would also be helpful to get updates about various issues in the system. The activities done for an issue can be tracked by means of comments added to it. It would also be nice to be able to chat with other users.

Part of the goal was addressed when we built the backend microservices. The services, when put together, provided the needed business logic and persistence of the domain model. Here's a logical view of a component-based angular app connected to the backend IMS microservices:

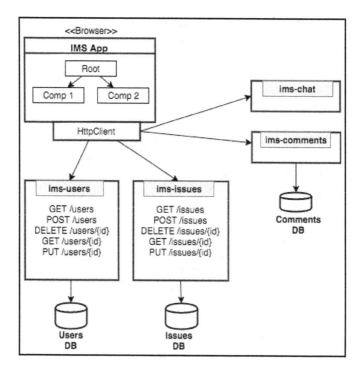

IMS angular app logical view with microservices

It is possible and often desirable to have the app development done independently from the actual microservices. The server-side team could have their own release cycles that may inadvertently impede the app team's progress. While you do need to connect with the backend, it's not a must during development, as we can use mock JSON data to simulate the server's response in some cases. Our aim will be to build the IMS frontend app with all its components and UI logic. The approach is to focus primarily on the user interface, which consists of navigation and components with data. The source of our data will be mock JSON data that the backend services would have sent; this allows us to build the UI independently wherever possible.

The IMS homepage will show notifications related to issues logged in the system and additionally display statistics such as the number of issues for the day. The issues page will be used to display the listing of issues with details, and additionally an option to delete an existing issue. Here's the issue listing page:

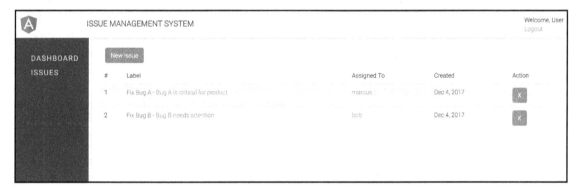

IMS issue listing

Setup

The project can be set up using the CLI and needed packages. For the IMS app, we will create the `ims-ui` project and install bootstrap as a dependency. This can be done by issuing the following commands on the command line:

```
ng new ims-ui --routing

//Then install bootstrap 3 from within the project folder

npm install bootstrap@3 --save
```

Structuring the project

Let's break the application into screens to be developed, where each screen is represented by a URL and a corresponding component which is loaded for the same. The application has two primary views:

- **Dashboard**: Homepage for the user, with a view showing the feed and statistics
- **Issues**: The issues view, which is a listing of the issues in the system

Apart from the primary view, we will also have a chat section on the UI. Within the issues view, we will have components that support the adding, updating, and deleting of issues. These can all be grouped under the issues module, which will be a feature module. The issues edit view will also display the comments regarding an issue. Comments can be developed as a separate component, but for the simplicity of understanding, we will be including this within the issue edit component itself. Let's look at the structure of the project for these features:

```
src/app
├──── app-routing.module.ts
├──── app.component.css
├──── app.component.html
├──── app.component.ts
├──── app.module.ts
├──── domain
│   ... Entities for our domain model
├──── shared
│   ... Shared singleton services
├──── home
│   ... Components related to home page
├──── issues
│   ... Components related to issue add/edit/listing
├──── chat
```

The code is organised into various folders with each catering to a specific concern within the application. For our services, we make these singletons, so they are shared between components. Here's the top-level folders and their purpose:

- domain: As the name suggests, this is our TypeScript classes for entities used in the app, such as Issue, User, Comment, and so on.
- shared: This holds the singleton services such as IssuesService, UsersService, and more, which are shared between components. These services will be passing and returning the domain classes.

- `home`: A logical grouping of components used for a dashboard-based view.
- `issues`: A feature module that is imported in the `AppModule` and declares the listing, editing, and adding of components for issues.
- `chat`: Component which uses WebSocket for enabling chat features in the app.

Looking at the `home` view, we can create two components; one acts as the landing page and another displays the notifications as feed data. Here's the structure for `feed` and `home` components, which are placed under the `home` folder. The home folder has `home.component.ts`, which is the parent for the `feed` component. The home folder is not a module in itself; instead, it is used to group together homepage-related components:

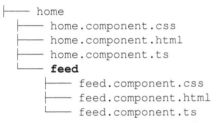

```
├── home
│   ├── home.component.css
│   ├── home.component.html
│   ├── home.component.ts
│   └── feed
│       ├── feed.component.css
│       ├── feed.component.html
│       └── feed.component.ts
```

Given the `Issue` module features, we require a view to list issues and to provide the ability to a user to add new and update existing ones. We use routing to navigate to `IssueAddComponent` for presenting the issue creation form and similarly we use another route to present the `IssueEditComponent` for updating an issue. Here's the issues-related module structure:

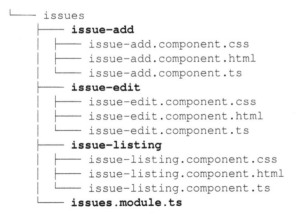

```
└── issues
    ├── issue-add
    │   ├── issue-add.component.css
    │   ├── issue-add.component.html
    │   └── issue-add.component.ts
    ├── issue-edit
    │   ├── issue-edit.component.css
    │   ├── issue-edit.component.html
    │   └── issue-edit.component.ts
    ├── issue-listing
    │   ├── issue-listing.component.css
    │   ├── issue-listing.component.html
    │   └── issue-listing.component.ts
    └── issues.module.ts
```

Unlike the homepage-based components, which were only grouped in a logical folder called `home`, the issue-based components are represented as a feature module. This is done by declaring the components as part of the `issues.module.ts` file and not directly referencing them in `AppModule`. Here's the `IssuesModule` code:

```
@NgModule({
  imports: [
    CommonModule,
    FormsModule,
    ReactiveFormsModule,
    RouterModule
  ],
  declarations: [IssueListingComponent,
                 IssueAddComponent,
                 IssueEditComponent]
})
export class IssuesModule { }
```

The issues module has three components that deal with issue-related features:

- `IssueListingComponent`: Used to display a tabular list of issues, with the option to add or edit an issue by navigating to the other component's URL.
- `IssueAddComponent`: This presents a reactive form for adding new issues. It also displays a dropdown to assign the created issue to a user within the system.
- `IssueEditComponent`: This component will load issue details based on the issue ID passed to it in the URL. It also queries and displays the comments associated with an issue.

We import the `IssuesModule` into our `AppModule`, along with registering the required services:

```
@NgModule({
  declarations: [
    AppComponent,
    HomeComponent,
    FeedComponent,
    ChatComponent
  ],
  imports: [
    BrowserModule,
    AppRoutingModule,
    HttpClientModule,
    FormsModule,
    IssuesModule
  ],
```

```
providers: [ IssuesService, UsersService,
             WebSocketService, AuthService ],
bootstrap: [AppComponent]
})
export class AppModule { }
```

The `providers [...]` declares the three services that are used by various components to interact with the backend.

To work with these views, we need to map the URLs to our components, which is done in the `app-routing.module.ts` file, as shown here:

```
const routes: Routes = [
  { path: '', redirectTo: 'home', pathMatch: 'full' },
  { path: 'home',          component: HomeComponent },
  { path: 'issues',        component: IssueListingComponent },
  { path: 'issues/create', component: IssueAddComponent },
  { path: 'issue/:id',     component: IssueEditComponent }
];
@NgModule({
  imports: [RouterModule.forRoot(routes)],
  exports: [RouterModule]
})
export class AppRoutingModule { }
```

Thus, for loading the homepage, a user would hit the /home URL, which would in turn load the `HomeComponent`. The empty path (' '), used in our routes, facilitates users landing on the root URL / to be taken to /home. We will cover the homepage in more detail in the next chapter, when we subscribe to updates from the backend.

Working independently of the backend

When working on the frontend, it is helpful to have dummy data during development. As we already know the expected JSON structure that our app will be getting, we can create the needed TypeScript classes and consume the JSON without hitting the microservices for now.

 Here's a site which helps with generating TypeScript code from JSON http://json2ts.com/.

Similarly, you could explore other options such as Swagger for code generation.

So, here's what a single `issue` JSON object looks like. We map it to our TypeScript `Issue` class. The JSON shown is an array containing a single `Issue` object, for reference:

```
[{
    "assignedTo":{
        "id":23,
        "name":"marcus"
    },
    "created":"2017-12-04T14:38:47.654Z",
    "description":"Bug A is critical for product",
    "id":7564,
    "label":"Fix Bug A"
}]
```

In this project, we maintain various JSON files under the `src/assets` folder, which will act as the mock data. The same will be returned by the service class, such as `IssuesService`, when queried by a component class. While this isn't really required as part of our project since we do have the backend microservices available, it's good practice to keep mocks handy for testing cases, without having to start up the fleet of services, which can grow over a period of time.

In Angular, we can look up the relative path of this JSON file using `HttpClient`. We will explore more details about the `HttpClient` and its options in the next chapter, but for now, here's the quick basics of it. A service class would first obtain the `HttpClient` via injection:

```
constructor(private http: HttpClient) { }

public get(id: number): Observable<any> {
    return this.http.get('/assets/issue.json');
}
```

The `HttpClient` is available, as we imported the `HttpClientModule` into the `AppModule`. The `get` method on the `HttpClient` is used to request the contents of `issue.json`, holding our dummy issue. The response is an `Observable` we can use to get to the underlying data.

Observable isn't an angular specific feature, but is popularized by libraries such as RxJS, which promote reactive-style programming. While RxJS and Observables have a lot to offer, it's enough to understand a few basics to get started with it.

Think of an observable as a stream of data that one can subscribe to. When new data arrives on this stream, it will be pushed (not pulled) to the subscribers of this observable. Another point to remember here is that data will be pushed only if you subscribe to the observable. So, the call to `get(..)` won't do anything unless some component code subscribes to it. We will look at more details on this when we get into the next chapter for integrating with microservices.

Data models

Here's the applications model in the Angular project, which is based on the backend services that are consumed. The domain classes are placed under the `src/app/domain` folder:

TypeScript classes: Issue and Comment	TypeScript classes: User and Chat
```export class Issue { id: number; label: string; description: string; assignedTo: User; created: Date; comments?:CommentInfo[]; }```	```export class User { id: number; name: string; email?: string; credential?:Credential; }```
```export class CommentInfo { byUserName: string; comment: Comment; } export class Comment { byUser: number; forIssue: number; id: number; text: string; }```	```export class Credential { username:string; password:string; } export class Chat { message: string; sender: string; created: Date; }```

The ? used for some data members is used to signify that these are optional properties.

Securing the application

Security concepts go beyond frameworks and applications in general. There are various strategies employed to secure both the frontend and backend. Solutions can range from **OAuth** to **JSON Web Tokens** (**JWT**) and more. As of now, our backend service doesn't have a security mechanism in place. We will look at security, which is better covered in the chapter aptly titled Securing the application.

There are identity platforms that can be leveraged to build security for our application. One such platform is **Auth0**, which solves identity use cases. The single-page application can follow an OAuth based-flow or use JWT token-based authentication for its authentication and authorization needs.

For our backend project, we will be using JWT for backend/API validation and for the frontend app we will store the issued token and pass it during each HTTP call. In this chapter, we will not be using any login/authentication features as that will only complicate the setup to begin with. Once we have a working model, we will expand and add the security layers for completeness. Nevertheless, in our case we do need a user to simulate the flow, which we can add by having it defined as a dummy data.

We define an `AuthService` in the application, which will return the current user. This, for this chapter's purpose, will be a dummy account that is returned. The sample service is shown here, and will later get replaced by an actual implementation:

```
const DUMMY: User = {
  id: 1,
  name: 'bob'
}

@Injectable()
export class AuthService {
  public get currentUser() {
    return DUMMY;
  }
}
```

Issue lists and details

The listing component, during its initialization, fetches the issue list by using the IssuesService class. It holds an Observable declared as issues$ which is initialized in the component's ngOnInit() life cycle hook. The listing component needs a reference to the router for navigating to different routes. It also makes use of IssuesService and UsersService for retrieving issues and getting additional information about the user to whom the issue is assigned.

Here's our IssueListingComponent code, present in the issue-listing.component.ts file:

```
export class IssueListingComponent implements OnInit {
  issues$: Observable<Array<Issue>>;

  constructor(private router: Router,
    private issuesService: IssuesService,
    private usersService: UsersService) { }

  ngOnInit() {
    this.issues$ = this.issuesService.getAll();
  }

  createIssue() {
    this.router.navigate(['/issues/create']);
  }

  editIssue(issue: Issue) {
    this.router.navigate(['/issue', issue.id]);
  }
  ....
}
```

The createIssue and editIssue methods are invoked from the component's template code to navigate to IssueAddComponent and IssueEditComponent respectively. For editIssue, we also pass the Issue ID in the URL that needs to be edited. The getAll() method is defined on the IssuesService class, which returns an Observable. The issues$ is an Observable containing an array of Issue instances, defined by Array<Issue>. The $ suffix is a naming convention used for variables of type *Observable*, which helps differentiate an observable variable from others.

Rendering data with templates

Here's the template for the `issue-listing.component.html` file:

```html
<div class="top-bar">
    <button class="btn btn-primary"
        (click)="createIssue()">New Issue</button>
</div>
<table class="table table-striped">
    <thead>
        ... omitted code for table headers ...
    </thead>
    <tbody>
        <tr *ngFor="let issue of issues$ | async">
            <td>{{issue.id}}</td>
            <td>
                <a (click)="editIssue(issue)">
                    <b>{{issue.label}}</b> - {{issue.description}}
                </a>
            </td>
            <td>
                <a *ngIf="issue.assignedTo
                        (click)="showUserInfo(issue.assignedTo)">
                    {{issue.assignedTo?.name}}
                </a>
                <small>{{issue.assignedTo?.email}}</small>
            </td>
            <td>{{issue.created | date}}</td>
        </tr>
    </tbody>
</table>
```

The `*ngFor` is used to loop and create dynamic table rows as per the number of issues found. The async pipe is used additionally here; the Angular framework manages the subscription for us. This takes care of subscribing and unsubscribing manually to the observable.

We only display the name of the user to whom the issue is assigned. Upon clicking the name, we make an additional call to fetch further details, such as the email ID of the user. Here's the code for `showUserInfo`, where we are manually subscribing to the observable returned and using the result to set the `email` property on the `User` type:

```
showUserInfo(user: User) {
    this.usersService.get(user.id).subscribe(res => {
        user.email = res.email;
    });
```

```
}
```

Injectable service

Our services are bound to the components via injection. These are added to the
`providers[..]` array of the `AppModule`. Services, as we learned earlier, can also be added
at a component level, but that will not make them singletons. In the IMS application, we
have some services that we can make use of:

- `IssuesService`: Exposes the `getAll`, get, add, update, and delete operations for
  an issue
- `UsersService`: Exposes the `getAll` and get operations for a user
- `WebSocketService`: Enables the chatting features in the IMS app

Here's the `UsersService` defined in the `users.service.ts` file:

```
import { Injectable } from '@angular/core';
import { User } from '../domain/user';
import { HttpClient } from '@angular/common/http';
import { Observable } from 'rxjs/Observable';

@Injectable()
export class UsersService {

  constructor(private http: HttpClient) { }

  public getAll(): Observable<Array<User>> {
    return this.http.get<Array<User>>('/assets/users.json');
  }

  public get(id: number): Observable<User> {
    return this.http.get<User>('/assets/user.json');
  }

}
```

The `User` type is imported from a relative path and the `HttpClient` is imported from the
`@angular/common/http` namespace. The `getAll()` operation makes use of generic types
for type information and returns an array of `User`, wrapped in an Observable. The default
JSON response and its mapping to the defined type is handled for us here. Similarly, the
`get(id)` method returns a single `User`, which is used for getting further details from issue
listing components and the `showUserInfo` method. We have used JSON files as our mock
data here.

Here's the `IssuesService` defined in the `issues.service.ts` file:

```
import { Injectable } from '@angular/core';
import { HttpClient } from '@angular/common/http';
import { Observable } from 'rxjs/Observable';
import { Issue } from '../domain/issue';

@Injectable()
export class IssuesService {

  constructor(private http: HttpClient) { }

  public getAll(): Observable<Array<Issue>> {
    return this.http.get<Array<Issue>>('/assets/issues.json');
  }

  public get(id: number): Observable<any> {
    return this.http.get('/assets/issue.json');
  }
  ... more methods omitted ...
}
```

The `getAll()` method is invoked from the `IssueListingComponent` to get all the issues within the system. Notice that this method is very similar to the `getAll()` defined in `UsersService`. This enables us to load a list of issues and display them in the UI.

Issue creation and updates

We make use of `ReactiveFormsModule` to build the form for adding and updating an issue. The `IssueAddComponent` is loaded when the route changes to the `/issues/create` URL. During the initialization of the component, the list of users is fetched for whom an issue can be assigned. The form presents a label and description that needs to be filled mandatorily, along with the selected user from the dropdown for assigning the issue. For simplicity and understanding, the add and edit forms are kept mostly the same, the only difference being that the `IssueEditComponent` form allows for deleting an existing issue as well:

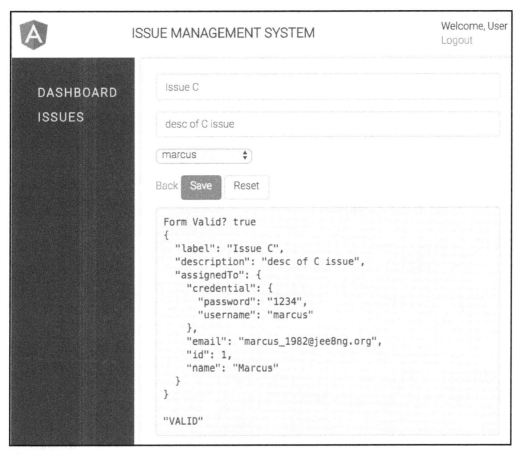

IMS app issue add components reactive form with debug information

Reactive forms

Here's how we construct our reactive form for the issue. The following code snippet is the same for `IssueAddComponent` and `IssueEditComponent`, which is used to build the form group for an issue:

```
//Within the class body
users: User[]; // drop down list of users
public issueForm: FormGroup;

constructor(private router: Router,
    private issuesService: IssuesService,
    private usersService: UsersService,
```

```
      fb: FormBuilder) {

      this.issueForm = fb.group({
        id: null,
        label: [null, // defaultvalue
                [Validators.required, Validators.minLength(2)],
                null], // no async validators
        description: [null, Validators.required],
        assignedTo: [null, Validators.required]
      });
  }

  reset() {
      this.issueForm.reset();
  }
```

Within the IssueAddComponent, we save the form by referencing the value of the form group (issueForm) and pass it to the service method:

```
onSave() {
    this.issuesService.add(this.issueForm.value).subscribe(res => {
      this.reset();
    });
}
```

To add a method on the service, we simply use the HttpClient post method to save the issue data. The response is used to reset the form, so a new issue can be added by the user.

In our IssueEditComponent, we need to consider an existing issue; thus, this component subscribes to the URL param for changes to the issue ID in the URL, and accordingly loads the issue. Here's the route subscription code that retrieves the ID value from the URL param:

```
this.route.params.subscribe((params: Params) => {
    let id = +params['id'];
  ...
  }
```

After getting the issue ID, the next step required is to load the issue details and also the comments against an issue, if any. Here, we have two choices—either we load them sequentially, as in the issue detail first and then the comments, or we load them both in parallel. Since we only need the ID of an issue for making both the calls, a parallel call will be more efficient to use:

```
import { forkJoin } from "rxjs/observable/forkJoin";
...
let issueDetail = this.issuesService.get(id);
let issueComments = this.issuesService.getComments(id);

forkJoin([issueDetail, issueComments]).subscribe(results => {
  this.issue = results[0]; //issue JSON without comments
  this.issue.comments = results[1];// comments JSON
  this.updateForm();
});
```

Our API return values stored in `issueDetail` and `issueComments` are Observables, which we further pass to the `forkJoin` RxJS operator. The `forkJoin` is best used for cases in which we group together Observables and capture the final value for each. Once both the Observables emit their value, the result is emitted by `forkJoin` as a single result containing our list of response values.

Next, within the `updateForm` method, we update our `issueForm` `FormGroup` instance with the loaded issue details by using the form's `patchValue` method:

```
updateForm() {
    this.issueForm.patchValue({
      id: this.issue.id,
      label: this.issue.label,
      description: this.issue.description,
      assignedTo: {
        id: this.issue.assignedTo.id,
        name: this.issue.assignedTo.name
      }
    });
}
```

The patch value accepts the JSON object, which maps to the `FormGroup` elements. This, as we have learnt, can also be used to patch partial values rather than the entire form, if required.

The `onSave()` operation for both `IssueAddComponent` and `IssueEditComponent` uses the value property of the `issueForm FormGroup`. While one calls the `add` method on the service, the other calls the `update` method. Post-updating, we can use the router to navigate to the `/issues` URL, which takes the user to the `IssueListingComponent` view.

On the edit form, a user can also delete an issue; this is done by placing the delete button on the issue edit template, which invokes the `delete` method on the component. Here, after confirming the operation, the issue is removed by making the delete call on the `IssuesService`:

```
deleteIssue() {
    if (confirm("Are you sure you wish to delete?")) {
        this.issuesService.delete(this.issue.id).subscribe(res => {
            this.router.navigate(['/issues']);
        });
    }
}
```

We will check the template and validation aspects next.

Validation

In our issue's reactive form template, we define two input fields for the label and description of the issue and a dropdown for selecting the user. These three inputs are marked as required, and thus we also need to display validation errors if the input has been touched and is invalid:

```
<form [formGroup]="issueForm" (ngSubmit)="onSave()">
...
    <input type="text" class="form-control" id="label"
           formControlName="label">
    <span *ngIf="issueForm.get('label').touched &&
issueForm.get('label').hasError('required')">
        Label is required
    </span>

    <input type="text" class="form-control" id="description"
           formControlName="description">
    <span *ngIf="issueForm.get('description').touched &&
issueForm.get('description').hasError('required')">
        Description is required
    </span>
...
</form>
```

These validations are as defined when we created our `issueForm FromGroup` using the `FormBuilder`. For the `assignedTo` property of an issue, we fetch the users and then show them in the dropdown. Since these are objects, we make use of `[ngValue]` as we want to save our selection as an object of type `User`. The initial option with `[ngValue]="null"` is used for showing a default selection of `Choose Assignee` when no user is chosen:

```
<select formControlName="assignedTo" id="assignedTo">
    <option [ngValue]="null" disabled>Choose Assignee</option>
    <option *ngFor="let assignedTo of users" [ngValue]="assignedTo">
        {{assignedTo.credential.username}}
    </option>
</select>
```

While this works for the add form, it needs to be tweaked further when using it as part of an edit form. In the case of an edit, we need to show the current user who is already assigned the issue. Thus, the dropdown needs to have the assigned user pre-selected. But since the option values are objects, Angular would by default perform object instance comparison, as we require it to perform field level comparison. This can be done by supplying a comparator to the select element that will compare the option values with the user's ID:

```
<select [compareWith]="compareUser" ....

//The method in component file
compareUser(user1, user2): boolean {
    return user1 && user2 ? user1.id === user2.id :
                user1 === user2;
}
```

Issue comments

The comments for an issue can be loaded in parallel, as we saw earlier, to issue details. While this is an option, we can also load it independently. Comments may have been put under their own component class and service class; that's when the logic and code grows, and we can keep it simple for this example. Here's how the comments can be loaded:

```
this.issuesService.getComments(this.issue.id).subscribe(result => {
    this.comments = result;
});
```

Similarly, we can create a simple form to capture the text input of the comment and save it. Given the simplicity of the form, we can use the template-driven form approach here. The `FormsModule` will have to be imported into the `IssuesModule`. Then, the form can be created with HTML 5 validations, as shown here:

```
<form #commentForm="ngForm" (ngSubmit)="onComment(commentForm)" >
    <input type="text" class="form-control" id="comment"
        required [(ngModel)]="comment" name="comment"
        minlength="5" maxlength="30">
    <button type="submit" class="btn btn-default"
            [disabled]="!commentForm.form.valid">Submit</button>
</form>
```

This will ensure a comment for `minlength` of 5 chars and for `maxlength` of 30 chars is allowed, and on submission, it's passed to the service for adding a comment against the issue. Before saving the comment, we initialize a `Comment` object with details of the comment text, for the `issue ID` and then by `user ID`, of the current user of the system:

```
let newComment = new Comment();
newComment.byUser = this.authService.currentUser.id;
newComment.forIssue = this.issue.id;
newComment.text = this.comment;
```

Chatting on an issue

We enable the chatting feature within the IMS project by providing a group chat that is available to all users of the app. A `WebSocket` object can be used to create and manage WebSocket connections to a server. This object provides attributes that can be used to listen for events such as `onopen`, `onclose`, and `onmessage`. We make use of these events to build our chat component. A `WebSocketService` in the project provides a `connect()` method that the chat component calls when it's initialized. Here's the `connect()` method of `WebSocketService`:

```
private socket: WebSocket;
private listener: EventEmitter<any> = new EventEmitter();

public connect() {
        const path = `ws://localhost:8084/ims-chat/chat`;
        this.socket = new WebSocket(path);

        this.socket.onmessage = event => {
            this.listener.emit({ "type": "message",
                                "data": JSON.parse(event.data) });
```

```
            }
    }

    public getEventListener() {
            return this.listener;
    }
```

We connect to the `ws://` URL of the chat endpoint and listen for new messages. The code for the `onmessage` event uses an `EventEmitter` to emit the event containing the message body. The `ChatComponent` class uses this service class's `getEventListener()` method to subscribe to events and push new messages represented by a `Chat` class instance on an array. Here's the complete code for `ChatComponent`:

```
export class ChatComponent implements OnInit {
  messages: Array<Chat>;
  chatBox: any;

  constructor(private socketService: WebsocketService) { }

  ngOnInit() {
    this.messages = [];

    this.socketService.getEventListener().subscribe(event => {
      if (event.type == "message") {
        let chatMessage: Chat = event.data;
        this.messages.push(chatMessage);
      }
    });
    this.socketService.connect();
  }

  public onSubmit(event: Event) {
    let chatMessage: Chat = new Chat();
    chatMessage.sender = this.authService.currentUser.name;
    chatMessage.message = this.chatBox;
    chatMessage.created = new Date();
    if (this.chatBox) {
      this.socketService.send(JSON.stringify(chatMessage));
      this.chatBox = '';
      event.preventDefault();
    }
  }
}
```

The component's `ngOnInit` method is used to initiate the WebSocket connection by invoking the service class's `connect` method. Then, as the `this.listener.emit(...)` is fired from the `WebSocketService` class, the `ChatComponent`, which has subscribed to the listener, receives the message for pushing on the messages array. The `onSubmit` simply creates a new `Chat` objectder, creating message data for sending over the WebSocket. The message is captured from a text input mapped to `chatBox` property using a simple form. We render the messages in our template using `*ngFor` to loop over the array and to display new messages as they are received.

Production-ready build

Angular applications, when built, are treated as JavaScript, which is hosted on a server. Typically, during development, we make use of the `ng serve` command to quickly start up our development server and work with the application. This is a convenient method, but doesn't cater to production needs. This development build running locally of the application can grow big, as can be seen from the page size that gets downloaded to the user's browser. The numbers can be greater than 10 MB or 16 MB, which is not something you want to push to the end users accessing the application.

When we are ready to build and distribute the application, we go through a process of build optimization. Running the `ng build` command will produce our output in the `/dist` folder of the application. This, and other aspects of the build process, can be tweaked using the `angular-cli.json` file. We need to pass the meta flag `--prod` to the `ng` command when creating the build, for performing all the optimizations:

```
ng build --prod
```

The meta flag will enable many other flags that are used during the build. Here's a table showing the difference from a `--dev` versus `--prod` build as published on the Angular CLI Wiki:

Flag	--dev	--prod
--aot	false	true
--environment	dev	prod
--output-hasing	media	all
--sourcemaps	true	false
--extract-css	false	true

--named-chunks	true	false
--build-optimizer	false	true

The `--prod` flag also triggers the running of **UglifyJS** on the code.

For more details, you may wish to visit the CLI Wiki link (`https://github.com/angular/angular-cli/wiki/build`).

You can now transfer the contents of the `dist` folder to your web server of choice. For example, here's the configuration for running the build on Apache:

```
<VirtualHost *:80>
        ServerAdmin webmaster@localhost
        DocumentRoot /var/www/html
        ServerName www.example.com

    <Directory "/var/www/html">
        AllowOverride All
        RewriteEngine on

        # Don't rewrite files or directories
        RewriteCond %{REQUEST_FILENAME} -f [OR]
        RewriteCond %{REQUEST_FILENAME} -d
        RewriteRule ^ - [L]

        # Rewrite everything else to index.html
        RewriteRule ^ index.html [L]
    </Directory>

    ErrorLog ${APACHE_LOG_DIR}/error.log
    CustomLog ${APACHE_LOG_DIR}/access.log combined

</VirtualHost>
```

The `Rewrite` options are used to ensure the page reloads are handled by directing it to the `index.html` page, since we have a single HTML file, `index.html`. Otherwise, you would run into 404 errors. We need to also ensure the dist folder contents are copied to the `/var/www/html` folder for serving the page.

Summary

We have seen the IMS app frontend project and the general features which cover the common cases, which needs to be addressed when building angular applications. The project-introduced feature module has its own set of components. We used reactive and template-driven forms to display and capture user input. We went over the basic use of `HttpClient` to retrieve our mock JSON data, allowing us to work independently of the backend team.

While this is not an exhaustive application, it does lay the foundations for dealing with CRUD applications with their own complexities. The separation of domains for entities and shared services is just the beginning for structuring the project. As the project evolves, more strategies such as core modules, lazy modules, and shared modules can be employed to allow for scaling the application. In the next chapter, we will explore integrating this frontend app with our backend microservices.

12
Connecting Angular to Java EE Microservices

You will now learn to fit both the pieces together—the frontend Angular application with the backend Java EE microservices. Having learnt the intricacies of both worlds, you can now feel confident integrating these solutions. This chapter goes over some of the necessities and real-world practices when working with UI and backend teams, such as:

- Integration with microservices
- Cross Origin Resource Sharing (CORS)
- JSON communication
- Observables in Angular
- Going to production:
    - Deploying on the cloud using AWS
    - Docker release

Integration with microservices

The IMS App, with its various components, can now be put to the test by integrating it with the actual backend services. In theory, a single developer could work on the microservice, as well as the application frontend; in practice it is often not the case. In real-world development scenarios, you may either have teams collocated and working together or they could be spread out geographically. Since the system is delivered as a whole, it's often required to run all the different parts or microservices together. For example, there could be different teams managing each of our backend microservices. A team focused on UI development using Angular may need a stable version of all the IMS microservices. A backend team owning the IMS Comments project may require a certain version of IMS Users to be available during their own development. Docker provides the much needed solutions to these burning needs by making it possible to run either the whole suite of services or parts of it as containers.

The IMS App project team could be given Docker images for each of the IMS backend microservices, which they can boot up in a few seconds without having to worry about the environment and necessary tooling for each. The whole gamut of IMS, shown in the logical view, can be run on a single machine for convenience for the developer:

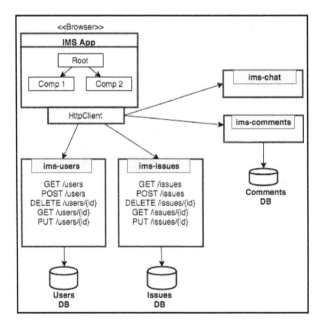

IMS Angular app logical view with microservices

Docker – focusing made easy

While working on local machines it is preferable to have things running locally rather than having remote machine dependencies. In microservice architecture, the number of services will always be one plus, making it desirable, if not a necessity, to automate the running of these processes. Irrespective of developers contributing to a project, you don't want to go about typing mundane commands just to get your services running, especially when this needs to be repeated often. Docker not only makes it easy to bundle and ship our microservices as images, but it also helps with running them locally.

A developer on a team could focus on Angular application aspects, while running multiple microservices as Docker containers. With the images present locally or pulled from the Docker registry, a single command such as `docker-compose` up will have all the needed processes running on the local machine. A Docker image is not limited to the bundling of just application servers; one could very well bundle the Angular application as an image too.

Let's recap our image building steps for the backend. Each of the IMS backend projects is first built as a WAR file, which is then used to create a Docker image. Here's the example commands for the IMS Users microservices, which are run from within the `/ims-users` directory:

```
mvn clean package
docker build -t org.jee8ng/ims-users
```

The `docker build` command will use the Payara Micro base image and add the `ims-users.war` as a layer to it. While it's possible to run the individual projects by using the `docker run ..` command, we will make use of the `docker-compose` command to boot up all the services. The *Users*, *Issues*, *Comments*, and *Chat-based* backend projects are defined in a `docker-compose.yml` file which makes it possible to issue a single command to have all of these up and running locally. From within the `/putting-together-ims` directory, which is the parent for each of the IMS backend projects, issue the following command:

```
docker-compose up
```

This should use the images built earlier and spawn container instances for our IMS microservices. Pressing *Ctrl + C* would shutdown the running containers.

When running the `docker-compose` command, the default path for the configuration file is `./docker-compose.yml` . This file is handy for tweaking the runtime environment for the services, such as limiting the hardware resource usage or having multiple copies of a service running together. These settings are beyond the scope of this book and better explained on `https://docs.docker.com/`.

Verifying the running services

When you do get the backend dependencies up and running, you want to try invoking some of them. The `postman` or `curl` commands can be your friends too; these come in handy when trying to perform the typical CRUD operations:

- `postman`: It offers a graphical interface with many useful features, making it arguably the most widely used REST client.
- `curl`: It is used commonly on Linux, is a command to transfer data to and from a server. It is meant to be run without user interaction and supports a variety of protocols.

Postman is a quick and easy way to build a collection of requests for IMS, which can be done by using this tool. You define a collection in the tool and add multiple requests to it. These can be saved and run with the click of a button. Using an account, you get the benefit of syncing, which allows you to get the data across devices:

Postman in action, shows the IMS request for adding a user

The `curl` command-line utility can be used as a client for URLs, and is available on almost every Linux system out of the box. Those not fond of graphical interfaces will appreciate the versatility this tool has to offer. To fetch all users of the project, a simple GET-based HTTP request can be made by running the `curl` command as follows:

```
curl -v -H 'Accept: application/json'
http://localhost:8081/ims-users/resources/users
```

Similarly, a user can be added via a POST-based request to the IMS Users web resource, like so:

```
curl -v -H 'Content-Type: application/json'
http://localhost:8081/ims-users/resources/users -d
'{
    "name": "sam",
    "email": "sam123@ims.org",
```

```
        "credential":  {"username":"prashant","password":"testing"}
    }'
```

There are multiple flags that can be passed to the command for tweaking its behavior. If you wanted to test the **Service Level Agreement (SLA)** of your REST APIs, you could pass the `--connect-timeout` and `--max-time` flags for specifying the maximum time to wait for a connection to the server and for the whole operation respectively. One could bundle such calls in a shell script for setting up the needed dataset and tests.

Our choices are not limited to only the `curl` and `postman` commands, as there are other capable REST clients as well. The simplicity of RESTful APIs opens up possibilities for easily testing it with a variety of tools. We will explore some of these in the next chapter when we look at the unit testing of IMS microservices.

Cross Origin Resource Sharing (CORS)

In the Angular service code, when you replace the dummy JSON data references with an actual REST endpoint URL, you would run into CORS errors.

No Access-Control-Allow-Origin header is present on the requested resource.

This is a commonly faced error when invoking resources hosted on a different domain than the currently hosted site. This requires your endpoints to say that they will allow calls from certain origins, which is done by passing additional HTTP headers.

CORS is a mechanism that uses additional HTTP headers to let a user agent gain permission to access selected resources from a server on a different origin (domain) than the site currently in use. For reference, visit `https://developer.mozilla.org/en-US/docs/Web/HTTP/CORS`.

Apart from allowing the requests from an origin, browsers will restrict certain HTTP methods as well. These too would be required to be flagged as allowed by the endpoints of IMS.

Given, this would be applicable across REST endpoints as a cross-cutting concern, it can be modified in a `ContainerResponseFilter` implementation as a provider. Here's the filter class which is common for IMS backend projects:

```
@Provider
public class CorsFilter implements ContainerResponseFilter {

    @Override
```

```
public void filter(ContainerRequestContext requestContext,
        ContainerResponseContext responseContext)
        throws IOException {
    MultivaluedMap<String, Object> headers
                            = responseContext.getHeaders();
    headers.add("Access-Control-Allow-Origin", "*");
    headers.add("Access-Control-Allow-Headers",
                        "Origin, Content-Type, Accept");
    //More headers can be configured here
    }

}
```

These headers on a resource enable us to inform the browser of which origins are allowed and what request headers the client can pass to the server. Using the `curl` command, we could examine the response headers for the IMS Users REST endpoint:

```
$ curl -v -H 'Accept: application/json'
http://localhost:8081/ims-users/resources/users

* Trying ::1...
* TCP_NODELAY set
* Connected to localhost (::1) port 8081 (#0)
> GET /ims-users/resources/users HTTP/1.1
> Host: localhost:8081
> User-Agent: curl/7.54.0
> Accept: application/json
>
< HTTP/1.1 200 OK
< Server: Payara Micro #badassfish
< Access-Control-Allow-Origin: *
```

Similar to allowing headers and an origin, we can also control the HTTP methods that are allowed on a resource by using the Access-Control-Allow-Methods HTTP header. This header will take a comma-separated list of HTTP Methods that will be allowed by the endpoint.

JSON communication

From a web browser, you could use an XMLHttpRequest object to make HTTP calls, but this is cumbersome to use and considered low-level API. Angular's HttpClientModule provides an HttpClient class that we can import and use for invoking the REST endpoints. This is a convenient class that provides methods equivalent to HTTP methods found for the web such as GET, POST, PUT, DELETE, and more. The methods provided are not only simpler to work with but also provide strong typing support. To use this class, we first import it into the Service classes:

```
import { HttpClient } from '@angular/common/http';
```

For the import to work we do need the HttpClientModule to be imported into our AppModule, as shown here:

```
@NgModule({
  declarations: [...],
  imports: [
    BrowserModule,
    HttpClientModule,
    ...
  ],
  ...
})
export class AppModule { }
```

Each of the service classes would then declare the HttpClient as a member, which is used to make the HTTP calls to backend microservices. From within our Service class methods, we reference the injected HttpClient instance and invoke its methods.

The this.http.get call doesn't trigger an HTTP call, instead it constructs an Observable for the request which, when subscribed (we do this from the component class), fires the request through the chain of interceptors defined, if any.

Here's a snippet of the code for invoking a GET request and printing the response to the console:

```
this.http.get('http://localhost:8081/ims-users/resources/users/1')
  .subscribe(data => console.log(data));
```

The `subscribe` method call is what triggers the HTTP invocation. The `data` variable holds our response returned by the REST endpoint URL passed, which would be User JSON, as shown in the following code:

```
{
    "credential":{
        "password":"test123",
        "username":"bobby"
    },
    "email":"bob@ims.org",
    "id":1,
    "name":"bob"
}
```

Typing `data.name` would give you an error in the editor as there is no type information associated with the variable. We need to specify the response type to be able to access the members of the `User` class. Here's how we can change the invocation code for that:

```
this.http.get<User>(
'http://localhost:8081/ims-users/resources/users/1')
    .subscribe(data => console.log(data.name));
```

For a `User` or `Issue` list, we would specify the response as an `Array` of the needed type. So our `Issue` list can be fetched by using the following snippet, which is part of the `IssuesService` class:

```
public getAll(): Observable<Array<Issue>> {
    return this.http.get<Array<Issue>>(
        'http://localhost:8082/ims-issues/resources/issues');
}
```

The `getAll` method within the `IssuesService` fetches all the issues from the IMS Issues microservice, and the response has a type parameter `Array<Issue>` for holding the `Issue` list returned by the REST endpoint. Unlike before, we did not subscribe to the method from within the service code, as that's something our `Component` code would do. Angular takes care of mapping the response JSON to `Array<Issue>` for us, without writing any extra lines of code.

Subscribing to any HTTP call can result in either a success response or a failure, which we should handle. For failure, we get back an `HttpErrorResponse` object, which has more details about the response. The code used for subscribing to the `Observable` returned can define the handlers, as shown here:

```
this.issuesService.getAll().subscribe(
    data => {
```

```
      console.log(data);
    },
    (err: HttpErrorResponse) => {
      console.log("Error occurred with STATUS CODE", err.status)
    }
  );
```

Similar to the GET method, we can use the other methods for operations such as POST, PUT, and so on. While in the GET-based call, we did not pass a request body, so we use the POST and PUT methods to pass JSON types such as Comment or Issue for adding and updating. Here's how you would invoke the POST operation for adding a new Issue object:

```
public add(issue: Issue): Observable<any> {
    return this.http.post(
    'http://localhost:8082/ims-issues/resources/issues', issue);
}
```

While the operation would succeed, the HttpClient code returns an HttpErrorResponse; this is because there is no JSON response returned but the client expects one. Thus, we can specify the responseType explicitly as text to resolve this error:

```
return this.http.post(
'http://localhost:8082/ims-issues/resources/issues', issue,
    { responseType: 'text' }
);
```

Here are a few other operations that are performed from the IMS App service code for adding a Comment against an Issue entry and for updating and deleting Issues in the system:

```
public addComment(id: number, comment: Comment) : Observable<any> {
    return this.http.post(
`http://localhost:8083/ims-comments/resources/comments/${id}`,
    comment ,
    { responseType: 'text' }
    );
}

public update(issue: Issue): Observable<any> {
    return this.http.put(
`http://localhost:8082/ims-issues/resources/issues/${issue.id}`,
    issue);
}

public delete(id: number): Observable<any> {
```

```
    return this.http.delete(
`http://localhost:8082/ims-issues/resources/issues/${id}`,
        { responseType: 'text' }
    );
}
```

In practice, we could define the endpoint base URLs as part of our environment configuration and not hard code it within each method. For more details on the `HttpClient` and its methods, you can refer to the Angular doc's website: `https://angular.io/api/common/http/HttpClient`.

Observables in Angular

You may already know that JavaScript is implemented as a single-threaded event loop, making it synchronous. Thus, no two script codes can run in parallel. Angular applications can make use of a `Promise`, which is part of **ECMAScript 6**, or Observables from RxJS, for handling asynchronous data. In the near future, Observables may also be made part of standard JavaScript.

A `Promise` allows you to define handlers for an asynchronous event's eventual completion. We used a `Promise` in `Chapter 10`, *Angular Forms*, too, for performing asynchronous validation. Here's a sample snippet for using a `Promise`:

```
return new Promise( (resolve, reject) => {
        if (/* some condition */) {
                resolve("success");
        }
        reject("failed");
});
```

The function passed to a promise is an executor function that would perform some asynchronous operations and, on completion, call resolve or reject based on success or failure respectively.

Observables are another option for asynchronous data handling in the form of an `Observable` from the RxJS library. An `Observable` argument is used when you can get multiple values emitted over time. Only subscribers to `Observable` are pushed to the data rather than a pull. If there are no subscribers then there won't be any actual execution. We can relate this to an observer pattern, where the subject keeps a list of observers that have subscribed to it and in turn notifies them when its state changes. There are two ways to get data from the `HttpClient` methods within Angular applications:

```
//Approach 1
user: User;
public getUser(id: number) {
    this.http.get( url ).subscribe( result => {
            this.user = result;
    } );
}

//Approach 2
user$: Observable<User>;
public getUser(id: number) {
    this.user$ = this.http.get( url );
}

// Somewhere in template code use async pipe
{{ (user$ | async) }}
```

Let's have a look at the two approaches mentioned in the preceding code:

- **Approach 1:** We manually subscribe to `Observable`, as shown, and get the resulting value. When using this approach, it's also required to manually unsubscribe in order to avoid memory leaks.
- **Approach 2:** Angular's `HttpClient` returns `Observable` which can be stored as a reference within the component without subscribing to it. This would then be used in the template with the `async` pipe. The advantage of using the pipe is that the subscription is managed by Angular for us, so there are no memory leaks. The output of `(user$ | async)` is the emitted value whenever it's available.

We need to import an `Observable` for referencing in the code, using the following code:

```
import { Observable } from 'rxjs/Observable';
```

Observables are a powerful concept and used heavily in the `HttpClient` code of Angular.

Dynamic updates using Observables

Let us look at the feed component, which displays the issue updates on the landing page (home component).

Here's the directory structure for home and feed components within the src/app folder:

```
├── home
│   ├── home.component.css
│   ├── home.component.html
│   ├── home.component.ts
│   └── feed
│       ├── feed.component.css
│       ├── feed.component.html
│       └── feed.component.ts
```

The home.component.html file simply references the feed component in its template:

```
<app-feed></app-feed>
```

The feed.component.html file displays the feed or updates of the newly added Issues in the system. The ngFor directive is used to loop over an Array of Issue objects:

```html
<table class="table">
    <thead>
        <tr>
            <th>#Id</th>
            <th>Label</th>
            <th>Assigned To</th>
            <th>Created</th>
        </tr>
    </thead>
    <tbody>
        <tr *ngFor="let issue of issues">
            <td>{{issue.id}}</td>
            <td>{{issue.label}}</td>
            <td>{{issue.assignedTo.name}}</td>
            <td>{{issue.created | date}}</td>
        </tr>
    </tbody>
</table>
```

The code for `FeedComponent` in the `feed.component.ts` file connects with the **Server-Sent Event (SSE)** endpoint published within the IMS Issues project. The SSE endpoint is an **Event Source** which can be consumed within our component.

MDN docs

The `EventSource` interface is used to receive server-sent events. It connects to a server over HTTP and receives events in text/event-stream format without closing the connection. For reference, visit `https://developer.mozilla.org/en-US/docs/Web/API/EventSource`.

Let's look at the following code:

```
import * as EventSource from 'eventsource';
...
export class FeedComponent implements OnInit {
  issues: Array<Issue>;
  url = 'http://localhost:8082/ims-issues/resources/feed';

  constructor() {
    this.issues = [];
  }

  ngOnInit() {
    this.getFeedData(this.url).subscribe(data => {
      this.issues.unshift(data.instance);
    }, err => console.error('Error occurred: ' + err));
  }

  getFeedData(url): Observable<any> {
    let observable = Observable.create(observer => {
      const eventSource = new EventSource(url);

      eventSource.onmessage = x =>
              observer.next(JSON.parse(x.data));
      eventSource.onerror = x =>
              observer.error(console.log('EventSource failed'));

      return () => {
        eventSource.close();
      };
    });
    return observable;
  }
```

Think of the `getFeedData` method as a source for our events, which we subscribe to in the `ngOnInit` method of the component. As we receive an `Issue` instance, we add it to the beginning of the issues `Array` using the `unshift` method. This code has been kept simple, but it can leverage a shared data approach using a service so the `Array` data is not lost during component initialization.

Within the `getFeedData`, we created `Observable` by using its `create` method. The code within `Observable` will emit new data by using the `observer.next` method call and passing the JSON parsed data. An observer can also return an error which is emitted using the `observer.error` method.

For example, we have looked at how to work with Observables which are returned by `HttpClient` as well as how to create one ourselves. These concepts are commonly found in the Angular world especially in the reactive style of programming. For more detailed coverage on the topic, here is a reference from the reactive docs `http://reactivex.io/documentation/observable.html`.

Going to production

A trending choice for production infrastructure is to make use of cloud-based services such as those offered by Google, Amazon, and others. Once we build our shippable code, we need a place to host and serve the application in a secure and scalable way. These infrastructure needs, which most DevOps engineers have to deal with, are easier to achieve with cloud-based offerings. We get fully automated solutions using which you need not manage the application server or database server. If you desire to have some control and keep things simpler, then you can use **Infrastructure as a Service (IaaS)** solutions.

We already covered how to run Docker containers; let's look at the steps for building an image and hosting it on a cloud environment.

Deploying on the cloud using AWS

AWS provides an on-demand cloud computing solution that many companies and individuals leverage for their needs. With an account, you can create EC2 machines, a service that is offered to developers for making it easy to set up computing machines with minimum upfront cost and effort.

The advantages of moving to the cloud are already documented in various references published online, thus, without duplicating the information, here are some benefits:

- Upfront cost becomes operational cost with pay-as-you-use models
- Capacity planning to scale up or down can be met as per business needs
- More control over the computing environment in AWS

Here's a logical view of our deployment that utilizes two EC2 instances, one for the web server and another for the backend services:

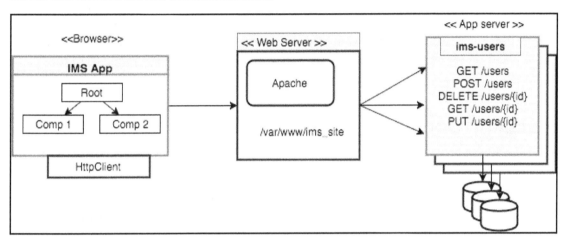

Deployment view of IMS App and backend services

Launching the Amazon EC2 instance

The Amazon console provides a step-by-step wizard to launch new EC2 instances. The typical steps are:

1. Choose an **Amazon Machine Image** (**AMI**), which is like choosing an OS.
2. Select the EC2 instance type, which will define the hardware needs such as memory and processing power.
3. Configure instance details, which allows for specifying the number of instances and network selection.
4. Add Storage, which is a choice regarding disk space needed. More storage can be associated with the instance as desired later.

5. Add tags and define the security group for the instance. A security group is a set of firewall rules that you define for securing access to the instance being launched.
6. Review and launch.

These steps are enough to start your EC2 instance. In an application such as IMS, we want to have two EC2 instances, one for the web server and another for the microservices. You should look at the Amazon docs for the specifics about the setup instructions.

Assuming you have got the instances and the connectivity details, you can connect or SSH into the box from a terminal of your choice. A clean installation would require you to set up the needed application services. We have two choices here—we can either opt for setting up the application server and web server software manually or use Docker images to run containers.

Installing Docker on Amazon EC2

The installation process of Docker is well documented here `https://docs.docker.com/engine/installation/`.

Let's install Docker on a 64-bit machine with Ubuntu 16.04, which is the LTS version. Docker recommends using its repositories for installation, so let's do that by running the commands here, listed after the ($) prompt:

```
$ sudo apt-get update

$ sudo apt-get install \
    apt-transport-https \
    ca-certificates \
    curl \
    software-properties-common
```

With the repository in place, we should now install Docker's official GPG key:

```
$ curl -fsSL https://download.docker.com/linux/ubuntu/gpg | sudo apt-key
add -
```

Next, we install the repository and then Docker CE, which is the Community Edition:

```
$ sudo add-apt-repository \
   "deb [arch=amd64] https://download.docker.com/linux/ubuntu \
   $(lsb_release -cs) \
   stable"

$ sudo apt-get update
$ sudo apt-get install docker-ce
```

That's it, you should now have Docker installed and ready to use.

> If you want to avoid the use of sudo when running docker commands, you need to add your username to the `docker` group, which is created as part of the installation. You do need to log out and log back in for the changes to reflect.

With Docker images, it's easy to pull and run the shipped image that would typically be uploaded to a registry accessible from the server. While we touched on the basics of setup, this is by no means a production-grade installation, which is beyond the scope of this book. Let's look at the steps needed for the creation of a Docker release.

Docker release

The Docker CLI can be used to push an image to a remote registry. The registry itself can be private-company hosted or a cloud-provided one. Docker Hub, from `https://hub.docker.com/`, allows one to pull and push images. We need to create a repository on the website, before pushing any image of our projects. Think of repository, as a collection of images which are versioned using tags.

Create an account on the site and then use that to log in with your Docker ID to push and pull images from Docker Hub. On the site click the "Create repository" option and fill the repository name, such as `ims-comments`. This repository would get created as <your-hub-username>/<repo-name>, you can now pull and push images from and to it. Similar repositories can be created for the rest of the projects.

On your machine which has the local images, open a terminal and log in to Docker Hub by typing `docker login` and entering your credentials when prompted. Here's the command sample, along with a successful output:

```
$ sudo docker login --username prashantpro
Password:
Login Succeeded
```

You need to replace the username with your own for accessing your account.

Before pushing any image, we should tag it by using the `docker tag` command, which has the given syntax `docker tag SOURCE_IMAGE[:TAG] TARGET_IMAGE[:TAG]`.

The `SOURCE_IMAGE` can be the local `IMAGE ID` or `REPOSITORY_NAME[:TAG]`; all these details will show up as part of running the `docker images` command. Here's the tag command which tags our local image to `<your-hub-username>/<repo-name>[:<tag>]`, which is the repository we created on the Docker Hub site.

```
$ docker tag org.jee8ng/ims-comments prashantpro/ims-comments:1.0
```

To see the tagged image, you can run the `docker images` command.

After tagging the image, we can push the same to our repository on Docker Hub by running `docker push`, as shown in the following command:

```
$ docker push prashantpro/ims-comments:1.0
```

Your image is now available for everyone to use. The access to the image can be restricted by using a private repository or having your own Docker registry.

To get the image on a Docker supported machine, such as our new EC2 instance, you would simply pull and run the image. For example, run the following command:

```
$ docker pull prashantpro/ims-comments:1.0
```

This is used for getting our pushed image downloaded to a machine. We can similarly pull all the project images as needed. If the image is pushed to a public repository, anyone could pull it, but for a private repository the user needs to first log in to the account using the `docker login` command as shown earlier.

To run the pulled images, we first create a user-defined network and then use `docker run` command to create our containers using this network, as shown here:

```
$ docker network create backend

$ docker run --rm -d -p 8081:8080 --name ims-users --network backend
prashantpro/ims-users:1.0

$ docker run --rm -d -p 8083:8080 --name ims-comments --network backend
prashantpro/ims-comments:1.0
```

This allows us to pull an image and run it as a Docker container. You may recall that `ims-comments` project required connecting with `ims-users` project's service, to fetch the username for a comment. For this communication to be possible, we make use of our backend user-defined network, to connect containers. Containers part of the same network can communicate using another containers name, thus `ims-comments` can lookup `ims-users` by name.

Summary

We have understood the gist of using Angular's `HttpClientModule` and its `HttpClient` class. It's a simple class that offers various HTTP method equivalents and returns `Observable` that can be used to perform operations on REST endpoints. REST clients, such as the `postman` and `curl` command, are very handy in a developer's kitty to quickly set up test data and verify services when required. We learned that JSON communication is made easy, both by Java EE 8 APIs and Angular's own `HttpClient` which adds strong type support.

Amazon's IaaS offers great choice for developers looking to quickly set up instances and tinker around with their choice of OS and hardware needs. EC2 instances are not only easy to set up by using online wizards, but can also be made robust and scalable when needed.

Docker has made fast-paced progress in the industry and is becoming a compelling choice for modern-day deployment needs. We learned that it can be leveraged by teams and individuals for sharing deployable software code as well as releasing it to a Docker Hub such as a registry.

In the next chapter, we will cover unit testing for our Java EE services in more detail.

13
Testing Java EE Services

Most developers do understand that writing tests is important, but more often than not, they are the most neglected of all. Those venturing into the testing arena can easily get overwhelmed with the jargon and tools that are doing rounds on the internet. It helps if you re-establish the gains that you have set out to achieve before picking up the tools. We will go over the testing strategies and how you can build and run the tests for a microservice-based architecture.

In this chapter, we will cover the following topics:

- Testing strategies for microservices:
    - Understanding the testing pyramid
    - Microservice testing challenges
    - Contract testing
    - Balancing act of tests
- Testing in practice:
    - Integration testing with Arquillian
    - Acceptance testing with Cucumber

Testing strategies for microservices

With the need for agility, development practices exhort the developer to write tests as part of the day-to-day development. Modern day development advocates testing from the start, as it isn't something you ignore till the very end. **Test-driven Development** (**TDD**) and **Behavior-driven Development** (**BDD**) are ways of ensuring that you write code the way your tests expect them to behave. Following these approaches arms us with a battery of tests that shields us from bugs that are hard to find in the tangled web of code.

Now that you have learned most of the basics for building microservices, let's go over it from a testing perspective. Testing typically revolves around two approaches:

- **Manual Testing**: Humans armed with a browser or other forms of tooling, which are typically GUI based, perform the tests. These tests tend to be more about business cases than the internals of a system.
- **Automated Testing**: We have reached the thing that programmers do—automate. Programmers and, sometimes, test engineers write test scripts using frameworks and tooling. This facilitates testing of both internal and external interfaces of a system.

While we will not cover the gamut of the testing universe, we will definitely build enough knowledge of the essentials for testing. Testing could mean unit, integration, performance, penetration, acceptance, and more. Rather than focusing on these terminologies, which can arguably become confusing, let's focus on understanding the basics of automation testing.

Understanding the testing pyramid

Testing a microservice architecture, which can be composed of multiple services, is different from how we test a monolith. But that doesn't mean that the knowledge and tooling used traditionally are no longer applicable. When you get into automated testing, you may come across the term **testing pyramid**.

The term **test automation pyramid** was introduced by Mike Cohn in his book, *Succeeding with Agile*. It is also commonly referred to as just a test pyramid.

This idea can be used to build a common understanding about the three kinds of tests we should write and the cost associated with each. Here's the pyramid with some hints about the number of tests and the cost for the layers shown:

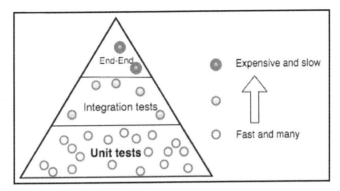

Test pyramid: Unit, integration and end to end

At the bottom of this pyramid or triangle, you will notice that **Unit tests** are given more weightage, followed by **Integration tests**, and finally **End-End** tests. Apart from these three, there are some more layers that get added for microservices. But before we talk about those additions, let's look at each of these three a little closer.

Unit testing

This is the simplest form of tests one would write to verify the finer details within the code. The subject of the test is usually a class or a couple of classes that collaborate with each other. The code can be tested without starting up a Java EE container, making it extremely fast to run. The pyramid's layer for unit tests shows that we should invest in building a larger number of unit tests than others, as these are easier to maintain, and it helps with faster feedback. Some popular frameworks for unit testing include **JUnit** and **TestNG**.

Since most of the Java EE components such as EJBs are just classes with annotations, it is easy to unit test them without a container. However, doing so does not aid in testing the component code in it's true Java EE container environment.

Integration testing

To verify that the modules within a microservice are working as expected, we need to perform coarser grained tests. These help in verifying the components' behavior in the desired manner in the target environment. We can use mocks for external dependencies, such as persistence and other external system calls, allowing the target code to be tested, rather than its external dependencies.

Integration testing is often performed by spawning a container, which is either embedded within the application during tests or referenced remotely. You can think of this as an in-container testing of components, which includes service layer components and REST endpoints of the microservice.

Arquillian is a popular framework that can be used to test code against a target application server.

End-End testing

Once the individual services are tested, it's time to test the whole solution that is delivered to the end users. Here, you are testing outside-in also termed as black-box testing, where end-end behavior is tested. These can also be called **acceptance testing**, as the system is tested against its external interface. In terms of microservice, this means testing scenarios in which multiple microservices could be participating to meet the desired goal.

The external dependencies such as a database could be an in-memory database for testing purposes, which can be disposed at the end of the tests. Another approach is to use dedicated environments to verify the systems put together, such as a staging environment, which replicates production to an acceptable level.

This strategy can benefit from BDD where the business scenarios are written as tests. Cucumber is a widely adopted choice for performing BDD.

In summary, each kind discussed is used to test some facet of code, but you need all three to test every facet of the application code. If you prefer simpler unit tests, then that's great but you do need integrated and end-end tests, as the unit tests aren't suited to verify larger modules and the system as a whole.

Microservice testing challenges

Most of the things we know about testing that exist in the Java EE world are still applicable, but we do need to consider a few new ones for microservices. While unit and integration testing should mostly be the same in the microservices world, the same can't be said for End-End testing. We no longer deploy one monolith; instead, we have multiple applications that can be deployed individually and they all need to work together. Let's assume that we have three microservices, A, B, and C, with some interaction between them. The dependencies between services would mean that testing service A might require service B to be running and if B depends on C, then C needs to be running as well.

Multiple teams could be involved in delivering the end solution, with each team owning either a single or couple of microservices. Putting together a release can be a challenge, as one team's failures could block another dependent team's testing. To reduce such cases, teams not only need to be the owner for development of a service, but also for testing the service independent of others. Another layer that gets added to the pyramid is **contract testing**.

Contract testing

In contract testing, the perspective changes from code within the service to the end consumer of a service. Looking at any microservice, the first thing that a client or user would see is that at the surface lies a web resource or REST endpoint that is published to the outside world. This could be a single REST endpoint or multiple, depending on the size of the microservice. Here, we focus on the service contract that is published as the interface to the outside world. This form of testing verifies that the external boundary of a service meets the consumer's expectations.

A contract test could be provided by the consumer who consumes the service to validate the expected response for given inputs to a service. These tests by each consumer could then be made part of the service maintainers test suite. It can help test both service response structure and time taken for a response.

Microservice delivers an API that serves a business feature, such as find all Issues in the IMS system. This would be consumed by a client such as our Angular frontend. A test is meant to give you feedback when you make changes, it can also act as a documentation of how to use a service.

Balancing act of tests

The test pyramid serves as a good reference and helps with getting the right balance of tests. Writing too many end-end tests may lead to slower build-test-release cycles as these are brittle and slow to run, while writing too few unit tests can leave unexpected bugs lurking in the code. In the rush to complete a feature, a team might not write any tests at all. These issues need to be addressed by putting checks in the deployment pipeline, as well as the development process. A team must decide for itself the goals and rules it plans to comply with, rather than following arbitrary ones that don't fit their needs. You do not want to get caught fighting with slow, meandering, and messy processes that hinder progress.

Building effective tests with good code coverage takes time. You need to be patient and not get disheartened if it doesn't finish quickly. The writing of tests isn't meant to finish, as these will grow along with your application code. As the number of tests grows, so does the confidence to make changes, knowing your tests have got you covered.

A failing acceptance test could indicate missing unit tests, so these can be used to add or improve the unit testing of code. The goal should be to harden the test suite based on failing tests, thereby promoting stability of the code. Continuous testing could be your bridge to take to reach the goal of continuous deployment.

Having discussed the techniques of testing all facets of code, let's look at some of these in action, starting with unit tests.

Testing in practice

With so many moving parts, it becomes necessary to maintain the quality of the application at hand. Tests not only ensure correctness of the currently running code but they also help to ensure that adding new code doesn't break earlier code. Tests should be written not only for the happy path of what you expect to happen, but also for the negative cases. When writing tests, you would set up a case and then verify how the code behaves in an expected manner.

Unit testing would usually be done at a class level or for one or more related classes. This is often the subject for TDD, which influences the implementation of code to be more testable. When testing a single class having other dependencies, it is desirable to isolate it from its dependencies.

A common need is to test part of a code without having to worry about its dependencies. But the code should not be changed directly, instead you hand it its dependencies, which could be fake or dummy objects that simulate an expected behavior. These kinds of objects are called **mock objects**, which help with isolating code under the test. The de facto tool to use for mocking is arguably **Mockito**.

Looking back at our IMS Comments project, we had code in the `CommentsService` EJB bean class to update the username for a given `CommentInfo` instance:

```
public CommentInfo updateName(CommentInfo info) {
        String name = getUserName(info.getComment().getByUser());
        info.setByUserName(name);
        return info;
}
```

The `getUserName` method used within the same class was making an external call to the IMS Users microservice. When testing the `updateName` method, we want to avoid such calls, thus we will use a mock here. To make the code more testable, we will move the `getUserName` method to its own class. This does two things:

- The responsibility of an external call to connect with another service is to push out as separate code, which becomes a dependency that can be swapped in future as needed
- This code separation makes the code more testable as we can mock the dependency during tests

The updated code would look like the one shown in the following code block:

```
@Stateless
public class CommentsService {
    @Inject
    public FindUserName findUserName;
    public CommentInfo updateName(CommentInfo info) {
        String name = findUserName.getUserName(
                            info.getComment().getByUser() );
        info.setByUserName(name);
        return info;
    }
    ...
}
```

The `FindUserName` instance is injected using CDI at runtime. The `CommentsService` class now doesn't care how the user name is fetched as that logic is encapsulated within another class. To write a unit test for this class, we need to add certain dependencies in our IMS Comments, the `pom.xml` file:

```xml
<dependency>
    <groupId>junit</groupId>
    <artifactId>junit</artifactId>
    <version>4.12</version>
    <scope>test</scope>
</dependency>

<dependency>
    <groupId>org.mockito</groupId>
    <artifactId>mockito-all</artifactId>
    <version>1.10.19</version>
    <scope>test</scope>
</dependency>
```

Now, we define our `Test` class within the `src/test/java` folder, under a package such as `org.jee8ng.comments.boundary`, which is similar to the package of `CommentsService`:

```java
//Testing imports required here
import static org.junit.Assert.*;
import static org.mockito.Matchers.*;
import static org.mockito.Mockito.*;
import org.junit.*;

public class CommentsUnitTest {
    CommentsService service;
    @Before
    public void setup() {
        this.service = new CommentsService();
        this.service.findUserName = mock(FindUserName.class);
        when(this.service.findUserName.getUserName(anyLong()))
                .thenReturn("prashant");
    }
    @Test
    public void testCommentInfoUpdatedByName() throws Exception {
        Comment comment = new Comment();
        comment.setByUser(11L);
        CommentInfo updatedInfo = service.updateName(
                            new CommentInfo(comment));
        assertNotNull(updatedInfo);
        assertThat(updatedInfo.getByUserName(),
                        equalTo("prashant"));
    }
```

```
}
```

The setup method annotated with @Before creates a mock for the FindUserName class, which is done using the mock method from Mockito. We then set this mock as the dependency for the service class. Additionally, we make use of the *when... then* construct to make our mock return a dummy name when its getUserName method is called.

The @Test annotation is the unit test that will run and invoke the updateName method, post which we use assertions to validate that the method returns the expected values.

This serves as an example of how testing influences writing more flexible code that is both testable and maintainable.

Integration testing with Arquillian

Arquillian is not a library like JUnit or TestNG, but it integrates with these for running the tests. You can use it for running tests in an IDE or as part of your builds, using tools like Maven. It provides a framework for running tests against an application server using a supported container. Let's write our tests using JUnit and Arquillian put together, considering that we want to test our service code running under a container.

We will need to update IMS Comments pom.xml to add the additional support for Arquillian:

```xml
<dependencyManagement>
    <dependencies>
        <dependency>
            <groupId>org.jboss.arquillian</groupId>
            <artifactId>arquillian-bom</artifactId>
            <version>1.1.15.Final</version>
            <scope>import</scope>
            <type>pom</type>
        </dependency>
    </dependencies>
</dependencyManagement>

<dependencies>

<dependency>
    <groupId>fish.payara.extras</groupId>
    <artifactId>payara-embedded-all</artifactId>
    <version>5.0.0.Alpha3</version>
    <scope>test</scope>
</dependency>
```

```xml
<dependency>
    <groupId>org.jboss.arquillian.junit</groupId>
    <artifactId>arquillian-junit-container</artifactId>
    <scope>test</scope>
</dependency>

<dependency>
    <groupId>fish.payara.arquillian</groupId>
    <artifactId>arquillian-payara-server-4-embedded</artifactId>
    <version>1.0.Beta2</version>
    <scope>test</scope>
</dependency>

... More dependencies of project omitted...
</dependencies>
```

As our service is run in Arquillian with embedded Payara server as a container, we need these dependencies of `payara-embedded-all`, `arquillian-payara-server-4-embedded`, and `arquillian-junit-container`. The versions would be updated by the time you use these, so always check for the latest stable version to use.

We now need to use an Arquillian JUnit runner, which is done by annotating our `Test` class with the `@RunWith` annotation:

```java
@RunWith(Arquillian.class)
public class CommentsIntegrationTest { .. }
```

Arquillian requires specifying the deployment details of the code that we want to test using the `@Deployment` annotation. This is for creating the needed artifact that gets run against our embedded container. This strategy allows us to focus on the classes we want to test:

```java
@Deployment
public static WebArchive createDeployment() {
        return ShrinkWrap.create(WebArchive.class,
                                        "ims-comments.war")
                .addClasses(CommentsService.class,
                        Comment.class,
                        CommentInfo.class,
                        FindUserName.class)
                .addAsWebInfResource(EmptyAsset.INSTANCE,
                                "beans.xml")
                .addAsWebInfResource("web.xml")
                .addAsResource("persistence.xml",
                        "META-INF/persistence.xml");
}
```

This code runs the `ShrinkWrap` library to create the archive, which is created by specifying all our dependencies, including the classes and resources required. The library can also create Java archives apart from web archives. The `arquillian.xml`, `web.xml`, and `persistence.xml` are placed under `src/test/resources`. The `arquillian.xml` file is used to configure `arquillian` and, for our purpose, it just contains the container reference specifying the use of `glassfish-embedded`, which is the same for the Payara server as it's based on Glassfish:

```
<arquillian....>
    <container qualifier="glassfish-embedded" default="true">
    </container>
</arquillian>
```

Given this code is part of in-container testing, we can actually use `@Inject` to get our EJB component and other resources. The invoked code would run within the container, making it more real. The `setupMock()` method is similar to our unit test code, where we mock the dependency of `FindUserName` to return a dummy value:

```
//Code within our test class
@Inject
private CommentsService service;

@Before
public void setupMock() {
    this.service.findUserName = mock(FindUserName.class);
    when(this.service.findUserName.getUserName(anyLong()))
                .thenReturn("prashant");
}

@Test
public void testAddComment() throws Exception {
    Comment comment = new Comment();
    comment.setByUser(11L);
    comment.setForIssue(200L);
    comment.setText("Test");
    comment.setCreated(LocalDateTime.now());

    service.add(comment);
    Optional<Comment> dbComment = service.get(comment.getId());

    assertTrue(dbComment.isPresent());
    assertThat(dbComment.get().getId(), equalTo(comment.getId()));
}

@Test
public void testCommentInfoUpdatedByName() throws Exception {
```

```
Comment comment = new Comment();
comment.setByUser(11L);
CommentInfo updatedInfo = service.updateName(
                          new CommentInfo(comment));

assertNotNull(updatedInfo);
assertThat(updatedInfo.getByUserName(), equalTo("prashant"));
}
```

These two test methods with the `@Test` annotation would be using an EJB instance that is provided by the container. This is different than the Unit test run earlier, which instantiated the `CommentsService` class using `new`, which made it work like any other POJO. The `assertXXX` methods are statically imported from the `org.junit.Assert` package, while `equalTo` is used from the `hamcrest` library. Given that it's an integration test running under a container, these are more expensive to run than our unit tests.

Arquillian serves as a testing platform, which uses supported containers for performing in-container testing. This helps with verifying components in their expected environment, which can't be done during unit tests. For example, you can't test an asynchronous behavior of EJB or verify that a CDI Producer is working as expected without performing container-based testing. You can look up more about Arquillian and its features using the following reference website:

- `http://arquillian.org/features/`
- `http://arquillian.org/guides/shrinkwrap_introduction/`

Acceptance testing with Cucumber

We make use of Cucumber for writing our acceptance tests. These tests are written in a language called **Gherkin**, which is used by Cucumber for describing the features and scenarios for our tests. The choice of Gherkin makes reading and writing tests simpler for both developers and non-developers, for example, testers and business analysts. In BDD, a term often used is **Living Documentation**. As developers, we tend to prefer reading and writing code, thus anything that helps to generate docs based on code is a plus.

Swagger uses annotation to produce documentation based on the REST API code. We saw this in Chapter 7, *Putting It All Together with Payara*, where we bundled the generated documentation (using the Maven Swagger plugin) within the IMS Users project. The additional benefit you gain is that the generated UI can also be used by developers for trying out the API. Here's the Swagger UI for IMS Users, with some of the supported web resource methods:

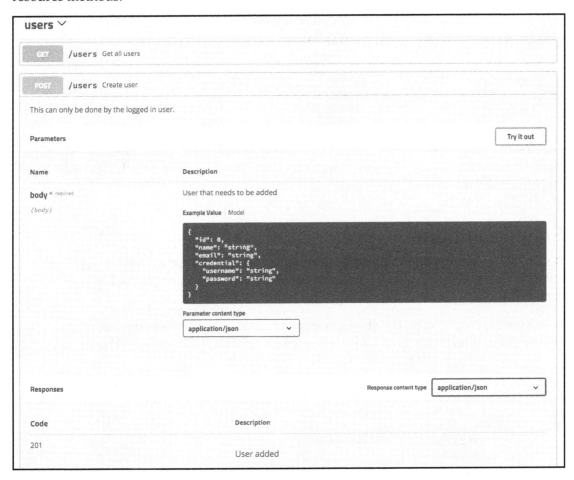

Swagger doc generated from IMS Users with UI showing POST action

Similar to Swagger, we can make use of **Serenity BDD**, which helps in writing acceptance tests that can later be used as documentation. We don't need to use Serenity for our tests and can stick to using just Cucumber.

There are two aspects to maintain with Cucumber: the feature files and the step definitions.

Feature file

Here's a sample feature file written in Gherkin, that is free from any Java code resulting in a friendlier syntax for all. This is written as statements describing a feature containing one or more scenarios that we want to test. This basically contains the *Given..When..Then* construct, which describes a condition and action followed by an expected outcome.

A feature file called `issues.feature`, present under `src/test/resources/feature` directory:

```
Feature: IMS Issues API - Test Env
  Scenario: Issues API Listing
    Given issues api is up and running
    When a request to the Issue listing is made
    Then a list of issues should be returned with 200 status code
```

The first line starts with a keyword, `Feature`, which is a feature description. Our sample feature file has a `Scenario` keyword called `Issues API Listing`, which is verified by executing the *Given..When..Then* steps.

Step definitions

We can set up a new project dedicated to running the tests against a microservice. Our microservices could run as standalone Payara Micro instances or as part of Docker containers.

Here's the Maven POM for our standalone Java project, which defines the `cucumber` dependencies along with some additional ones for working with JAXRS APIs.

```xml
<dependencies>
    <!-- JAXRS support -->
    <dependency>
        <groupId>org.glassfish.jersey.core</groupId>
        <artifactId>jersey-client</artifactId>
        <version>2.25.1</version>
    </dependency>
    <dependency>
        <groupId>org.glassfish.jersey.media</groupId>
        <artifactId>jersey-media-json-processing</artifactId>
        <version>2.25.1</version>
    </dependency>
    <dependency>
        <groupId>org.glassfish</groupId>
        <artifactId>javax.json</artifactId>
        <version>1.1</version>
```

```xml
        </dependency>

        <!-- Cucumber support -->
        <dependency>
            <groupId>info.cukes</groupId>
            <artifactId>cucumber-java</artifactId>
            <version>1.2.5</version>
            <scope>test</scope>
        </dependency>

        <dependency>
            <groupId>info.cukes</groupId>
            <artifactId>cucumber-junit</artifactId>
            <version>1.2.5</version>
            <scope>test</scope>
        </dependency>

        <!-- JUnit -->
        <dependency>
            <groupId>junit</groupId>
            <artifactId>junit</artifactId>
            <version>4.12</version>
            <scope>test</scope>
        </dependency>

        <!-- To ease our REST API testing and validation -->
        <dependency>
            <groupId>io.rest-assured</groupId>
            <artifactId>rest-assured</artifactId>
            <version>3.0.6</version>
            <scope>test</scope>
        </dependency>

        <!-- Easily parse JSON documents -->
        <dependency>
            <groupId>io.rest-assured</groupId>
            <artifactId>json-path</artifactId>
            <version>3.0.6</version>
        </dependency>

    </dependencies>
```

Cucumber also provides a support for Java 8 Lambdas. If you wish to use lambda expressions when writing the step definitions, then you could use `cucumber-java8` dependency instead of `cucumber-java`.

```xml
<dependency>
    <groupId>io.cucumber</groupId>
    <artifactId>cucumber-java8</artifactId>
    <version>1.2.5</version>
    <scope>test</scope>
</dependency>
```

We define a test class containing the steps described for our feature. We need to translate the feature file statements into the Java code that gets executed. The test file uses annotations with similar names to map these statements, as shown in the following code:

```java
//Cucumber imports for Given, When, Then
import cucumber.api.java.en.*;

//Client API for JAXRS
import javax.ws.rs.client.*;
import javax.ws.rs.core.*;

//Assertions
import static org.hamcrest.CoreMatchers.is;
import static org.junit.Assert.assertThat;

public class IssuesSteps {
 private WebTarget targetAPI;
 private Response resp;

 @Given("^issues api is up and running$")
 public void given() throws Throwable {
     Client client = ClientBuilder.newClient();
     this.targetAPI = client.target(
     "http://localhost:8082/ims-issues/resources/issues");
 }

 @When("^a request to the Issue listing is made$")
 public void when() throws Throwable {
     this.resp = this.targetAPI
                     .request(MediaType.APPLICATION_JSON)
                     .get();
 }

 @Then("^a list of issues should be returned with (\\d+) status code$")
 public void then(int status) throws Throwable {
     assertThat(this.resp.getStatus(), is(status));
```

```
    }

}
```

Assuming that we have our IMS Issues microservice running, we can try out the test. Running a Cucumber test can be done similar to JUnit tests from an IDE or as part of build steps. If we run the test from an IDE like Eclipse, here's how the test results may appear:

RunCucumberTest file results, shown when run from within Eclipse IDE.

Here, you may have noticed that we used a regex-like syntax to capture the dynamic parameters described in the feature file:

```
@Then("^a list of issues should be returned with (\\d+) status code$")
```

When `Cucumber` runs, it will parse the `(\\d+)` value, which was defined as 200 in the `issues.feature` file. To be able to run these tests, we do need to add a `Cucumber` test runner by using the `@RunWith` annotation:

```
@RunWith(Cucumber.class)
@CucumberOptions(
        plugin = {"pretty", "html:target/cucumber"},
        features = {"classpath:feature"}
)
public class RunCucumberTest { }
```

A report for the tests gets generated under the `target/cucumber` folder, since we passed the plugin option to `Cucumber`.

Testing a REST API is not that complex; you can make use of tools such as Cucumber that can make your tests readable and more fluid.

Reference: `https://cucumber.io/docs`

Summary

Testing facilitates change. If you are using unit testing, integration testing, and acceptance testing, then you are doing the right thing.

Unit tests run fast and are used to test the smallest unit of code such as a method or class. You could test a unit in a solitary environment by mocking all its other dependencies, which could be in the form of other classes that it may require. We could also test a unit along with its collaborating dependencies making it more real. Some components such as EJBs or Persistence code require a container-like environment to function, thus these are candidates for integration tests.

Microservice testing is challenging and brings with it new ways of testing code. Contract testing changes the perspective to be more consumer driven. It's possible to perform integration and acceptance testing using Arquillian and Cucumber.

In the next chapter, we will build the security layer for IMS frontend and backend.

14
Securing the Application

Building any application without security is a potential risk not only to the consumers of the application but also to the business owners. Web-based applications not only need to store data but also transmit it over the wire. Most of these applications would contain valuable information for a business, thus requiring them to be secured. Whether an application is for internal use or publicly available, securing it cannot be ignored. Even for internal applications within a network, security cannot be taken for granted. With the growing number of security threats, it would only take one of these to seep through the security holes and cause damage.

In the sections to follow, we will walk through the steps required to secure our backend and frontend using token-based security. You will learn to secure your applications and understand the basics of securing an Angular Single Page Application. We will also see how a **JSON Web Token** (**JWT**) can be used as a tool to secure your frontend and backend communication. You will be able to utilize JWT to implement security in REST APIs and exchange these with Angular frontend.

In this chapter, we will cover these topics:

- Securing the application
    - JSON Web Tokens (JWT)
        - Token structure
        - Generating the token
        - Verifying the token
        - Consuming the token in Angular
    - Route Guards
    - Exchanging tokens
        - Injecting an authorization header

- Neither in Java EE nor MicroProfile
- General tips

Securing the application

To secure web-based applications, we would need to first establish the user's identity and then maintain this authenticated state in some kind of session. Here's a simplified view of the steps for establishing authentication with the session-based or cookie-based approach:

1. The client sends a request to a server-side application along with user credentials.
2. The server validates the credentials against a database and creates a session ID, which is persisted on the server and sent as part of the response.
3. A cookie is set in the user's browser having the session ID.
4. The series of requests that follow would contain the same ID that gets validated by the server against its own database of active session IDs. The server then remembers who the user is.

This allows for a stateful conversation between client and server, which is typical of traditional web applications. But with the separation of frontend and backend applications, this approach needs a revisit. Since microservice backend with RESTful APIs are stateless, we will not be maintaining any state on the server, such as a user's session ID. This does not mean that the client needs to keep passing user credentials with each REST API call. The server needs to somehow authenticate and authorize each request in a stateless way. This is where token-based authentication shines for securing APIs. JWT is a popular choice for working with tokens and has gained momentum owing to the rise of Single Page Applications.

JSON Web Tokens

We employ token-based security for the IMS App, which is a technique for authenticating users with a server-provided token. JWT is an open standard, defined in RFC 7519 as follows:

> *"JWT is a compact, URL-safe means of representing claims to be transferred between two parties."*

The token allows us to identify who is the user and also what resources the user is allowed to access. Knowing this information from the token itself helps reduce database lookups. The idea of a token is often used in OAuth 2.0 specification as access and refresh tokens. With a token in each request, the server no longer needs to maintain session ID in its database and deal with session replication across multiple nodes. Not having to replicate sessions also aids in horizontal scaling. The client would obtain the token for a user and then use the same in subsequent calls to the backend APIs, thus it's the client who is responsible for maintaining the logged in state for a user.

Token structure

The token is a string containing three distinct parts separated by a dot. It contains a header, payload data, and JWT signature. The token itself is signed, but not encrypted.

So what does it mean when we say the token is signed, but not encrypted? A few things to consider --sensitive information must be kept in the token, as it can be read; but any change to the values of a token will get rejected by the issuing party (server) as the signature would not match. This facilitates passing data between parties, without allowing for any tampering of the data. Let's look at a token's distinct parts:

- **Header**: This contains metadata for the token along with type of algorithm used for the signature.
- **Payload**: These are claims or any information that you set. It can contain information regarding authorization or scope of access granted.
- **Signature**: This is the signature generated by using the algorithm specified in the header, for both header and payload values.

Here's an encoded form of the token, as a sample:

```
eyJhbGciOiJIUzUxMiJ9.eyJzdWIiOiJwcmFzaGFudC5wcm9AZ21haWwuY29tIiwidXNlcklkIj
oyMywiaXNzIjoiaHR0cDovL2xvY2FsaG9zdDo4MDgwL21pY3JvLXBhcnRpY2lwYW50cy9yZXNvdd
XJjZXMvYXV0aGVudGljYXRlIiwiaWF0IjoxNTE0NDkzMDI4LCJleHAiOjE1MTQ0OTMzMjh9.CiO
ieXZGGAZs4csZoTZu0VgBLsZxfll71LbAmNQ7tALF6Z4gQLx9WYhd0MciKBFeXmHBdet_K1abdY
ohIQd6rQ
```

The format is `header.payload.signature` without the quotes, if we decode (not decrypt) this token, we would find the following information from it:

Token Part	Contents
Header	```{ "typ": "JWT", "alg": "HS512" // Short version for HMAC SHA-512 }```
Payload	```{ "sub": "prashant.pro@gmail.com", "userId": 23, "iss": "http://localhost:8080/micro-participants/resources/authenticate", "iat": 1514493028, // Fri Dec 29 2017 02:00:28 GMT+0530 (IST) "exp": 1514493328 // Fri Dec 29 2017 02:05:28 GMT+0530 (IST) }```
Signature	This contains the digital signature created using a secret key, which is the last part appended to the token.

The header indicates that `HS512` is the algorithm that was used to generate the signature, while the payload contains information about when the token was issued (`iat`) and its expiry time (`exp`) along with other metadata. All of these distinct parts of a token are URL encoded for transmitting over the network. A secret key would be used to calculate and verify the signature; the key itself would not be transmitted over the network and is to be kept secured.

Generating the token

There are many libraries that can be made use of for working with JWT. The following are two such open source libraries to consider:

- **JJWT**: As per the site, this library aims to be the easiest to use and understand for creating and verifying JWTs on the JVM. It is available at `https://github.com/jwtk/jjwt`.
- **Java JWT**: This is a Java implementation of JWT. It is available at `https://github.com/auth0/java-jwt`.

Both of these libraries allow for creating and verifying tokens. In IMS backend, we need to perform two actions—one is to issue a token when a login request is made and another to verify the token in subsequent requests. Both of these functionalities are added to a library project, namely IMS Security.

IMS Security

We set up this Java library project with `artifactId` as `ims-security`, which will be added as a dependency to each of our microservice projects. The IMS Security library itself depends upon the JJWT Maven dependency, as shown here:

```
<dependency>
    <groupId>io.jsonwebtoken</groupId>
    <artifactId>jjwt</artifactId>
    <version>0.9.0</version>
</dependency>
```

IMS Security project would contain a `TokenIssuer` class, which is used to issue JWTs. The issued JWT would have an expiration date time set on it along with the subject name, which is part of the token payload data. The token is also signed with a `"secret"` key before returning to the caller. We have used `HS256`, which stands for **HMAC-SHA256**, a hashing algorithm that uses a secret key to calculate the signature:

```
import io.jsonwebtoken.*;
import java.security.Key;
import java.time.LocalDateTime;
import java.time.ZoneId;
import java.util.Date;

public class TokenIssuer {
    //Expiration time of token would be 60 mins
    public static final long EXPIRY_MINS = 60L;

    public String issueToken(String username) {
        LocalDateTime expiryPeriod = LocalDateTime.now()
                                  .plusMinutes(EXPIRY_MINS);
        Date expirationDateTime = Date.from(
                expiryPeriod.atZone(ZoneId.systemDefault())
                    .toInstant());

        Key key = new SecretKeySpec("secret".getBytes(), "DES");
        String compactJws = Jwts.builder()
                .setSubject(username)
                .signWith(SignatureAlgorithm.HS256, key)
                .setIssuedAt(new Date())
```

```
                     .setExpiration(expirationDateTime)
                  .compact();
          return compactJws;
     }
   }
```

In the code, the `Jwts` builder also provides methods for adding multiple claims to the token. While we could add many claims, it's best to keep in mind that this leads to larger tokens, which could be a concern when transmitting them often.

The IMS Security library would then get imported into a microservice such as IMS Users, which would be responsible for authenticating the user and issuing the JWT in its response. We will publish a URI such as `/users/authenticate` for authenticating the user. Here's the method added to the `UsersResource` class within the IMS Users project:

```
//Class from IMS Security library
@Inject private TokenIssuer issuer;

@Inject
private UsersService service;

@Path("/authenticate")
@POST
public Response authenticate(Credential creds) {
        boolean valid = service.isValid(creds.getUsername(),
                                         creds.getPassword());
        if (valid) {
            String token = issuer.issueToken(creds.getUsername());
            return Response.ok(token).build();
        }
        return Response.status(Response.Status.UNAUTHORIZED)
                .build();
    }
    ...
```

This code simply uses the `username` and `password` to verify the user record and accordingly uses `TokenIssuer` to issue the JWT as part of a success response.

Here's a sample `curl` command for calling and getting the token from this service:

```
curl -v -H 'Content-Type: application/json'
http://localhost:8081/ims-users/resources/users/authenticate -d
'{"username": "random@jee8ng.org", "password":"random@jee8ng.org"}'

eyJhbGciOiJIUzI1NiJ9.eyJzdWIiOiJqYW1lc29uQHNzLmNvbSIsImlhdCI6MTUxNDU1MzExMC
wiZXhwIjoxNTE0NTU2NzEwfQ.1vQVF-T4-I1u6RPz2CR9V0iWZywgehoQrCAPnBOPtGQ
```

With a valid account, we would get back the token, and a 401 response would be returned for an invalid account by the service. Now that we have issued a token to the caller/client, we would also need some way to verify the token when the same client passes the token in its request.

Verifying the token

We need to ensure that each request to our protected resource has a valid token present in the `Authorization` request header. There are other ways of passing the token, but it's fairly standard to use the `Authorization` request header. Since our backend is represented by multiple microservice applications, we don't want to duplicate the verification logic in each of them. A possible choice is to make use of an API Gateway, which acts as a filter or facade for the backend services. The API Gateway would intercept every request and validate the JWT before passing the request further to the target microservice. For the Issue Management System, a simpler strategy would be to use a request filter in the form of JAXRS `ContainerRequestFilter`, which would validate the JWT. But we won't be copying this filter code in each microservice; instead, we code it as part of our IMS Security library.

The IMS Security library with the JWT filter for dealing with a token is shared by the backend services. The filter is registered as a `Provider` and gets activated by merely making it part of the microservice. Since we want to secure our RESTful APIs, we would require a marker annotation that can be placed on resource methods, needing to be secured. Here's the code for the `JWTRequired` annotation under the IMS Security project:

```
@javax.ws.rs.NameBinding
@Retention(RUNTIME)
@Target({TYPE, METHOD})

public @interface JWTRequired {
}
```

Here's the `@JWTRequired` annotation placed on a resource method of the Issues REST API:

```
@GET
@JWTRequired

public Response getAll() { ... }
```

We then have an authentication filter, which gets invoked before the resource method is called, so we can perform the required checks. We use `@Priority(Priorities.AUTHENTICATION)` on the filter to ensure that it gets triggered before any other filters:

```
@Provider
@JWTRequired
@Priority (Priorities.AUTHENTICATION)
public class JWTFilter implements ContainerRequestFilter {

    @Override
    public void filter(ContainerRequestContext requestContext)
        throws IOException {
        String header = requestContext
                .getHeaderString(HttpHeaders.AUTHORIZATION);

        if (header == null || !header.startsWith("Bearer ")) {
            throw new NotAuthorizedException(
                    "Authorization header must be provided");
        }
        // Get token from the HTTP Authorization header
        String token = header.substring("Bearer".length()).trim();

        String user = getUserIfValid(token);
        //set user in context if required
    }
}
```

The filter is primarily responsible for extracting the `Authorization` request header value, which is then passed to the `getUserIfValid` method, where we utilize the JJWT provided classes to verify the token. The JJWT library is part of IMS Security, thus available to IMS Issues as well due to transitive dependency.

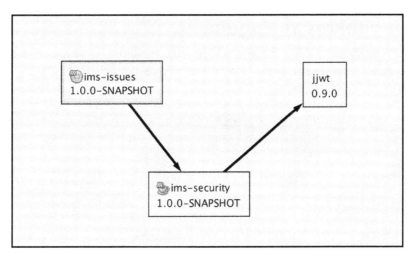

IMS Issues has transitive dependency on JJWT

Here's the library in action within the `getUserIfValid` method present in the `JWTFilter` class:

```
private String getUserIfValid(String token) {
    Key key = new SecretKeySpec("secret".getBytes(), "DES");
    try {
        return Jwts.parser().setSigningKey(key)
                .parseClaimsJws(token)
                .getBody()
                .getSubject();
    } catch (Exception e) {
        //don't trust the JWT!
        throw new NotAuthorizedException("Invalid JWT");
    }
}
```

It's important that the code uses the same `"secret"` key that was used to generate the token. Since we had set the username, in the payload of the generated token, we can now get back the same by reading the payload/claims. Here, that would mean that the `getSubject()` method returns our `username`. On finding the username for a valid token, the method doesn't throw any exception, thus allowing further processing by the actual resource method.

Consuming token in Angular

We need to present the user a login form, which will be used to post the credentials to our authentication API. A successful login would return a response containing the issued token that we can store in the client browser's local storage. Let's assume that we have our login component with the fields of `username` and `password` created. On login submission, we need to send a POST request to the `/users/authenticate` URI:

```
/* src/app/domain/credential.ts */
export class Credential {
 constructor(public username?: string, public password?: string) {}
}

/*
 Code on login submit under, login.component.ts
*/
this.authService.login(
    new Credential(
        this.loginForm.value.username,
        this.loginForm.value.password
    )
);
```

The `login` component code submits the form, then the `authService.login` method gets the token and saves in browsers local storage. The code serves as an example login call, but in the real world, you would have error handling code around this for dealing with failed logins. We also need to check in our application components whether the user is authenticated, that is, logged in. To do so, we would need to check for presence of the token and its validity.

To work with JWT, we can make use of the `angular-jwt` library by installing it in the IMS Application. We need to issue the following command from the project directory to add this library:

```
npm install --save @auth0/angular-jwt
```

Next, we need to import the `JwtModule` library into our `AppModule` class (`app.module.ts` file) and configure it, so it can fetch the saved token when needed:

```
import { JwtModule } from '@auth0/angular-jwt';

export function tokenGetterFn() {
  return localStorage.getItem('token');
};

@NgModule({
```

```
    declarations: [... ],
    imports: [
      JwtModule.forRoot({
        config: {
          tokenGetter: tokenGetterFn
        }
      })
    ...
  })
export class AppModule { }]
```

We then update the `AuthService` code to get the `JwtHelperService` library and provide an `authenticated()` method, which tells us if the user has a valid token that hasn't expired. This class also has code for the login and logout behavior. Here's the complete class for `AuthService`:

```
...
import { JwtHelperService } from '@auth0/angular-jwt';

@Injectable()
export class AuthService {
  private BASE_URL = 'http://localhost:8081/ims-users/resources';
  private user: User;

  constructor(private jwtHelper: JwtHelperService,
              private http: HttpClient, private router: Router) { }

  public get authenticated(): boolean {
    const token = this.jwtHelper.tokenGetter();
    if(token) {
        // Check if saved token has not expired
        return !this.jwtHelper.isTokenExpired(token);
    }
    return false;
  }

  public login(userCreds: Credential) {
      let url: string = `${this.BASE_URL}/users/authenticate`;
      return this.http.post(url, userCreds,
              { responseType: 'text' }
      ).subscribe(tokenResult => {
          localStorage.setItem('token', tokenResult);
          this.user = new User();
          this.user.name = userCreds.username;

          this.router.navigate(['issues']);
      });
```

```
    }

    /* Logout in AuthService simply removes token */
    public logout() {
        localStorage.removeItem('token');
        this.router.navigate(['login']);
    }

    public get currentUser(): User {
      return this.user;
    }
  }
}
```

On the Angular side, thus far, we have code for login, which will get us the token for a valid user account and code for validating the token. Next, we need to restrict our user's access to certain components or views, which the user may navigate to.

Route Guards

The IMS App makes use of routes to navigate to different views within the application. Angular provides Route Guards, which can be used as interceptors when routing to views. We will make use of the CanActivate interface, which is an interface that a class implements to be the guard deciding whether a route can be activated. Here's the AuthGuard service class located at src/app/shared/auth-guard.service.ts:

```
import { CanActivate, Router, ActivatedRouteSnapshot }
from '@angular/router';

@Injectable()
export class AuthGuardService implements CanActivate {

    constructor(private router: Router,
                private authService: AuthService) { }

    canActivate(route: ActivatedRouteSnapshot): boolean {
        //logic to check if user is logged In
        if(this.authService.authenticated) {
            return true;
        }
        this.router.navigate(['login']);
        return false;
    }
}
```

This class would also need to be registered in the list of providers within the `app.module.ts` file.

With the `CanActivate` guard defined, we can reference it within our routes, where we need access control to be enforced. Here's the updated route defined in the `app-routing.module.ts` file:

```
const routes: Routes = [
    { path: '', redirectTo: 'home', pathMatch: 'full' },
    { path: 'home', component: HomeComponent },
    { path: 'issues', component: IssueListingComponent,
      canActivate: [ AuthGuardService ] },
    { path: 'issues/create', component: IssueAddComponent },
    { path: 'issue/:id', component: IssueEditComponent },
    { path: 'login', component: LoginComponent }
];
```

Our `AuthGuardService` would get invoked just before the user navigates to the `/issues` route, allowing for the needed login check. We could similarly put the `canActivate` guard against other all other routes that need to be secured.

Let's quickly look at what we have achieved here:

- We added a URI for authenticating a user and issuing tokens within the IMS Users microservice. This was done by making use of IMS Security's `TokenIssuer` class.
- Additionally, we secured our IMS Issues GET all issues URI by using the `@JWTRequired` marker annotation.
- The `JWTFilter` code is used to validate the token before the call is forwarded to the target API.
- On the client side, we created a login component that hits the authentication URI for obtaining the token. The JWT is stored in the local storage of browser.
- We utilized `angular-jwt` to validate the token, which is done in the `AuthService` code.
- Lastly, we created a Route Guard to control access to certain routes using the `CanActivate` interface.

These steps have enabled security for IMS project. We could also make use of the `decodeToken` method of `JwtHelperService` from the `angular-jwt` library, which can be useful for reading the claims within the token. What remains is to pass the generated token as part of the request when making a call to the IMS Issues API, which is secured.

Exchanging tokens

The client needs to send the JWT token as part of every request to the server. This is typically done by setting the token in the `Authorization` header. Here's a sample request header:

```
Authorization: Bearer
eyJhbGciOiJIUzI1NiJ9.eyJzdWIiOiJ0ZXN0IiwiaWF0IjoxNTE0NTU3ODA2LCJleHAiOjE1MT
Q1NjE0MDZ9.kA2mP2jZN-zbtzAmD1BZWkz7XPlV0NM3gcv6RLbOuf0
```

To set this as part of the HTTP call from Angular, we have a couple of choices:

- Use an `HttpInterceptor` so that all outbound HTTP calls can be manipulated to have our token in them. This way, you need not pollute each call in the service code with logic to extract the token and set it in the request header.
- Use the service class to extract the JWT (token) and set it as part of the HTTP call. This is useful if the number of such calls are kept low.

For IMS App, we have only secured the Issues API call, thus it's simpler to go with the second option for our requirements.

Injecting an authorization header

We do have the token, but for us to be able to invoke the IMS Issues resource method of `/issues`, we now need to pass the `Authorization` request header. To do so, we will update our `getAll()` method within `IssuesService` to pass the token as part of the request:

```
@Injectable()
export class IssuesService {

  constructor(private http: HttpClient) { }

  public getAll(): Observable<Array<Issue>> {
    return this.http.get<Array<Issue>>(
        'http://localhost:8082/ims-issues/resources/issues',
        {
         headers: new HttpHeaders().set(
         'Authorization', `Bearer ${localStorage.getItem('token')}`
         )
        });
  }
//Other methods omitted
}
```

The second argument to the `http.get` call are the options that we can pass to set the headers on this request. We use it to retrieve the `'token'` that is saved in the browser's local storage and then set its value as part of the `"Authorization` header. We have prefixed the token value with `Bearer` and the resulting HTTP call would look like this:

```
GET /ims-issues/resources/issues HTTP/1.1
Host: localhost:8082
Connection: keep-alive
Accept: application/json, text/plain, */*
Origin: http://localhost:4200
Authorization: Bearer
eyJhbGciOiJIUzI1NiJ9.eyJzdWIiOiJOZXN0IiwiaWF0IjoxNTE0NTU3ODA2LCJleHAiOjE1MT
Q1NjE0MDZ9.kA2mP2jZN-zbtzAmD1BZWkz7XPlV0NM3gcv6RLbOuf0
```

With this code in place, now we have completed our last step for using the token to make calls to our services.

Neither in Java EE nor MicroProfile

While JWT is not a part of Java EE or the MicroProfile, it has become a de facto for token-based authentications. RESTful services, being stateless, require dealing with security with each request. So, clients typically would be sending some form of a token along with each request. This allows the API to create the needed security context for the caller and perform role-based checks as needed. As token-based authentication is widely adopted and standards such as OpenID Connect and OAuth2.0 are also token-based, it makes sense to get the approach standardized.

There is also a proposal to include **JWT Role Based Access (JWT RBAC)** for MicroProfile, so in the near future, we may see this get adopted as a standard. This would allow for working with authentication and authorization policies using tokens in a standard manner. The strategy of passing security tokens is not just limited for frontend clients to services, but also between service to service communication. JWT's simplicity of using JSON structure to define the token format along with the needed security signature and compactness adds to its growing adoption.

Reference: `https://github.com/eclipse/microprofile-jwt-auth`.

General tips

While there's nothing that prevents you from setting your tokens within params or headers or the body of a request, it's best to stick to a standard, such as in the `Authorization` header with the `Bearer` keyword. Given that these tokens are not encrypted, ensure that you avoid storing sensitive information in them. You'd most likely rely upon a JWT implementation to validate or generate the tokens, so it pays to look up if it really is the best one considered for the task.

Consider creating your tokens with scopes that allow for finer-grained security. Scopes defined within a token are used to tell us the capabilities or access this token has:

```
/* Generate token with claims containig scope */
String compactJws = Jwts.builder()
                 .setSubject(username)
                 .claim("scope", "admin approver")
                 .signWith(SignatureAlgorithm.HS256, key)
                 .setIssuedAt(new Date())
                 .setExpiration(expirationDateTime)
                 .compact();

/* When verifying check the scopes within the passed token */
Jws<Claims> claims = Jwts.parser().setSigningKey(key)
                    .parseClaimsJws(token);
//Get scope here, which would be "admin approver"
String scope = claims.getBody().get("scope", String.class);
```

We have set the scope to `"admin approver"` while generating the token and the same can be verified during the parsing of claims. In our example of `TokenIssuer`, we had a fixed secret key, which is far from what you would want in the real-world project. Ideally, you would have a pair of an API key and a secret key per client or tenant, which is used for signing the token. The API key is public and shared with the client, but the secret key is not shared.

As the popularity of the application grows among users, so does the probability of it becoming a victim to attacks from different corners of the internet. Using cookies as an authentication mechanism works, but these are susceptible to CSRF attacks. CSRF is also known by other names such as XSRF or session riding. In this form of an attack, a user who's logged into the application (site) is directed to another malicious website, which then tries to impersonate requests to the application site on behalf of the user. To mitigate such threats, both the client and server need to participate in securing the communication. Angular already has in-built support when using `HttpClient` to handle the client-part of CSRF protection. It's also best to secure data transmission by using the HTTPS protocol instead of plain HTTP.

Cross-site scripting (**XSS**) is another common attack faced by web applications. In this form of an attack, the attacker would inject a script within the running application content (DOM) to gain access to sensitive information. For example, the application input fields can be used to insert scripting code such as `<script>..</script>` block to run arbitrary JavaScript in the code. These vulnerabilities need to be fixed to prevent XSS attacks. The good news is that Angular offers built-in security, which intercepts inserted values through the view that makes use of interpolation or any input bindings. These values are, by default, not trusted and thus sanitized and escaped by Angular before rendering it on the DOM. This does not safeguard us from server-side generated HTML templates, thus it's best to avoid such techniques.

While Angular does provide built-in security checks for XSS and CSRF along with XSSI (cross-site script inclusion), the onus of application level security for authenticating and authorizing a user belongs to the developer.

Summary

We gained an understanding of how security tokens are exchanged between web-based Angular applications and backend APIs. JWT is a standard for representing claims securely between two parties. The simplicity of JWT makes it a compelling choice as the preferred token format for use in any token-based authentication solution. There's already a proposal for including it as part of the MicroProfile standard.

Angular comes with built-in security for various kinds of attacks, but still the developers need to pay attention to not break these. We saw how security can be implemented on the server side using JWT filters for securing RESTful APIs that are at the boundary of a microservice. We also saw how the client can obtain a token and then pass it in subsequent requests, using the `HttpClient` for Angular. Access control to certain views can be defined using the `CanActivate` interface for guarding routes. It's also possible to decode the JWT to perform role-based checks. All of these features have helped us build a layer of security for the IMS application, not only for the backend, but also for the frontend.

Other Books You May Enjoy

If you enjoyed this book, you may be interested in these other books by Packt:

Java EE 8 Application Development
David R. Heffelfinger

ISBN: 978-1-78829-367-9

- Develop and deploy Java EE applications
- Embrace the latest additions to the Contexts and Dependency Injection (CDI) specification to develop Java EE applications
- Develop web-based applications by utilizing the latest version of JavaServer Faces, JSF 2.3.
- Understand the steps needed to process JSON data with JSON-P and the new JSON-B Java EE API
- Implement RESTful web services using the new JAX-RS 2.1 API, which also includes support for Server-Sent Events (SSE) and the new reactive client API

ASP.NET Core 2 and Angular 5
Valerio De Sanctis

ISBN: 978-1-78829-360-0

- Use ASP.NET Core to its full extent to create a versatile backend layer based on RESTful APIs
- Consume backend APIs with the brand new Angular 5 HttpClient and use RxJS Observers to feed the frontend UI asynchronously
- Implement an authentication and authorization layer using ASP.NET Identity to support user login with integrated and third-party OAuth 2 providers
- Configure a web application in order to accept user-defined data and persist it into the database using server-side APIs
- Secure your application against threats and vulnerabilities in a time efficient way
- Connect different aspects of the ASP. NET Core framework ecosystem and make them interact with each other for a Full-Stack web development experience

Leave a review - let other readers know what you think

Please share your thoughts on this book with others by leaving a review on the site that you bought it from. If you purchased the book from Amazon, please leave us an honest review on this book's Amazon page. This is vital so that other potential readers can see and use your unbiased opinion to make purchasing decisions, we can understand what our customers think about our products, and our authors can see your feedback on the title that they have worked with Packt to create. It will only take a few minutes of your time, but is valuable to other potential customers, our authors, and Packt. Thank you!

Index